Civilian Control of the Military

Civilian Control of the Military

The Changing Security Environment

MICHAEL C. DESCH

The Johns Hopkins University Press   Baltimore and London

© 1999 The Johns Hopkins University Press
All rights reserved. Published 1999
Printed in the United States of America on acid-free paper

Johns Hopkins Paperbacks edition, 2001
9 8 7 6 5 4 3 2 1

The Johns Hopkins University Press
2715 North Charles Street
Baltimore, Maryland 21218-4363
www.press.jhu.edu

Library of Congress Cataloging-in-Publication Data
will be found at the end of this book.
A catalog record for this book is available from
the British Library.

ISBN 0-8018-6639-1 (pbk.)

Make peace! And what will you do with the generals?
Will they cultivate greens?

PAUL VICOMTE DE BARRAS, *Member of French Directory*

Nothing is so dangerous as an army in the midst of an unwarlike nation; the excessive love of the whole community for quiet continually puts the constitution at the mercy of the soldiery.

ALEXIS DE TOCQUEVILLE, *Democracy in America*

Contents

Figures and Tables

Figures

Tables

Acknowledgments

John Mearsheimer planted the seeds of this book. He used to open every national security course he taught at the University of Chicago with a discussion of the various subfields of national security studies, illustrated as a pie chart divided into thirds. The first third contained nuclear deterrence issues; the second, conventional forces and grand strategy; the third, military-and-society issues. John always gave me the impression that he thought the first two thirds had been pretty well worked over by other scholars and that the most interesting, but least studied, questions generally fell in the last third. As always, I look to John not only for interesting questions but also for help in finding answers.

My interest in military-and-society issues grew during the two years I spent as a John M. Olin Post-Doctoral Fellow in National Security at the Center for International Affairs at Harvard University. Samuel Huntington was the director of the CFIA during my first year and director of the John M. Olin Institute for Strategic Studies the second. Anyone writing in the area of civil-military relations has to reckon with his *The Soldier and the State*. I have tried to do that in this book, building on those many parts of Sam's work that I think have stood the test of time and challenging a few parts that I think have not. I am deeply indebted to Sam for advice and support during the writing of this book.

I also would like to express my gratitude to two other institutions for their generous support of this project. In 1990 I was awarded a fellowship by the Center for International Studies and the University of Southern California on the basis of a proposal for what I hope will become another book, about the wartime impact of prewar planning. For a variety of reasons, I decided at the last minute to begin this project instead. In something of a "bait and switch," I told CIS's director, John Odell, that I would come but wanted to work on this new project. I am deeply grateful to him for his flexibility and hope that this book merits his indulgence. I am also grateful to the chairs of the Department of Political Science of the University of California at Riverside, Grace Saltzstein and David Lanoue, both for research support during the years I taught there and for granting me a very generous leave to return to the Olin Institute to finish the book.

I presented an early draft of the theory chapter at the September 1995 American Political Science Association Annual Convention. A later version of it was published as "Soldiers, States, and Structures: The End of the Cold War and Weakening of U.S. Civilian Control," *Armed Forces and Society* 24, no. 3 (1998): 389–406. I presented early drafts of the chapter on the United States at a workshop sponsored by the Social Science Research Council, "The Politics of Strategic Adjustment: Ideas, Institutions, and Interests," at the University of Texas at Austin in April 1994; at the Olin Institute's "Strategy and National Security" conference at the Wianno Club in June 1994; and at seminars at the U.S. Naval War College in December 1994 and the Defense and Arms Control Studies Program, MIT, in April 1995. I vetted early drafts of the Soviet Union and Russia chapter at workshops and seminars at Oxford and in Seillans, France, sponsored by the Ford Foundation Project at the University of Birmingham, U.K.; and at workshops at the Russian Research Center, Harvard University, and the Harvard-Russian Institute of International Affairs, Moscow. A very early version of this chapter was published as "Why the Soviet Military Supported Gorbachev but Why the Russian Military Might Only Support Yeltsin for a Price," *Journal of Strategic Studies* 16, no. 4 (1993): 455–89. Finally, I presented an early draft of the chapter on southern Latin America at USC's Center for International Studies in November 1990.

I owe great debts to many other colleagues who read drafts of the various chapters in this book. I would particularly like to thank Roy Allison, Deborah Avant, Richard Betts, James Burk, David Burrelli, Eileen Crumm, Kurt Dassel, Steven David, Chris Davis, Brian Downing, Lynn Eden, Peter Feaver, Emily Goldman, Ted Hopf, Stuart Kaufman, Grant Klein, Richard Kohn, Paul Kowert, Abraham Lowenthal, Sarah Mendelson, Mike Mochizuki, Will Moore, Charles Moskos, Henry Nau, Max Neiman, Robert

Pape, David Pion-Berlin, Bruce Porter, Barry Posen, Dani Reiter, Edward Rhodes, Tom Ricks, Harvey Sapolsky, Mark Shulman, Marc Trachtenberg, Peter Trubowitz, Stephen Van Evera, Stephen Walt, and James Wirtz. I was especially fortunate to have been able to run drafts of the whole manuscript past two very tough groups of critics: first, the 1995/96 John M. Olin Fellows in National Security, James Davis, Colin Elman, Hein Goemans, Geoffrey Herrera, Alexander Kozhemiakin, Jeffrey Legro, Thomas Mahnken, Laura Miller, Brian Taylor, and Rick Villalobos; second, the International Security Policy Studies group at the University of Chicago, David Edelstein, Kier Lieber, Sean Patrick Lopez, and David Yingling. Henry Tom, George Scialabba, and Nancy Trotic gave me terrific editorial advice.

I would also like to acknowledge the very important institutional support I have received directly or indirectly from the Academic Senate of the University of California, the Institute for Global Cooperation and Conflict, the Ford Foundation, the John M. Olin National Faculty Fellowship in the Social Sciences, the Lynde and Harry Bradley Foundation, and the Smith-Richardson Foundation.

My wife, Mary Jo, provided astute commentary on the manuscript and, even more important, love and affection. My daughter, Sophie, arrived just in time to see the book off.

Chapter 1

Introduction

How has the changed international security environment of the post–Cold War era affected the relationship between civilian and military leaders? This new security environment is bringing about changes in civil-military relations globally. For example, in both of the Cold War protagonists, the end of the Cold War coincided with a deterioration in the relationship between civilian authority and the military. The United States and Russia, once models of military subordination to civilian authority,[1] have both experienced a weakening of civilian control. Since the August 1991 coup attempt in the Soviet Union, there have been recurrent concerns about whether the Soviet and then Russian militaries have been fully under civilian control.[2] More recently, some observers in the United States have suggested that there is a "crisis" in U.S. civil-military relations.[3] In neither country is there much danger of a military coup d'état or even outright insubordination by the military. Nevertheless, in both countries once-ideal patterns of civilian control changed for the worse with the end of the Cold War.

This development is surprising. Much of the theoretical and conceptual literature on civil-military relations focuses almost exclusively on domestic influences on civil-military relations, such as the character of individual civilian and military leaders, the structure and norms of the military organization, the institutions of civilian government, and the nature of society. And the small part of the literature that looks to international variables shares Harold Lasswell's premise that the military should be harder to control in a challenging international threat environment than in a relatively benign one.[4] The end of the Cold War, according to Lasswell's logic, should make it more, rather than less, likely that civilians will maintain control of their military organizations. In this book I explain why the opposite is true. The root of the problem, at least in the Russian and American cases, is that neither military quickly found new doctrines and missions as conducive to firm civilian control of the military as were their Cold War doctrines and missions.

Historically, interest in civil-military relations, at least in the United States, has been most intense at times when the international security environment seemed to be changing. The first wave of Cold War scholarship on the subject was prompted by concerns about how a prolonged period of "neither peace nor war" might affect U.S. civil-military relations.[5] A second wave of scholarly interest emerged in the mid-1970s, when many thought that détente might inaugurate an enduring period of reduced international threat.[6] The post–Cold War renaissance of interest in civil-military relations constitutes a third wave.[7] This coincidence between international change and intensified scholarly interest in civil-military relations is in line with my theory that changes in the structural threat environment ultimately shape the relationship between the military and civilian leadership. I trace the actual causal relationship in the cases I examine in this book.

One might ask why, if there is so much scholarly interest in post–Cold War civil-military relations, this issue is not more prominent in the public debate in the United States. There are four reasons. First, civilian leaders, especially those in the Clinton administration, have little interest in publicizing their ongoing problems with the American military because these problems make the civilian leaders look weak.[8] Second, the American military also does not want to highlight this weakening of civilian control because the notion of subordination to civilian authority is so deeply embedded in its professional culture that it is difficult for most military officers to admit publicly their changed attitudes toward civilian control.[9] Yet it is clear that these attitudes *have* changed.[10] I heard an active-duty Russian Army officer minimize the extent of post–Cold War civil-military tension in his country by arguing that the actions of Russian generals in challenging civilian policies with which they disagreed were no different from those of American generals such as Colin Powell.[11]

Third, the U.S. public's interest in military issues has waned dramatically since the end of the Cold War, so the short-term consequences of this weakening in civilian control of the military are not readily apparent.[12]

Finally, many believe that problems with civil-military relations are exclusively a Third World phenomenon and that if there is no danger of a military coup d'état, everything is fine. The confluence of these four factors explains why this issue has so far remained largely an inside-the-Beltway and academic-specialist concern.

Civil-military relations is a very complicated issue. Analysts disagree about how to define and measure civil-military relations as the dependent variable. These disagreements have two causes. First, it is not always clear when issues involve civil-military conflict rather than intracivilian struggles, intramilitary fights, or civil-military coalitional wars. Few issues clearly pit civilians against military officers.[13] In pluralist democracies, civilian leaders may be divided over an issue—especially in the United States, where the institutions of civilian rule are divided and the Constitution assigns responsibility for control of the military to both the executive and the legislative branches.[14] Ironically, legislative assertiveness in this area, while constitutionally sanctioned as an important check on executive power, is likely to dilute executive authority and thereby weaken civilian control of the military. The theory I offer in this book would lead us to expect greater civilian and military disunity, and a consequent weakening of civilian control, in less challenging external threat environments.

A second cause of disagreement in analyses of relations between civil and military establishments is that even when we are sure the issue is one of civil-military relations, it is often not clear whether these relations are good or bad. There is a remarkably broad range of ideas on what constitutes "good" or "bad" civil-military relations.

Most people think about civil-military relations strictly in terms of coups: if there are coups, then civil-military relations are bad, and if not they are good. But there are many other aspects to civil-military relations.[15] As Samuel Huntington notes, "the problem in the modern state is not armed revolt but the relation of the expert to the politician."[16] One can have poor civil-military relations without the threat of a coup.

Some analysts use the extent of military influence in areas beyond strictly military issues as a measure of civil-military relations.[17] By this indicator, good civil-military relations exist when the military concerns itself exclusively with military affairs. The problem with this standard is that sometimes the military takes on nonmilitary functions at the behest of civilians.[18] Moreover, the line between the civilian and military spheres is not always clear.

Others may argue that excessive military influence on national policy debates is a potential problem: for example, military support for the Committee on the Present Danger's critique of the SALT II treaty may have skewed public perception of the soundness of that agreement. There may be a problem here, but not necessarily one of civil-military relations. There is in principle nothing wrong with the military's participating in national debates on important issues in which it has substantial interest and expertise. When its influence in these debates is disproportionate, it is likely to be due to civilian deference rather than inappropriate military influence.

Some observers look to the frequency of conflict between military and civilian leaders as an indicator: a state has good civil-military relations when there are few conflicts. This criterion also is misleading, since some conflict is inevitable and perhaps even desirable in a pluralistic political system.[19]

Still others suggest that the state of civil-military relations should be measured by how much civilians and military officers like and respect one another. But it is not necessary for military officers to like and respect civilian leaders in order for them to obey these leaders.[20] Disrespect is not a problem in itself, though it could reflect deeper problems.

Another possible definition is that good civil-military relations are whatever results in effective military policies.[21] The objective of civilian control is not, however, just to produce good military policy. Civilian control of the military, like the separation of powers among the civilian branches of the U.S. government, was clearly a compromise between increased military or political effectiveness and the preservation of domestic liberty.[22] Good civil-military relations will usually produce good policy, but not always. During the Vietnam War, for example, the U.S. military, despite its grave reservations, obeyed civilian orders that led to disaster. Conversely, Gen. Charles de Gaulle made the right choice in breaking with the Vichy Republic in June of 1940 but established an unfortunate precedent for later French civil-military relations.

In an ideal world, of course, there would never be any threat of a coup, the military would always stay clearly within the "military" realm and make only constructive contributions to national policy debates, there would be few civilian-military conflicts, top military and civilian leaders would respect and even like one another, and effective national policies would result. But in the real world, the bottom line for developed democracies is civilian control: can civilian leaders reliably get the military to do what they want it to?

The best indicator of the state of civilian control is who prevails when civilian and military preferences diverge.[23] If the military does, there is a problem; if the civilians do, there is not. To determine whether the military plays an important role in a society's political decision-making, one should identify a number of issues that pitted military preferences against those of civilians and show who prevailed.[24]

There are four potential, but not ultimately insurmountable, problems with this approach. First, initial civilian and military positions may be strategic and not reflect real preferences. However, this ought to be true of both sides, so it should still be possible to judge whose preferences prevailed based on the outcome. Second, parties in a dispute may resolve their differences if members of one side change their minds about the issue. If this genuinely occurs, this outcome should not be coded as a victory for either side. The best way to tell whether one side has really persuaded the other is to observe whether the issue is a recurrent source of civil-military conflict. Third, the two sides may compromise. Often, however, "compromises" conceal a victory by one side or the other. Moreover, it is not indicative of firm civilian control that civilian leaders have to bargain with the military. Fourth, it is conceivable that looking only at disputes might bias my study toward finding more conflict than there really is. But if the outcomes of civil-military conflict vary with changes in the international and domestic security environments, we have at least established a causal link, even if the magnitude of conflict is somewhat overstated.

The level of civilian control can be determined by whether or not civilians prevail in disagreements with the military. Civilian control is weak when military preferences prevail most of the time; the most extreme example is military rule or military coups that oust one civilian regime and install another. It is a less serious problem for civil-military relations when military preferences prevail only some of the time, though civilian control is still not firm. Finally, civilian control is firm when civilian preferences prevail most of the time.

Obviously, the prospects for successful democratization in the former Soviet Union and other areas of the world are inextricably linked to reliable civilian control of the military. As Robert Dahl has argued, the "circumstances most favorable for competitive politics exist when access to violence . . . is either dispersed or denied to oppositions and to government."[25] Military institutions are inherently undemocratic, because they are hierarchically organized. Moreover, they have a near monopoly on coercive power in a state. If it is not under firm civilian control, the military can represent a serious threat to democracy. Given that most political violence during recent years has been domestic, rather than interstate, and domestic violence has been one of the primary precipitants of the complete breakdown of civilian control of the military in various coun-

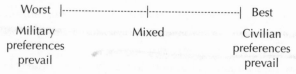

FIGURE 1   Measures of Civilian Control (the Dependent Variable)

tries, inadequate civilian control of the military will likely remain a crucial issue in the years to come.

Not only is civilian control necessary to preserve domestic liberty (not in danger in the contemporary United States), but *on balance* it also produces better national policy, since civilian leaders are less subject to organizational biases and have a more "national" perspective on defense issues.[26] As Carl von Clausewitz argued early in the nineteenth century, "The subordination of the political point of view to the military would be contrary to common sense, for policy has declared the War; it is the intelligent faculty, War only the instrument, not the reverse. The subordination of the military point of view to the political is, therefore, the only thing which is possible."[27] When democratic civilian leaders make bad policy decisions, they can be replaced. It is more difficult for the public to hold military leaders directly accountable for failure.[28]

This does not mean that civilian leaders should be deeply involved in every tactical or technical military decision. Usually a natural division of labor will emerge, with the military enjoying substantial autonomy in military-technical matters. The issues likely to divide civilian from military leaders are the larger military-political questions, including the use of force, budgets, and procurement.

Although various theories might explain the changing patterns of civilian control of the military in the post–Cold War world, in my view the case studies undertaken in this book show that it is easiest for civilians to control the military when they face primarily international (external) threats and it is hardest for them to control the military when they face primarily domestic (internal) threats. Structural incentives in states facing both external and internal threats (or neither) are less decisive. In order to account for these patterns, we need to look to other variables. Certain aspects of a state's military doctrine take on a greater independent role in strengthening or weakening civilian control in less structurally determinate situations.

The cases studied in this book cover all four combinations of threats—high or low, external or internal—and they show that each combination tends to produce the level of civilian control of the military predicted by my theory. From this examination, we can draw some policy prescriptions for how civilians can maintain firm control of the military in a changing international security environment, and we can explore some of the theory's implications about how international change affects domestic politics.

Chapter 2

Civilian Control of the Military in Different Threat Environments

Alternative Theories of Civilian Control of the Military

The individual characteristics of civilian and military leaders have been used to explain changes in civilian control of the military. Charles Moskos and others hold that America's post–Cold War problems with civil-military relations are a result of the Clinton administration's insensitivity to military norms and values. Conversely, many scholars of the French civil-military crisis during the Algerian war attributed its successful resolution to de Gaulle's skillful leadership. Others assign great weight to Douglas MacArthur's and Colin Powell's personalities in their respective civil-military conflicts. On this view, the level of civilian control of the military should vary with the personality, character, and experience of the individual civilian and military leaders.[1] The problem is that these arguments beg the question of why different types of civilian or military leaders come to power at particular times.

Another possible explanation centers on changes in military organization. Employing Morris Janowitz's military organizational model,[2] for example, one would expect that civilian control of the U.S. military would have begun to deteriorate after the enactment of JCS (Joint Chiefs of Staff) reform through the Goldwater-Nichols legislation of the mid-1980s. Richard Kohn has attributed the post–Cold War difficulties to the increasing unity of the American military since Goldwater-Nichols.[3] Alternatively,

Samuel Huntington has argued that the higher the military's level of professionalization, the better the civilian-military relationship.[4] Either of these views predicts that institutional changes in the military—such as increasing or decreasing unity, changes in organizational culture, or changes in the level of professionalism—will strengthen or weaken civilian control. In my opinion, however, these organizational perspectives are also inadequate, because the strength of civilian control of the military cannot be understood merely by examining military institutional variables. We need to ask, what ultimately accounts for the particular organizational structure and professional culture of a military?

A third explanation holds that changes in the civilian institutions of government affect civilian control of the military. For example, Huntington argues that when civilian authority is divided, as it is in the United States because of the separation of powers, the military will be able to play civilians off one another and achieve greater autonomy. The increasing assertiveness of Congress, this argument goes, has diluted the authority of the executive branch and given the military more freedom from civilian control. In contrast, when civilian authority is relatively unified, as it is in parliamentary systems such as that of the United Kingdom, control over the military will be easier.[5] This argument has been resurrected by the new institutionalist "principal/agent" approach to studying American civil-military relations.[6] This is logical, since this approach was initially developed by rational choice scholars studying the American Congress. But it has serious limitations: it remains more a framework than a theory; logically, it should predict constant rather than variable civil-military tensions; and it is not clear that it will work well beyond the American case. We need, therefore, an explanation of variation in the level of unity of civilian authority.

A related argument is that weak state institutions are less effective tools of civilian control. In *Political Order and Changing Societies*, Huntington contrasted "civic societies"—those with a high level of institutionalization and a low level of participation—with "praetorian societies," which have a low level of institutionalization but a high level of political participation. In the former, stable civil-military relations are part of a larger, more orderly political system, while in the latter the "wealthy bribe; students riot; mobs demonstrate; and the military coup."[7] However, this distinction leaves unanswered the question of what determines whether a state has strong civilian governmental institutions or not.

Yet another argument holds that the method of civilian control determines its strength. Under "objective control," the military is given a large measure of autonomy in its narrow technical sphere in return for complete political subordination to civilian authority. In contrast, "subjective control" means that civilians try to control the military at all levels and make it look more like civilian society. Huntington has suggested that objective control mechanisms are most conducive to stable civil-military relations.[8] But what determines which method of control the civilian leadership embraces?

An important societal argument is that sharp differences in civilian and military ideas and cultures weaken civilian control of the military.[9] Some have begun to argue, for example, that since the abolition of the draft in 1973—which meant fewer Americans would serve in the military—civilian and military political and social attitudes have increasingly diverged.[10] This divergence could have implications for both domestic resource allocation and the international use of force. Unfortunately, this societal argument does not explain what causes convergence or divergence of military and civilian cultures and ideas.

A few analysts have suggested that changes in the international environment are ultimately the cause of the post–Cold War problems.[11] However, the most rigorous theoretical statements of how international factors might affect civilian control of the military are contradictory. Stanislaw Andreski has argued that an increasing external threat should improve civilian control of the military: "'The devil finds work for idle hands': the soldiers who have no wars to fight or prepare for will be tempted to interfere in politics. Taking a long-term view, it seems that there is an inverse connection between strenuous warfare and pretorianism."[12] Harold Lasswell, on the other hand, suggested that a challenging external threat environment should undermine civil-military relations by creating the "garrison state." "Only the iron heel of protracted military crisis can subdue civilian influences and pass 'all power to the general.'"[13] While Huntington has articulated the most comprehensive and influential framework for the study of civil-military relations, even he does not clearly explain the effect of international variables. In some places he seems to take a Lasswellian line; in others, his argument is more in line with Andreski's.[14] The question remains: how should the less challenging international security environment of the post–Cold War era affect civilian control of the military?

A Structural Theory of Civil-Military Relations

Factors relating to individual leaders, military organizations, state structures, and societies undoubtedly influence the ability of civilians to control their militaries. The question is, what in turn affects these intervening variables? This book provides a theory of civilian control of the military that considers the role of individual, military, state, and societal variables as they respond to domestic and international threats. In other words, it treats them as intervening variables. This approach has been employed in analyses of the role of the military in individual countries; Alfred Stepan, for example, has suggested in his pathbreaking work on the Brazilian military that a "central task of the political sociology of the military is to look at both the military institution and the political system and to determine how the special institutional characteristics of a particular military establishment shape its response to influences coming from the political system."[15] So far, however, this perspective has not been applied more broadly across a number of different cases and incorporated into a general theory that also includes international influences.[16]

A theory of civilian control of the military with broad explanatory and predictive power will have to incorporate some elements of the theories discussed above. My argument is that the strength of civilian control of the military in most countries is shaped fundamentally by structural factors, especially threats, which affect individual leaders, the military organization, the state, and society. The variables emphasized in other theories have their effects primarily as intervening variables shaped by different combinations of international and domestic threat environments. Such a structural theory holds that the causes of patterns of civilian control are not completely reducible to the internal attributes of a particular state; rather, the patterns of civilian control are shaped by the interaction of these internal attributes with the external environment. My theory anticipates, therefore, that differently configured units (a unit being a particular country's society and military with their particular attributes) in similar structural positions will usually behave similarly. Like other structural theories, it cannot predict individual coups or other manifestations of a breakdown in civilian control of the military; it can only specify the general conditions under which civilian control is likely to deteriorate or improve.[17]

Structure does not determine outcomes directly. It operates indirectly through three mechanisms: socialization, emulation, and competition. As

Kenneth Waltz notes, states are not forced to adopt any particular pattern of behavior by the international structure. But they observe that states that conform their behavior to the structure of the international system do better in competition with other states, and so they will gradually learn to do so as well. On balance, similarly positioned states will behave in similar ways.[18] Waltz cautions that "one must ask how and to what extent the structure of a realm accounts for outcomes."[19] The degree of structural influence can vary: in some cases structure explains much about a state's pattern of civilian control of the military, while in other cases we must look to different variables. I offer a theory that integrates domestic and international independent variables and shows when one or the other is more important.

The problem with structural theory, as Peter Gourevitch points out, is that while the "world sets constraints and offers opportunities . . . explanation of the variance within those limits . . . requires analysis of internal politics."[20] Since the determinacy of structure varies, under certain conditions domestic variables can play a larger role in the outcome of civil-military conflict. In particular, military doctrines come to play an important independent role in structurally indeterminate threat environments such as the post–Cold War era. While international structure is not always decisive, international variables are nevertheless the place to begin in order to understand the strength of a state's civilian control of the military.

Threats, my independent variable, can be external (international) or internal (domestic) to the state and can vary in intensity (from high to low). They affect three major domestic actors: the military, the civilian government, and the rest of society.[21] Wars and periods of heightened international tension, such as World War II and the Cold War, present greater external threats; détentes and periods of peace, including the post–Cold War era, present lower external threats. External threats have obvious effects: they threaten the entire state, including the military; they usually produce increased unity within the state; and they focus everyone's attention outward.

Internal threats have more complex effects upon the various actors within a state. An internal threat that affects only state and society, not the military, is unlikely to adversely affect civilian control. A threat from society to the military and civilian institutions could lead to a military-supported civilian dictatorship, as in Alberto Fujimori's Peru. A threat from the state to the military and society is likely to produce a military coup that installs a different civilian leadership, as in France in May 1958.

Finally, a threat from the state and society to the military is apt to lead to military rule, as in Brazil in 1964 or Chile in 1973. Domestic threats divide the state and focus everyone's attention inward. The most important aspect of domestic threats for my theory is how they affect the military. The domestic priorities of the military institution that can be threatened are (in ascending order of importance) protection of budget share, preservation of organizational autonomy, maintenance of cohesion, and survival of the institution.

What really counts with threats, of course, is how actors perceive them. As Lewis Coser notes, "If men define a threat as real, although there may be little or nothing in reality to justify this belief, the threat is real in its consequences."[22] Clearly, when a state is at war, it is hard to argue that the threat is subjective. In peacetime, however, threats may indeed be subjective. In structurally determinate situations (where there is just one optimal behavior), threats are objective; in indeterminate environments (where there are a number of optimal behaviors), they are more subjective. In the latter case, military doctrines can play a significant role in determining what is considered a threat.

My structural theory of civilian control of the military is premised upon some simple assumptions. The structural threat environment should affect the character of the civilian leadership, the nature of the military institution, the cohesiveness of state institutions, the method of civilian control, and the convergence or divergence of civilian and military ideas and cultures. Any complex organization is likely to experience internal conflict and divisions. Sociologists have demonstrated that under certain conditions a common threat will mask these divisions, making members of a group more cohesive.[23] Threats to the organization also orient it in a particular direction. Unity or cohesiveness is not always desirable: for example, in an externally oriented military, cohesiveness is the sine qua non of military effectiveness, but in a military facing a domestic threat, it could make that organization a serious contender for control of society.[24] From these assumptions, we can deduce a number of simple hypotheses and predictions about the strength of civilian control of the military in different structural threat environments. These deductions will be illustrated with historical and contemporary evidence.

A state facing high external threats and low internal threats should have the most stable civil-military relations (fig. 2, quadrant [Q] 1). A challenging international security environment is more likely to bring to power a civilian leadership experienced in and knowledgeable about national security affairs.[25] Civilian institutions are also likely to be more cohesive

		External threats	
		High	Low
Internal threats	High	Poor (Q3)	Worst (Q4)
	Low	Good (Q1)	Mixed (Q2)

FIGURE 2 Civilian Control of the Military as a Function of Location and Intensity of Threats

because of the "rally 'round the flag" effect of external threats.[26] Civilians are more likely to rely on objective control mechanisms, trusting in the greater competence of the military to fight wars. An external threat will also tend to unify potential and actual military factions, orienting them outward. An externally oriented military will have less inclination to participate in domestic politics, especially if the state is supplying sufficient resources to execute the military's external missions. Furthermore, in an age of total war, the military must count on the complete support of the state in fighting a major war. "An embattled nation," Gerhard Ritter concludes, "sharing in the war down to the lowest rungs in the ladder, simply cannot be governed by authoritarian methods."[27] Armed forces recently used for internal repression would not have a high level of popular support or the military skills requisite for external wars.[28] Finally, civilian and military ideas will tend to be in harmony in such a threat configuration. One important reason that civilian control of the military in Europe and North America has been so firm is that the majority of threats these states have faced have been external.[29]

In contrast, a state facing low external and high internal threats should experience the weakest civilian control of the military (fig. 2, Q4). The civilian leadership is less likely to be attentive to national security affairs. In such a situation, civilian institutions are also likely to be weak and deeply divided.[30] Civilian factions may be tempted to impose subjective control mechanisms in order to gain military support in internal conflicts. As Huntington notes:

> Antigovernmental war encourages civil-military relations different from those stimulated by inter-state conflict. Other things being equal, the more a state achieves a system of objective control the more effective it is in providing for its external security and in conducting foreign wars. Domestic war, on the other hand, demands subjective control. In particular, in the post–World War II period the strategies of deterrence and of limited war

not only required types of military forces that were of little use in internal wars, but they also tended to demand a relationship between military institutions and the government opposite to that required by internal war.[31]

An internal threat to the military institution from the state and society will unify it, but with an inward orientation, making direct military intervention in politics more likely. There is some evidence that increasing factionalization within the military leads to more coup attempts, but the bulk of the evidence suggests that cohesion, successful coups, and military rule are highly correlated.[32] Finally, civilian and military ideas and cultures will be at great variance. Given that most of the threats to states in the Third World are internal, it is not surprising that civilian control of the military there has been so uncertain and military intervention into politics so frequent.[33]

Sustained military intervention in politics gives rise to something of a paradox, however. While threats to the military institution increase its cohesion and thereby its ability to seize power, the task of ruling eventually reduces that cohesion and results in the military's withdrawal from power.[34] The explanation of the paradox appears to lie in the nature of coalitional politics within the military. It appears to be relatively easy to forge a consensus among military officers on questions of "high politics" (e.g., protection of the institution and its core values), but it is more difficult to achieve consensus on matters of "low politics" (e.g., economic development strategies and the nature of the political regime). As Stepan puts it:

> Military unity . . . is weakest in regard to . . . detailed political and economic development policies, because these normally lie outside the professional domain of the officers, and as such, outside the realm of unquestioning obedience or established military doctrine.
>
> Military unity . . . is strongest when one of its central principles, such as military discipline, is threatened from outside.[35]

What this suggests is that not only do increasing threats produce greater cohesion, but decreasing threats undermine cohesion. The reason is that factions, even in highly professional armies, do not simply disappear. They are papered over during times of high perceived threat to the institution, only to reappear when that threat is gone.[36] When factionalism reappears, it is difficult for the military to continue ruling without further institutional decomposition.

The most difficult cases for a structural theory involve states facing indeterminate threat environments, such as low external and low internal

| | | External threats | |
		High	Low
Internal threats	High	Experienced leaders? Divided civilians Unclear control? Unified military? Unclear orientation? Divergent ideas? (Q3)	Inexperienced leaders Divided civilians Subjective control Unified military Internal orientation Divergent ideas (Q4)
	Low	Experienced leaders Unified civilians Objective control Unified military Outward orientation Convergent ideas (Q1)	Inexperienced leaders? Divided civilians Unclear control? Divided military Unclear orientation? Divergent ideas? (Q2)

FIGURE 3 Predictions of Structural Theory for Intervening Variables

| | | External threats | |
		High	Low
Internal threats	High	|---------|---------| military civilian (Q3)	| military (Q4)
	Low	| civilian (Q1)	|--------------------| mixed civilian (Q2)

FIGURE 4 Anticipated Range of Outcomes for Civilian Control of the Military

threats (fig. 2, Q2) or high external and high internal threats (Q3). A state facing low internal and external threats may have a civilian leadership without knowledge, experience, or interest in military affairs. Civilian policy-makers may abandon objective control. Civilian institutions may not be very cohesive. Factionalism can also emerge within the military institution, and the military's orientation may be uncertain. The lack of clear threats may reduce the military's cohesiveness, making it less capable of concerted collective action. Civilian and military ideas may not remain in harmony. Hence, we should expect low-level civil-military conflict to emerge. The problem is likely to be one of coordination rather than insubordination, because not only will the military, the state, and society be divided from one another, but they will also be divided internally. This means that many conflicts will pit one civilian-military coalition against another, rather than simply civilians against the military. Civilian control of the military in these circumstances can range from good to mixed.

Civilian control of the military in a high internal and high external threat environment is also complicated. A challenging security situation may bring experienced and knowledgeable civilian leaders to power, but it may not. A heightened internal threat may lead civilians to adopt subjective control mechanisms. Competing internal and external threats may cause splits within and among civilian institutions. A high level of threats may unify the military, increasing its capacity for effective action. But because it faces both internal and external threats, the military's orientation may not be clear. The military may recognize that if it ignores the external threat and seizes power, the nation will likely suffer military defeat, and for this reason soldiers will probably be inclined to remain outside politics. Civilian and military ideas may not be in harmony. On the other hand, civilian leaders may embrace the military's view of international politics, and civilian and military ideas may remain in harmony. In this case, then, we should expect to find serious problems with civilian control, but fewer than in a low external and high internal threat environment. The reason is that while the military's orientation may be uncertain, the presence of intense internal and external threats can render the military more unified and more capable of concerted action.

Figure 3 shows the expected values of the intervening leadership, organizational, state, and societal variables, while figure 4 provides the anticipated level of civilian control for each threat environment.

Military Doctrine

Although knowledge of structural circumstances is necessary for explaining different patterns of civilian control of the military, at times it is not sufficient. Structure tends to establish parameters; actual outcomes are sometimes determined by other factors. In quadrants 1 and 4, structure shapes outcome to a large extent directly. In quadrants 2 and 3, structure is not fully determinate; other possible determinants are domestic ideational variables such as military doctrine. Doctrine determines which military resources will be employed, how they will be used, and where. There has been widespread attention in the security studies literature to the external consequences of military doctrine,[37] but little discussion of the internal consequences.[38] Military doctrine can affect civilian control in structurally indeterminate environments by one of three routes. Acting as a proxy for structural threats, doctrine can influence the structure of military institutions, provide normative "road maps" for military behavior, or serve as a focal point for agreement between civilian and military leaders.[39]

Military doctrines can affect civilian control by shaping the structure of military organizations. As Andreski notes:

> There exists an intrinsic incompatibility between the internal and the external uses of armed forces. In other words: the more often the armed forces are used internally, the less capable they become of waging a war; and secondly (when the military participation ratio is high) the more intensely they are—or have recently been—involved in a war, the less amenable and dependable they become as tools of internal repression.[40]

Training and resources geared toward one mission are generally not immediately applicable to another. One clear implication of my argument is that internally oriented militaries should be harder to control than externally oriented ones. Therefore, externally oriented military doctrines should be more conducive to civilian control, while internally oriented doctrines should undermine it. External orientation is a necessary, though not always sufficient, condition for firm civilian control of the military.

Another way military doctrine can affect civilian control is through its effect upon the military's organizational culture. Organizational culture is the "pattern of assumptions, ideas, and beliefs that prescribe how a group should adapt to its external environment and manage its internal affairs."[41] One important component of military organizational culture is norms of subordination to civilian control. If these norms are deeply embedded, civilian control will be much stronger.[42]

Finally, military doctrine can affect civilian control of the military as a focal point for the convergence or divergence of civilian and military ideas about the use of force and the international environment. Huntington has argued that much about civil-military relations in the United States can be explained by the clash of two fundamentally different mind-sets: military realism and civilian liberalism. The former is premised on a skeptical view of human nature, rates the needs of society above those of the individual, values order and hierarchy, assumes the centrality of the nation-state and military force in international relations, advocates the discriminate use of force, and affirms a strict separation between the "military" and "civilian" realms. In contrast, civilian liberalism usually opposes the use of force, advocates either no use of force or the maximum use of force, and regards the military as a potential threat to liberty, prosperity, democracy, and peace.[43] In a challenging external security environment, civilian and military ideas will converge on realism. In a less threatening environment, civilian liberalism is more likely to emerge and come into conflict with military realism, weakening civilian control.

Selection of Cases for Study

intuition behind my structural theory is the observation that cl____ g external threat environments (defined by participation in war) an____ ivil-military relations (defined by absence of coups) seem to go han____ d. States in regions with relatively challenging external threat envir____ s and relatively benign internal threat environments tend to have ____ ilitary coups.[44] Of course, coups are not the only, or even the best, measure of civilian control, especially in developed democratic states. In fact, by focusing just on this most extreme breakdown of civilian control of the military, analysts risk biasing their findings.[45] We need a more fine-grained analysis, which can only come through in-depth case studies. Case studies will also allow us to go beyond simple correlation and illustrate causation through process tracing.[46]

There are four clusters of cases in this book, each of them illustrating the consequences of a different structural threat environment.

(1) During the Cold War, the United States and the Soviet Union faced few internal threats but significant external ones (fig. 5, Q1). This threat environment produced the most consistent and reliable civilian control of the military. I shall argue that this was also the case with Japan in 1945 and Brazil and Argentina after the Falklands War.

(2) In the post–Cold War period, the United States and Russia face declining external threats (fig. 5, Q2). These cases, plus Argentina (1955–66), Brazil (1961–64 and 1974–82), Chile (1970–73 and 1978 to the present), and Japan (1922–32), illustrate how the shift from a challenging external threat environment to a more benign one weakens civilian control of the military. They also demonstrate how military doctrine affects civilian control of the military in structurally indeterminate threat environments.

(3) Germany during World War I, France during the Algerian crisis, Japan during the interwar period, and the Soviet Union for a brief period

| | External threats | |
	High	Low
High	SU 1986–91 Ger 1914–18 FR 1954–62 Japan 1932–1945 (Q3)	ARG 1966–72 ARG 1976–82 BRA 1964–74 Chile 1973–78 (Q4)
Low	US 1941–45 US 1948–89 SU 1955–86 Japan 1945 BRA 1982– ARG 1982– (Q1)	RUS 1991– US 1945–47 US 1989– ARG 1955–66 BRA 1961–64 BRA 1974–82 Chile 1970–73 Chile 1978– Japan 1922–32 (Q2)

Internal threats (row label, left side)

FIGURE 5 Detailed Case Studies

in the late 1980s all faced significant external and internal threats (fig. 5, Q3). Because of the structural indeterminacy of such a threat environment, various aspects of a state's military doctrine can play a greater independent role than they otherwise would: civilian control of the military will be firm if the military's primary focus is the external threat; it should weaken if the main focus shifts to the state's internal problems. The military's perception of which threat is more pressing will be a function of its doctrine.

(4) From the mid-1960s to the late seventies and early eighties, the southern Latin American states of Argentina, Brazil, and Chile faced few external threats but many internal ones (fig. 5, Q4). This threat environment produced the antithesis of civilian control of the military: military rule.

These four clusters provide us with a total of twenty-three cases.[47] Within these cases, there are 127 data points. Three of the clusters have obvious policy relevance, and all are of clear historical interest. But the primary reason for their selection was to have sufficient variation on the independent variable—threat.[48] In addition, the majority of these countries represent "most likely" cases for Lasswell's "garrison state" theory: they are all highly developed states, most with long histories of involvement in international conflict. Like the United States and the USSR, Germany and France were both involved in major wars and periods of international tension. Interwar Japan would also seem to be a "most likely" case for Lasswell's garrison state theory. The southern Latin American countries, although technically part of the Third World, are among the most highly developed of Third World states and have historically been parties to serious international conflict, so they should also be hard cases for my theory. Thus, if my structural theory of civilian control of the military holds up when applied to these cases, it will have earned at least a modicum of credibility.

In sum, although this book is not strictly an exercise in comparative theory-testing because many of the domestic-level theories are subsumed in my structural theory, the cases examined can help us evaluate Lasswell's and Andreski's very different arguments about the impact of a challenging international threat environment on civilian control of the military. The cases in the following chapters do two things. First, they show that there is a correlation between the various combinations of my independent, or causal, variables (the internal and external threat environments) and changes in the dependent, or caused, variable (the strength of civilian control of the military), as predicted by my theory.[49] Second, they show through process tracing how different combinations of external and internal threats affect the intervening individual, military, state, and societal variables in the manner the theory anticipates.

Chapter 3

Losing Control?

Civil-Military Relations in the United States during and after the Cold War

The end of the Cold War coincided with a marked deterioration in the relations between civilian authority and the military leadership in the United States. While characterization of this as a "crisis" in civil-military relations is unwarranted, it is clear that civilian control of the U.S. military is weaker than in the Cold War period. This seems surprising from the Lasswellian perspective: the United States was a model of stable civil-military relations during the Cold War, and it should have become easier for civilians to control the post–Cold War U.S. military rather than harder.

To explain this puzzling development, most of the scholarly literature on U.S. civil-military relations and much of the current policy debate employ one or another domestic explanation of the kind discussed in the previous chapter. However, these explanations by themselves do not quite fill the bill. Major changes have occurred in the international system since 1989; individual leaders, military organizations, state institutions, and society are affected by external developments, so it makes sense to investigate whether and how the changing international security environment may have affected patterns of civilian control of the military.

I propose that the U.S. executive branch's firm control of the military during World War II and the Cold War was largely a function of the more challenging international threat environment (fig. 6, Q1). During these periods, the United States had civilian leaders who were knowledgeable about, and attentive to, military affairs. The institutions of civilian government were strong. Civilian leaders generally relied upon objective control mechanisms. The military was highly cohesive, but it was externally focused. Finally, civilian and military ideas about the use of force and the nature of international politics were compatible.

The post–Cold War period has seen a number of cases in which military preferences prevailed over those of civilians, and this, I believe, is a result of the less challenging international threat environment (fig. 6, Q2). The United States now has a civilian leadership with much less interest in, and experience with, military affairs. The institutions of government are far less effective. Civilian leaders are relying increasingly on subjective control mechanisms. The American military has become more deeply divided, and its orientation is now less clear. Finally, civilian and military cultures and ideas are widely at variance.

The following sections will examine U.S. civil-military relations during World War II, the Cold War, and the present. World War II was a high external and low internal threat environment (fig. 6, Q1); the Cold War was generally a moderately high external and low internal threat environment (Q1); and the post–Cold War period is a lower external and low internal threat environment (Q2). In none of these periods did the United States face significant domestic threats. In each case, the patterns of civilian control correspond to the dynamics of the structural theory laid out in chapter 2. In addition, I will go beyond correlation and show through process tracing that individual, military organizational, and state and societal institutional variables in these periods had the characteristics that the structural theory anticipates.

The Threat Environment and Civilian Control of the U.S. Military

For most of its history, the United States has conformed to the general patterns of civilian control of the military predicted by the structural theory. The Founding Fathers expressed anxieties about a standing military; Samuel Adams argued that

> a Standing Army, however necessary it may be at some times, is always dangerous to the Liberties of the People. Soldiers are apt to consider themselves as a Body distinct from the rest of the citizens. They have arms always in their hands. Their Rules and Discipline is severe. They soon become attached to their officers and disposed to yield obedience to their Commands. Such a power should be watched with a jealous Eye.[1]

| | | External threats | |
		High	Low
Internal threats	High	(Q3)	(Q4)
	Low	1941–45 1948–89 (Q1)	1945–47 1989–present (Q2)

FIGURE 6 The U.S. Threat Environment since 1941

From the beginning of the republic, American political leaders took steps to ensure that a standing army would not pose a threat to domestic liberty. But in the less challenging international security environment immediately after the Revolutionary War, civilian control of the nascent American military was shaky. In 1783 a group of former army officers hatched the abortive "Newburgh conspiracy" with the objective of crowning George Washington king. In the same year, the Society of the Cincinnati was formed by other Revolutionary War veterans to press their claims for preferential treatment, causing much civilian consternation. Finally, in April 1783, troops in Pennsylvania revolted in protest against wage arrears. Things did not improve until after 1790, when the Indians and the Barbary pirates became significant external threats.[2]

The Civil War period, a complex security environment characterized largely by internal threats, saw a number of serious civil-military conflicts. Not only was there the famous exchange between President Lincoln and Army of the Potomac commander General George McClellan about the latter's reluctance to launch offensives against the Confederate Army, but there were also concerns about General Ambrose Burnside's activities in Ohio. Even the Confederacy experienced problems with civil-military relations.[3]

The U.S. experience in the latter half of the nineteenth century was different, however. Samuel Huntington characterizes the years between the Civil War and the Spanish-American War, when there were few internal or external threats, as a "golden age" for U.S. civil-military relations because the military was so small and isolated that it could professionalize without civilian interference.[4] The U.S. military embraced as its model the externally oriented Prussian military;[5] this affected its relationship with civilian leaders, which was so harmonious that many scholars today assume that civil-military relations have never been a major concern for American policy-makers. As Walter Millis and his coauthors have ob-

served, the main concern for civilian leaders in the United States historically has not been to prevent a coup, but rather to limit military influence
upon national policy.[6] But to fully assess my theory, we need to look at
three more recent periods in some detail.

Civil-Military Relations during World War II

Before World War II, there was widespread concern that American democracy and a large standing army were incompatible. The best-known
articulation of these fears was, of course, Harold Lasswell's "garrison
state" thesis. Many scholars believe that the American military ran the
war, with Roosevelt merely a passive observer. Millis and his coauthors
noted that "Roosevelt rarely overruled JCS [Joint Chiefs of Staff], apparently only two or three times."[7] But the truth is that civilian control was
never in question during World War II.[8]

One notable example was the debate between FDR and his military
advisors over Operation Torch, the decision to invade North Africa rather
than Europe in 1943. Army chief of staff General George C. Marshall and
most of the other senior American military leaders vigorously opposed the
North African invasion, but FDR overruled their objections. Torch succeeded in capturing 275,000 Axis troops (more than the Soviets took at
Stalingrad), diverted thirty Axis divisions to Italy, and postponed Operation Overlord (the invasion of France) by a year, ensuring its success.[9] In
this and many other civil-military debates, FDR regularly prevailed over
military objections and generally made the right strategic decisions.

In the appendix, I have identified most of the significant disagreements
between U.S. civilian leaders (primarily Roosevelt) and military leaders
(usually the JCS) during the World War II period. Despite the increasing
influence of the military as a result of the buildup for war, the preferences
of civilian authorities prevailed in all twenty-eight cases. From major decisions, such as which theater should have priority, to minor ones, such
as whether the U.S. military representative in the Soviet Union should be
promoted, Roosevelt and other civilian leaders succeeded in getting the
JCS and other military leaders to do what they wanted. The United States
was a model of military subordination to civilian authority in this period.

The reasons for this were consistent with my structural theory. The
challenging international threat environment brought to power a civilian
leadership experienced in, and attentive to, military affairs. The civilian
government was highly unified under Roosevelt's wartime leadership. For
the most part, FDR relied on objective control mechanisms. The military

leadership under Marshall was quite cohesive, and the services were externally focused. Finally, there was little divergence between military and civilian attitudes toward the use of force and the nature of the international system.

Civil-Military Relations between World War II and the Cold War

A good example of how a less challenging international threat environment weakened civilian control was Truman's effort to combine the services immediately after the war: the president was forced to accept a compromise. According to his advisor George M. Elsey:

—President's intention was merger
—We are not getting merger . . .
—We have three services, headed nominally by a 'Secretary' with no staff, no tool, no control.[10]

By the time of the famous March 1948 meeting at Key West, Florida, Secretary of Defense James Forrestal finally forced the JCS to draft "Functions of the Armed Forces and the Joint Chiefs of Staff," which would define the "roles and missions" of the four services.[11] But it was not until the 1949 revision of the National Security Act that the strengthening of the Department of Defense became the major focus in efforts to unify the services. As the Cold War heated up, civilian efforts to consolidate control of the military were somewhat more successful. Even so, the famous "revolt of the admirals" in 1949—which was precipitated by Secretary of Defense Louis Johnson's decision to cancel the Navy's supercarrier in favor of the Air Force's B-36 heavy bomber and which led a number of high-ranking Navy officers to criticize Truman's defense reorganization plans in Congress and through the media—made clear just how deeply divided the newly joined military services were.[12]

Civilian efforts to improve the status of black Americans in the military gave rise to another conflict. Despite considerable de facto integration during the war, it was not until Truman's Executive Order 9981 of July 1948 that civilian leaders undertook a sustained effort to end racial segregation in the military. Truman's motives were largely political: he needed black support in the 1948 elections. Desegregation faced stiff military, congressional, and public opposition. Military leaders resisted integration for fear that it would undermine unit cohesion. But the manpower shortages of the Korean War forced them to experiment with integrated units, which fought as well as all-white units and far better than all-black units. In the early 1950s, military resistance to desegregation ended, though public and congressional opposition continued.[13]

Civil-Military Relations during the Cold War

The Cold War witnessed some variation in the level of external threat, but it was generally a challenging international environment. It was also a period of relatively firm civilian control. The appendix identifies thirty instances of civil-military conflict during the Cold War. In only three or four cases did military preferences prevail; more than 90 percent of the time, civilian control was firm.

The most famous case was President Truman's relief of General Douglas MacArthur during the Korean War after MacArthur took it upon himself to dictate terms for an armistice to the Chinese.[14] This incident is usually portrayed as one of the most serious breakdowns of civilian control in U.S. history, but on closer examination it actually demonstrates the robustness of civilian control. In the final analysis Truman had the complete support of the JCS, and the general's significant congressional and public support was not decisive.[15] Truman prevailed and the conflict never represented a real threat to civilian control.

During the early years of the Cold War, when military influence ought to have been at its pinnacle, civilian leaders were regularly able to force the military to accept lower defense budgets than it requested (see table 1). In fact, this was the case throughout the Cold War. Even though the Chiefs routinely pleaded their case before a sympathetic Congress, the more austere presidential defense budgets were rarely amended in any direction but downward.[16] The politics of Cold War defense budgeting testify to the strength of civilian control.

Yet another instance of Cold War civilian-military disagreement concerned the conduct of the war in Vietnam. The military was not enthusiastic at first about the commitment of U.S. ground forces in Southeast Asia.[17] And even after the civilian leadership persuaded them that vital national interests were at stake, military leaders had serious reservations about civilian strategies for the ground and air wars. For the ground war, they would have preferred that President Johnson mobilize the reserves; for the air war, they advocated attacking all priority targets immediately. In both cases they were overruled.[18] Johnson did not mobilize the reserves, and he capped U.S. ground-force commitments at 525,000 troops. The president and his civilian advisors also withheld authorization to attack

TABLE 1

U.S. Military versus Civilian Defense Budgets (in billions of dollars)

Fiscal Year	Military	President	Actual Budget
1949 (supp.)	9	3	3.48
1950	29.4	15	16.9
1951	13.5	13.5	12.2
1952	56	56	56
1953	71(JCS) 55(DoD)	52	47
1960	50(JCS) 43.8(DoD)	40	40

Sources: Lawrence J. Korb, *The Joint Chiefs of Staff: The First Twenty-five Years* (Bloomington: Indiana University Press, 1976), 97–111; and Stephen E. Ambrose, *Eisenhower: Soldier and President* (New York: Touchstone Books, 1990), 478.

all the priority targets at once, hoping that a gradually escalating air campaign would bring the North Vietnamese to the negotiating table.[19] In both cases, civilian preferences for a strategy of limited war prevailed over military preferences for all-out war. Military discontent became so intense that the JCS reportedly considered resigning en masse in the summer of 1967. The Chiefs ultimately decided not to take this drastic step in the middle of a war.[20] Like the Truman-MacArthur conflict, the Vietnam War demonstrated the strength of civilian control, not weakness. (It also provides evidence that firm civilian control does not always produce effective national policy.)

A few times during the Cold War, military preferences appear to have prevailed over civilian preferences. As discussed above, in the ambiguous external threat environment between the end of World War II and the Korean War, civilian control was less firm. Likewise, some analysts have detected evidence of increasing civil-military tension during the period of détente.[21] One example was military resistance to SALT I.[22] Another was President Carter's decision to withdraw U.S. military forces from the Korean peninsula in May of 1977: military resistance ensured that few troops were ever actually withdrawn.[23] Détente did not last long enough to produce many instances of civil-military disagreement, but such tensions continued in the 1980s. For example, the JCS seem to have been successful in thwarting the Reagan administration's efforts to prepare to fight a protracted nuclear war.[24] Some scholars also believe that resistance by the U.S. military dissuaded the Reagan administration from using force against the Sandinista regime in Nicaragua and the Castro regime in Cuba in the early 1980s,[25] though biographer Lou Cannon claims that Reagan himself ruled out using military force against either Cuba or Nicaragua.[26]

But when one considers the complete record of civilian-military conflict from World War II to the end of the Cold War, it is remarkable that despite considerable friction, civilian preferences nearly always prevailed. Looking back over the Cold War, one is forced to agree with military historian Allan Millett:

> [One] cannot assert that military organizational preferences or the advice of senior military officers have dominated foreign policy decisions, let alone domestic policy. . . . Despite successive buffetings administered by civilian leaders and foreign enemies, the American system of civilian control has shown a resilience and strength that few predicted thirty years ago.[27]

During the Cold War, the United States generally had a top civilian leadership that was experienced with, and attentive to, military affairs. The civilian leadership was unified, the president exercising control of the military largely with the support of Congress. U.S. presidents during the Cold War generally relied on objective control mechanisms. The top military leadership was also unified, but it was externally oriented. Finally, civilian and military ideas about the use of force and the nature of international politics were generally in sync.

Civil-Military Relations in the Post–Cold War Period

Some analysts believe that there is a serious crisis in post–Cold War U.S. civil-military relations. They point to a number of alarming developments. Late in the Bush administration, former JCS chairman General Colin Powell assumed an unprecedented political role, publishing opinion pieces in the *New York Times* and giving interviews on issues that ought to have been decided by civilian leaders, such as whether the West should intervene militarily in Bosnia.[28] More recently, President Clinton was forced to retreat from his efforts to change the U.S. military's exclusionary policy on gays and was the object of harsh personal criticism from many members of the uniformed services, including sailors who heckled him on the USS *Theodore Roosevelt* and a high-ranking Air Force officer in Europe who called him a "dope-smoking . . . skirt-chasing . . . draft-dodging" commander in chief.[29] A member of Clinton's transition staff reportedly snubbed another high-ranking Army officer.[30] The country was treated to the spectacle of Clinton's secretary of defense–designate, retired admiral Bobby Inman, accepting the nomination only after deciding that his "level of comfort" with the president was high enough.[31] Senator Jesse Helms, chairman of the Senate Foreign Relations Committee, questioned Clinton's fitness to serve as commander in chief and hinted that military hostility toward the president was so intense that if Clinton went ahead with a planned visit to a military installation in North Carolina, he "better have a bodyguard."[32] These incidents suggested to some analysts that the relationship between U.S. civilian and military leaders was at an all-time low. Are the pessimists correct?

From one perspective, there is no crisis because there is little danger that the U.S. military will launch a coup d'état and seize power. Nor is it likely to become openly insubordinate and disobey direct orders. Many of the issues of civil-military friction cited above are minor and likely to be transitory. Moreover, U.S. civil-military relations are unlikely to become as bad as those of the coup-plagued regions of the Third World, or even as prickly as in contemporary Russia, because although the institutions of civilian authority in the United States have come under strain, they are still comparatively robust. There also remain external missions for the U.S. military, and even the new nonmilitary missions being pushed by civilians only faintly resemble those being foisted upon the new Russian Army or those usurped by the "New Professional" armies of Argentina, Brazil, Chile, and Uruguay during the 1960s and 1970s. Finally, the "Powell Doctrine" (which limits the use of the U.S. military to short, decisive conflicts with overwhelming public support) continues to emphasize an external focus for the U.S. military.

But while the United States was a model of stable civilian control of the military during the Cold War, there are compelling reasons for thinking that this has changed since the Cold War's end. The new era has seen the rise to power of a generation of American civilian leaders having little experience with, or interest in, military affairs. This came at a time in which the institutions of civilian government have weakened. Civilian leaders also seem inclined to try to politicize the military. Military unity has decreased, while interservice rivalry has increased. The major external missions that served to keep the U.S. military outwardly focused and subordinate to civilian authority have become less important. Though there are certainly many external threats remaining, they possess neither the scope nor the magnitude of the Soviet threat. Finally, civilian and military ideas about the use of force and the nature of the international system have diverged. The troubling side of the Powell Doctrine is that it asserted a greater military role in decisions about when, where, and how to use force; undermined long-standing norms of military subordination to civilian authority; and highlighted how different civilian and military ideas about the use of force have become. In short, with the end of the Cold War, a number of the pillars of firm civilian control of the military have begun to crumble.

The markedly less challenging post–Cold War international security environment witnessed mixed civilian control of the military. On the one hand, the civilian leadership succeeded in getting the military to accept significant reductions in defense spending.[33] Also, the Bush administration was able to overcome military reservations about an early commitment to offensive operations during the Persian Gulf War.[34] Bush also ignored military concerns about diverting military aid to Israel during the war.[35] Bush and Defense Secretary Richard Cheney had little trouble firing Air Force chief of staff General Michael Dugan after he made some unauthorized remarks about coalition air strategy in the Gulf.[36] Bush put a quick end to the ground war despite General Norman Schwarzkopf's objection that the Iraqi army had not yet been completely destroyed.[37] The Clinton administration eventually overcame the military's resistance to intervention in Haiti.[38] Finally, Clinton's Republican secretary of defense, former senator William Cohen, defeated Air Force chief of staff General Ronald Fogelman's efforts to protect a subordinate's career after a Department of Defense (DoD) investigation concluded that he was negligent in the Khobar Towers bombing in Saudi Arabia that killed a number of American military personnel.[39] To be sure, the U.S. military has not had things all its own way since the Berlin Wall came down.

On the other hand, in comparison to the Cold War period, there have been more instances when military preferences prevailed. Two social issues deeply divided civilians from military leaders. The perennial debate about women in combat sprouted again during the Clinton administration. Secretary of the Army Togo West pushed for a complete end to restrictions on women in combat. The JCS made a few token concessions, chiefly opening more specialties to women, while simultaneously calling for a "pause" in further concessions in the combat arms of the services.[40] The case of the women-in-combat debate should be classified as an instance in which civilians had only mixed success in getting the military to do what they wanted. In addition, an acrimonious debate erupted in the Navy over the role of women on combat ships and aircraft.[41] Finally, a series of sexual harassment scandals rocked the Army.[42] In the case of Air Force Lieutenant Kelly Flinn's separation from service for adultery, the top Air Force leadership was able to pressure Air Force Secretary Sheila Widnall into not giving her an honorable discharge.[43]

A more clear-cut case was the bitter struggle to get the military to end its exclusionary policy on homosexuality. During the 1992 election campaign, candidate Bill Clinton advocated ending all restrictions on homosexuals in the military. Elizabeth Drew suggests that this policy was not forced on a reluctant Clinton by gay rights advocates, but was something to which he was personally committed.[44] Once in office, he continued to push for change. Clinton ran into stiff military opposition (based primarily on fears that open homosexuals in the military would undermine small-unit cohesion in combat)[45], which had some support among influential members of Congress. The president was forced to accept the "compromise" policy of "don't ask, don't tell"—initially formulated by General Powell—which was supposed to make it possible for discreet homosexuals to continue to serve.[46] In fact, both critics and supporters agree that this new policy represents little real change.[47] Some also believe that this episode set the tone for Clinton's subsequent relationship with military leaders and that he has spent much effort since then trying to appease them.[48] Nothing could illustrate this more clearly than Clinton's subsequent appointment of General Barry McCaffrey as "drug czar": McCaffrey was the officer snubbed by Clinton's transition staffer, and once the issue had been made public, Clinton went out of his way to try to make up for it.

The military seems to be prevailing not just on social issues, but on operational matters as well. There is mounting evidence that military foot-dragging on direct intervention in Bosnia forced civilians in the Clinton administration to delay plans for a larger U.S. military role in that conflict for nearly four years and until conditions met the military's terms for going in. In his memoirs, former Secretary of State James Baker characterized a June 1992 meeting to discuss military options in Bosnia as "one of the most spirited [he] had ever attended as Secretary of State."[49] He clashed head-on with Powell, who not only vehemently opposed any use of force in Bosnia but was willing to publicly fight that battle with the civilian leadership more stridently than any of his predecessors. And even after agreeing to go in, the military still resisted civilian pressure to pursue war criminals vigorously.[50]

In addition, the military withstood congressional pressure to seriously rethink service roles and missions.[51] Military dissatisfaction with former secretary of defense Les Aspin's post–Cold War military strategy of "win-hold-win" resulted in the United States' adopting a more ambitious strategy of "win-win," which is probably not sustainable under the current defense budget.[52] Powell stated that he "was determined to have the Joint Chiefs of Staff drive the military strategy train."[53] Indeed, there has been a growing consensus that despite the Pentagon's Quadrennial Defense Review, the United States is still spending far more than it needs to on defense.[54] Finally, both President Clinton and Vice President Gore, both supporters of a ban on land mines, have been unwilling to challenge JCS opposition to such a ban.[55]

Admittedly, we can draw only tentative conclusions so early in the post–Cold War period, and some of these issues are relatively minor. But this preliminary review suggests that while there is no crisis, civilian control of the military has weakened after the Cold War. Also, many instances of successful post–Cold War civilian control came during the Gulf War; during periods of true peace, civilian control looked much worse. This trend is alarming because a number of serious issues—further deep cuts in budgets and force posture and additional interventions—loom ahead. If civilians could not win on social issues, such as "gays and gals," they are unlikely to prevail on operational ones, such as strategy and force posture.

Assessment of the Theory

What explains this post–Cold War weakening of civilian control? While changes in the political and military leadership, in the military organization, and in state and societal institutions are important, these changes are ultimately rooted in the altered international threat environment. The predictions of my structural theory about the effect of a changing international threat environment on military and state institutions have been borne out.

It is tempting to blame the current problems exclusively on the Clinton administration. Among post–World War II administrations, it has been one of the least adept at dealing with the U.S. military, precisely at a time when the top military leadership has become far more politically savvy.[56] However, it seems unlikely that a candidate with no military credentials, such as Clinton, would have been elected in a high external threat environment such as the Cold War. Foreign and defense policy issues played little role in the 1996 presidential election.[57] Harry Truman likewise had trouble imposing his will upon the U.S. military in a less challenging external threat environment. Finally, even Republicans—such as William

Cohen, Clinton's second-term secretary of defense, and Republican members of Congress—also experienced some post–Cold War difficulty in dealing with the military.[58]

Some observers claim that the most important reason for the post–Cold War difficulties is the increased power of the chairman of the JCS after the passage of the Goldwater-Nichols legislation of 1986.[59] It is true that this reform has played a part in the problems of civilian control, but it does not completely explain them. Throughout the Cold War, even after the enactment of Goldwater-Nichols, civilian control was seldom challenged. During the Gulf War, as we saw, George Bush had little trouble bending the military to his will when it came to prewar and wartime strategy. The difficult issues in recent U.S. civil-military relations—intervention in Bosnia, post–Cold War U.S. military strategy, and the integration of women and gays into the military—all occurred in the lower external threat environment of the post–Cold War period. Institutional change in the military cannot by itself account for the problem. We need to look to international explanations as well.

Others argue that because Congress has played a key role in many issues central to the post–Cold War difficulties, the problem is not really one of civil-military relations but is primarily a conflict between civilian branches of government.[60] There is also merit to this argument. The Constitution gives Congress some authority to regulate the military in peacetime, and the new Republican Congress was eager to challenge the Clinton administration over national security policy.[61] But although congressional resistance to presidential dominance of military policy has been constant, it has not always weakened the chief executive's authority.

During the Cold War, Truman prevailed on the divisive issue of integrating blacks into the military; Clinton clearly failed to get substantial change in the military's exclusionary policy on homosexuality after the Cold War. On both black and homosexual integration, powerful members of Congress opposed change, but this opposition played a role only in the latter case.[62] Truman finally prevailed during the Korean War, Clinton did not after the Cold War. And had there not been serious military opposition to changing DoD policy on homosexuals, Congress could not have thwarted Clinton on this issue: congressional efforts to prevent retention of HIV-positive soldiers failed in the face of unified presidential and JCS opposition to the measure.[63] As another example, when MacArthur tried—with substantial congressional support—to expand the Korean War, he was thwarted and then relieved by Truman. But in the post–Cold War period, Powell, also with congressional support, succeeded in limiting U.S. military involvement in the Bosnian civil war.

Much of the current congressional activism is doubtless a result of the "congressional revolution" of the 1970s. But if that were all, civilian control of the military should have been weakest in the post-Vietnam era, which was the apogee of congressional assertiveness in foreign and defense policy. Behind the increasing post–Cold War activism of Congress is the reduced international threat environment.

Important changes have also occurred in American civilian governmental institutions. Though still fairly robust, these institutions have come under some strain in recent years. Many scholars are convinced that this is a result of the end of the Cold War.[64] Weak civilian governmental institutions certainly complicate civilian control of the military.

In addition, civilian leaders now seem to be embracing subjective control of the military, moving to exert influence in a number of areas previously regarded as being within the military's exclusive purview. From the major effort to get the military to redefine the concept of "civil-military relations" to Clinton's use of the "campaign flags" during the 1992 election, the evidence suggests that civilians are trying to politicize the military.[65]

The American military is becoming more internally divided over such issues as the shrinking budget and future "roles and missions." The military is also now plagued by the same culture wars that are deeply dividing American society.[66]

The U.S. military's traditional external focus also seems to be changing. Civilian leaders have asked the military to take greater responsibility for such internal missions as antiterrorism activities, narcotics interdiction, disaster relief, and riot control, which are less conducive to military professionalism on the old pattern. There is increasing discussion within the military about domestic operations in the United States.[67]

Finally, decreased external threats have allowed civilian and military cultures and ideas about the use of force and about international politics to diverge markedly.[68] Nothing could illustrate this divergence better than the acrimonious debate about the Powell Doctrine, the U.S. military's post–Cold War blueprint for the use of force under very restrictive conditions.

Military Doctrine

In the structurally indeterminate threat environment of the post–Cold War era, military doctrine has played a major role in weakening civilian control of the U.S. military. A clear example is the military's willingness to use force only under the conditions elaborated in the Powell Doctrine.[69] While the Powell Doctrine is for the most part externally focused, it has nonetheless undermined civilian control, by asserting a greater domestic role for the military in foreign policy decision-making. This has led Robert Kaplan to conclude that the American military, "in all but a technical sense, is no longer ordered anywhere. It is a self-interested bureaucracy with the power of negotiation."[70] Moreover, the Powell Doctrine undermines military organizational norms of subordination to civilian authority. As Powell notes in his memoirs, the U.S. military learned an important institutional lesson from the Vietnam period:

> As a corporate entity, the military failed to talk straight to its political superiors or itself. The top leadership never went to the secretary of defense or the President and said, "This war is unwinnable the way we are fighting it." Many of my generation, the career captains, majors, and lieutenant colonels seasoned in that war, vowed that when our turn came to call the shots, we would not quietly acquiesce in half-hearted warfare for half-baked reasons that the American people could not understand or support.[71]

This lesson did not cause intense civil-military conflict until the post–Cold War era led civilians to push for the use of the military in operations other than war. Finally, the Powell Doctrine makes clear that civilian and military ideas about the use of force have diverged substantially. General Powell not only vehemently opposed any use of force in Bosnia, but he was willing to make his case far more forcefully against civilians than were previous military chiefs.[72]

Clearly, the less challenging international threat environment of the post–Cold War period has weakened civilian control of the U.S. military. While explanations based on leaders' personalities and on changes in military organization, state institutions, and society can account for some of the variance, they are not sufficient; the overarching causal factor is the changed international security environment. All of the structural theory's predictions about how the changed international security environment should affect the intervening variables of military and state institutions seem to have been accurate in the case of the United States.

Two possible objections might be raised against my argument. First, some believe that the security environment has become more, rather than less, challenging with the end of the Cold War. John Mearsheimer argues that the shift from bipolarity to multipolarity and the continuing anarchical nature of the international system will make it less peaceful and therefore more threatening.[73] However, most other analysts believe that although we are not witnessing the end of history, the contemporary international security environment is indeed less threatening.[74] During the Cold War, the United States was locked in an intense ideological struggle with an adversary possessing significant nuclear and conventional forces. Today that ideological struggle has largely been won, and while the United States still faces conventional and unconventional threats to its security, the stakes are widely recognized to be far smaller. A report issued by the House Armed Services Committee under Congressman Les Aspin in 1992 concluded that there had been a "decline in the magnitude of the military threats America faces."[75] While pessimists such as Mearsheimer may be vindicated in the long run, for the foreseeable future the end of the Cold War means a significant reduction in international security competition among the developed states of the world.

Second, others have challenged the view that civilian control of the military has deteriorated since the end of the Cold War. Powell himself dismissed reports of civil-military conflict, while General William Odom, former director of the National Security Agency, said that although there was conflict, it was nothing new.[76] "Since coming to this job this past year," observed former JCS chairman General John Shalikashvili in 1994, "I'd say the relationship between the military and the President has only improved."[77] Many active-duty officers I have spoken with share these sentiments, and at least some civilian analysts agree.[78] But the evidence I have presented in this chapter makes it clear that civilian control of the U.S. military has weakened in the post–Cold War period.

Conclusions

A state facing a significant external threat and few internal threats is likely to have firm civilian control of the military: the military will regularly do what civilian leaders want it to do. In contrast, a state facing a diminishing external threat and few internal threats is likely to have less firm civilian control of the military. The danger is not that the military will launch a coup or engage in outright insubordination; it will simply be harder for civilians to get the military to do what they want when civilian and military preferences are in conflict.

During World War II and the Cold War, the United States faced a relatively challenging external security environment and was able to maintain relatively firm civilian control of the military. As it entered the less challenging threat environment of the post–Cold War era, controlling the military became more difficult. Things have not been all bad: though civilian leaders have had trouble getting the military to undertake significant social changes and to think seriously about changing roles and missions, they have succeeded in obtaining deep cuts in force postures and spending levels. In short, post–Cold War civilian control of the military has been a mixed bag, as my structural theory predicts.

Chapter 4

Controlling Chaos

Civilian Control of the Soviet and Russian Militaries

During the Cold War, the Soviet Union, like the United States, was a model of civilian control of the military.[1] Some Western scholars assumed that this historical legacy would persist after the breakup of the Soviet Union.[2] This optimistic assessment has not been shared by all analysts, however. Paul Goble notes that "the Russian Army, or at least its senior leaders, have enormous and relative to Soviet times, autonomous power relative to the society and to the current political elite even though the military is mired in all too obvious financial and organizational difficulties."[3] This has also been a recurrent theme in respected Western periodicals such as the *Economist*.[4]

Most Russian civilian leaders have been even more pessimistic. In January 1995, former Acting Prime Minister Yegor Gaidar decried President Boris Yeltsin's growing dependence on the military.[5] In May 1995 Duma Defense Committee chairman Sergei Yushenkov suggested that recent changes in conscription and foreign policy and increases in the defense budget signaled the growing influence of the Russian military.[6] Yekaterina Lakhova of the Party of Women argued that the Duma has little real control of the military.[7] Both former foreign minister Andrei Kozyrev and former CIS (Commonwealth of Independent States) defense minister Yevgenii Shaposhnikov maintained that the Russian military is not fully under civilian control.[8] Russians from across the political spectrum—including Sergei Shakrai, Yegor Gaidar, Aleksandr Lebed, Vladimir Zhirinovsky, and Gennadii Zyuganov—have warned of the danger of a military coup d'état.[9] Russian journalists, too, have noted the weakening of civilian control. "Never before in Russian history," Aleksandr Zhilin argues, "has the army been so close to the helm of the ship of state."[10]

My position is that while the Russian Army is unlikely to launch a coup, civilian control of the Russian military, compared to that during the Soviet period, has been at best mixed. The firm civilian control of the Soviet military was in large measure a result of the challenging external threat environment of the Cold War (fig. 7, Q1). Such a threat environment was conducive to civilian control because it fostered a civilian leadership that was attentive to military affairs, highly cohesive, and reliant upon objective control mechanisms. It also produced a military that was unified but externally oriented. Finally, it led to a convergence of civilian and military ideas about the use of force and the nature of the international system.

We should not be surprised, then, that with the end of the Cold War, the military has become less amenable to civilian control. Russia now has a civilian leadership that is far less experienced in, and concerned about, military affairs. Civilian leaders are far less unified now than in the Soviet period, and they increasingly rely on subjective control mechanisms. The Russian military is also less unified than was the Soviet military, and its orientation is uncertain. Finally, civilian and military ideas about the use of force and the nature of the international system are now widely at variance. This leads me to expect that civilian control of the Russian military will continue to be mixed,[11] with consequences less dramatic than a coup d'état but still significant in terms of manpower levels, budgets, conscription, the use of force, foreign policy, military doctrine, the political role of the military, and military reform.

The Cold War and Civilian Control
of the Soviet Military

The Cold War was for the Soviet Union a period of few domestic but significant international threats. As the structural theory predicts, Soviet civilian leaders were generally able to exercise firm control over their military.[12] Despite his important support for Nikita Khrushchev against Khrushchev's political rivals, Marshal Georgii Zhukov was dismissed in 1958. In 1961, chief of the General Staff Marshal V. D. Sokolovskii and commander in chief of the Warsaw Pact Marshal I. S. Konev were fired for opposing Khrushchev's conventional force reductions. The civilian leadership also overruled defense minister Marshal Andrei Grechko's suggestion

		External threats	
		High	Low
Internal threats	High	1986–1991 (Q3)	(Q4)
	Low	1955–1986 (Q1)	1991–present (Q2)

FIGURE 7 Soviet and Russian Threat Environments

to launch a preemptive strike on the nascent Chinese nuclear program in 1969. Throughout the 1970s, the civilian leaders overcame military opposition to various arms control agreements. In 1979 they overruled military objections to greater Soviet military involvement in Afghanistan. In 1982, at the height of the second phase of the Cold War, Communist Party General Secretary Leonid Brezhnev denied the military larger budgetary allocations. In 1984 Marshal Nikolai Ogarkov was fired for his criticism of the civilian leadership's failure to increase defense spending. While there are some examples of military influence—such as Zhukov's support for Khrushchev in 1957, and the appointment of Marshal Grechko rather than the civilian Dmitri Ustinov as minister of defense in 1967—the general pattern during the Cold War was firm civilian control. Clearly, the Cold War was not a period of military predominance, as the Lasswellian model would suggest.

Why did the Cold War strengthen civilian control? For one thing, the civilian leaders tended to be quite attentive to military issues. For the most part, the civilian institutions of the Soviet regime—especially the Communist Party of the Soviet Union (CPSU)—were robust.[13] Soviet civilian leaders generally relied on objective control measures.[14] Though the Soviet military had occasionally played a role in domestic politics, either in power struggles or in internal policing, it was mainly externally oriented.[15] Finally, Soviet civilian and military cultures were largely in sync. In these circumstances, firm civilian control of the military was overdetermined. But circumstances changed dramatically with the end of the Cold War.

The Soviet Military's Ambivalent Response to Perestroika

The period of *perestroika* (restructuring) saw both external and internal threats to the Soviet military (fig. 7, Q3). The Cold War was a continuing

TABLE 2
Outcomes of Soviet Civil-Military Conflicts

Issue	Civilians	Unclear	Mixed	Military
Zhukov supports Khrushchev			X	
Zhukov ouster	X			
Sokolovskii, Konev ousters	X			
Grechko MoD				X
China nuclear	X			
Détente arms control	X			
Ustinov MoD	X			
Afghanistan	X			
1980s budgets	X			
Ogarkov ouster	X			
Perestroika	X			
August 1991			X	

external threat. The numerous fundamental changes fostered by perestroika constituted something of an internal threat to the military's core values: maintenance of political order, skepticism about the political process, intense Russian nationalism, and a Hobbesian view of both domestic and international politics.[16] *Glasnost* (openness) allowed antimilitary voices to speak freely. It also facilitated the rise of nationalist and ethnic movements, which threatened the viability of the Soviet Union. Gorbachev began to assert civilian authority in military affairs, such as doctrine and force posture,[17] and significantly reduced military spending.[18] His foreign policy led to numerous unilateral Soviet arms control initiatives, the breakup of the Warsaw Pact, the loss of forward positions in Eastern Europe, and the unification of Germany.[19] All these developments threatened the institutional interests of the Soviet military. Why, then, did the military refrain from actively opposing perestroika and, in some cases, even go along enthusiastically?

The answer is that because of its externally oriented military doctrine, many in the military shared Gorbachev's desire to reform the stagnant civilian economy of the Soviet Union; and many officers were sincerely interested in exploring some of the same programs that civilian reformers were advocating. True, there were very different motives on each side, so the alliance was bound to be only temporary.[20] The motives of Gorbachev and his coterie of "new thinkers" have been thoroughly analyzed elsewhere; suffice it to say that from their point of view, perestroika meant a whole new way of doing business both internationally and domestically.[21]

To the extent that perestroika was instrumental, it was intended mostly to save money.[22] For most military officers, on the other hand, reform and a relaxation in tensions were means to obtain a breathing space in the on-going military competition with the West, which they believed was moving in an entirely new direction.[23]

This new direction in the arms race was the result of a perceived change in the international distribution of technological capabilities caused by what the Soviets called the *nauchno-tekhnicheskaia revoliutsiia* (NTR), or scientific-technological revolution.[24] According to one Soviet military officer,

> a revolution in the material basis for conducting war has occurred out of the scientific and technical progress. . . . In the past, the development of military affairs was chiefly influenced by individual discoveries or inventions. At present, the relationship between scientific-technical progress, weapons production and the organizational development of the Armed Forces has become immeasurably more diverse and profound than was the case previously. . . . The new scientific-technical discoveries and advances encompass literally all types of weapons and military equipment, forming a unique causal chain between science and production.[25]

What made the NTR especially important for the Soviet military was its potential for changing the nature of warfare.

The NTR aroused consternation among Soviet officers because they perceived that in many areas of high technology, the West was pulling far ahead of them. These fears were reasonable, because the United States was superior in sixty-seven categories of militarily relevant technology, there was rough parity in thirty-one, and the Soviets were ahead in only twenty-eight.[26] Soviet concerns about this were evident as early as the 1973 Yom Kippur War and were intensified by the lopsided outcome of the Israeli-Syrian air battle over the Bekaa Valley in 1982.[27] The threat was really brought home to the Soviets as they watched the incorporation of conventional high technology into NATO's strategy of AirLand Battle, and it was dramatically reconfirmed by the outcome of the Gulf War.[28]

Initially, some analysts thought that the Soviet Union's technological backwardness would strain relations between civilian and military authorities.[29] In fact, the NTR led many Soviet officers to support domestic reform despite its threat to their institutional interests. The Soviet military reacted both externally and internally to the perceived shift in the international distribution of military capabilities, with important consequences for both international relations and domestic civil-military relations.

The appropriate response was not immediately clear, however. Some in the Soviet military advocated balancing the West's qualitative lead by a quantitative buildup. This was the Soviet strategy from roughly the late 1960s until the late 1970s. But it was costly and unsuccessful, perhaps even counterproductive. The Soviet military's next response, advocated by chief of staff Marshal Nikolai Ogarkov and his followers, was to try to incorporate high technology and change Soviet conventional strategy to match.[30] This also failed; the Soviet Union lacked the requisite technology. The final response, which took shape in the late 1980s and continued until recently, was to support, however reluctantly, both domestic reform and Gorbachev's policy of accommodation with the West.

Other changes wrought by perestroika that at first glance might have seemed to cut against military interests were in fact compatible with them. Although the motives of military proponents of defensive operations were very different from those of the "new thinkers," there was some convergence on actual policy. Many Soviet officers undoubtedly mourned the demise of the Warsaw Pact, but others realized that the costs had long exceeded the benefits of keeping Eastern Europe within the Soviet empire. Brigadier General John Reppert, U.S. military attaché at the U.S. Embassy in Moscow in the early 1990s, told me that he had had many conversations with Soviet military officers about their belief at the time that withdrawal from Eastern Europe was "inevitable." He said that they did not oppose it for three reasons: First, there was agreement that the cost of maintaining the empire was too high. Second, chief of staff General Mikhail Moiseyev and other officers believed that they could defend Soviet national interests without Eastern Europe, especially given the size of the Soviet nuclear arsenal. Finally, Soviet military officers anticipated that the disintegration of the Warsaw Pact would be followed by the collapse of NATO.[31] Interestingly, the major objections raised by Soviet military leaders focused mainly on whether cuts and withdrawals should be unilateral or bilateral, rather than whether they should take place at all.[32] Many in the Soviet military were thus probably content to let civilian reformers take the lead in addressing the serious problems facing the country. Moreover, Gorbachev's diplomacy gave even inveterate Cold Warriors in the military a breathing space to find a way to catch up with the West.

In short, the domestic threat to the military from perestroika was balanced by the external threat from the West's lead in high technology. The Soviet military was still animated by an outwardly oriented military doctrine, which fostered a professional culture that accepted civilian control. Civilian and military leaders agreed on the need for dramatic economic and political reform, although for very different reasons. Thus, despite the chaos of perestroika, civilian control of the Soviet military remained relatively firm.

Evidence of Increasing Civil-Military Conflict during the Late Gorbachev Period

By the end of the Gorbachev period, the marked easing of the Cold War, combined with continuing internal problems, led to increased civil-military tensions. As a result of perestroika, the Soviet military became deeply politicized at all levels. This politicization gave the military an increasingly internal focus. In addition, certain aspects of perestroika now began to seem more threatening to the military. In a speech to a closed session of the Soviet parliament in June 1991, Defense Minister Dmitrii Yazov pointed out that as a result of rising nationalism in the various Soviet republics, the army was short 350,000 conscripts that year. More than 15,000 officers were without apartments because of withdrawals from Eastern Europe.[33] These developments led even military officers originally promoted by Gorbachev to oppose him.[34] On January 25, 1991, Gorbachev ordered Soviet military units to begin supporting the militia in maintaining domestic order not only in the republics, but in Russia itself.[35] All these factors set the stage for the August 1991 coup attempt.

There were two major precipitants of the coup attempt. There was, of course, long-standing hard-line opposition to perestroika. The mood of hard-liners was clearly conveyed by Colonel Viktor Alksnis, a member of the Soyuz faction of the Supreme Soviet: "Indeed, our country, which was once listed as a superpower only a short while ago and made its voice heard on the world scene, is on its knees. Over the past six years the series of blunders and miscalculations by the architects of *Perestroika* has led to a situation in which our country resembles a disaster area hit by a destructive storm."[36] The immediate reason for the coup, however, was hard-line dissatisfaction with the so-called Novo-Ogarevo process, which was leading to a new treaty of union and would have replaced the heads of the military and the KGB.[37]

The exact role of the Soviet military in the August coup is still uncertain. Initial press reports suggested that the coup leadership was dominated by the military.[38] Scenes of tanks and troops on the streets of Moscow seemed to support this contention. Although the coup was planned and executed mainly by the KGB and its chief, Vladimir Kryuchkov,[39] some

Soviet military officers also participated. Defense Minister Yazov was the chairman of the Committee for the State of Emergency, which sought to replace Gorbachev.[40] Ground Forces chief General Valentin Varennikov— whose command stood to lose much as a result of the reforms—was part of the group that visited Gorbachev in the Crimea demanding either his support for the committee or his resignation.[41] Even Gorbachev's personal military advisor Marshal Sergei Akhromeyev was so deeply compromised that he committed suicide after the coup failed.[42] The General Staff chief Moiseyev was on "vacation" when the coup began. Gorbachev later admitted that significant portions of the Soviet military either actively or passively supported the coup.[43] Only RSFSR Defense Committee chairman General Konstantin Kobets, Airborne Forces commander General Pavel Grachev, Air Force commander Colonel General Yevgenii Shaposhnikov, and, after some hesitation, Leningrad Military District commander General Viktor Samsonov actively opposed the coup.[44]

There are many reasons why the coup should have succeeded, including the economic crisis, increasing hard-line disenchantment with Gorbachev, and the military's loss of prestige and resources. Given all these, the question is why the coup failed and why the Soviet military did not play a more active role.

Several explanations have been advanced.[45] Some Western commentators and Russian leaders, such as Boris Yeltsin, suggested that widespread popular resistance brought the coup down.[46] In fact, the evidence indicates that most Russians—like the bulk of the military—sat on the sidelines and passively awaited the outcome.[47] Others, including Gorbachev, argued that it was the extent of democratization that "predetermined" the failure of the coup.[48] But considering the course of political developments in the Soviet Union in late 1990 and early 1991, during which Gorbachev moved decidedly to the right, it is not clear that democratization was advancing across the board. A few Western analysts of the Soviet Union argued that it was the professionalization of the Soviet military that kept it out of the coup.[49] There is some truth to this explanation, but it fails to account for the involvement of some senior military officers in the attempt to seize power. A full explanation for the failure of the coup must include other factors.

Another possible explanation is that the military remained deeply divided over perestroika and its alternatives and therefore could not play a decisive role one way or the other.[50] Certainly, had large sections of the military decided to support the coup, they could have overwhelmed any opposition. According to Yeltsin's military aide General Konstantin Kobets, "If [Yazov] wanted, he could pulverize everything standing in the way of the armed forces."[51] But the military failed to act collectively at important moments. For example, the Russian Parliament was never stormed because the fifteen-member Collegium of the Defense Ministry refused to withdraw its troops from Moscow. Some units even defected to Yeltsin's side.[52]

The Soviet officer corps was faced with a painful choice. If the officers supported the Emergency Committee, they risked splitting the army along political and ethnic lines. But if they allowed the coup to fail, the Soviet Union might disintegrate. Given the available evidence, the failure of the August coup must be attributed to lack of military support, a result of residual military professionalism and a lack of unity. This lack of unity was caused by conflicting institutional interests in a changing domestic and international threat environment, which failed to provide clear guidance one way or the other to the Soviet officer corps. For all that, the Soviet military did play a role in the transition from Gorbachev and the Soviet Union to Yeltsin and the Commonwealth of Independent States (CIS).[53]

Prospects for Civilian Control of the Russian Military

The end of the Cold War and the breakup of the Soviet Union have left Russia facing few external threats but some potential internal threats (fig. 7, Q2, but close to the border with Q4). There is widespread recognition that the external threat environment has become less challenging. One former General Staff officer noted, "I don't see any real, any serious threat from the Western Powers."[54] So far, the Russians have not identified any new external threats comparable to that from the West during the Cold War.[55] The external missions of the Cold War have largely evaporated, removing a powerful reason for military subordination to civilian authority.

One of the few remaining external missions is the defense of ethnic Russians in non-Russian areas of the former Soviet Union.[56] This might be characterized as a new external mission, since it involves military activity outside the territory of Russia. On the other hand, it does not entail operations against other militaries, and because it involves issues central to contemporary Russian domestic politics, it is much more akin to an internal military mission. An appropriate historical analogue might be the role of the French Army in Algeria between 1954 and 1962. Unfortunately,

these latter-day missions are likely to have similarly deleterious consequences for civilian control of the military. The problem is not only that
many Russian Army units are still in these regions as a result of Soviet
deployments, but also that the fate of ethnic Russians has become a cause
célèbre for hard-line Russian politicians.[57]

Although the Russian military is facing a more benign external threat
environment, the internal threat environment is potentially challenging.
As the Chechen uprising demonstrates, the threat of secessions remains
significant.[58] Other potential internal threats from crime, social instability, and political chaos, in combination with the inward-looking military
doctrine put forward in November 1993, could set the stage for even
greater problems of civilian control.[59] As with the United States, we may
ask: When Russian military and civilian preferences diverge, who prevails?
While the record of post–Cold War civilian control of the military in Russia has been mixed, it seems clear that the Russian military has been less
amenable to civilian control than was the Soviet military.[60]

Size of the Armed Forces

The Russian military clearly did not get what it wanted in terms of levels
of manpower. Since the spring of 1992, the position of civilian politicians
in the Supreme Soviet, the Duma, and even the Yeltsin administration has
been that the Russian Army should number no more than 1 percent of the
population of the Russian Federation, or about 1.5 million men and
women. In October 1993, after the assault on Parliament, former minister of defense General Pavel Grachev said that the minimum size of the
army should be 2.1 million. In March 1994 Grachev argued that 1.9 million was the absolute minimum. In July he amended this number again,
stating that he could live with 1.9 million until the end of 1996, after
which 1.5 million would be acceptable. In October 1994 he lowered his
estimate yet again—to 1.7 million until the end of 1995, after which 1.5
million would be the target. Thus it has been the position of the Russian
military, and especially Grachev's position, that has had to change. This
continued to be the trend under Grachev's successors, Generals Igor
Rodionov and Igor Sergeyev.

But the overall predominance of civilian preferences in this area must
be qualified. For one thing, in December 1994 Yeltsin said he would cut
the Ministry of Defense (MoD) staff by 30 percent, yet it remains nearly
twice the size of the Soviet MoD. For another, the number of generals in
the Russian Army has grown (to more than 1,800), despite the shrinking

of the total forces. This has left the Russian Army with one general for each one thousand troops, an extremely high ratio. Manpower levels are on the rise again. Finally, it is not clear that the military has been completely forthright with the civilian leadership about the true size of the armed forces.

Defense Spending

Defense spending is another issue on which the Russian military has not had things its own way. That is a little surprising, since the MoD expected increased defense spending after supporting Yeltsin against Parliament in October 1993. Since then, the military has not gotten a substantial increase in spending, but instead has gone deeply into debt, has had power shut off at various installations for nonpayment of electric bills, has experienced recurrent problems paying its employees, and has even had some of its budgeted funds withheld by the Ministry of Finance (MoF).

In fiscal year 1994, the MoD requested 87 trillion rubles. The Duma eventually approved a budget of 37.1 trillion rubles, ultimately increased to 40 trillion. Grachev was so unhappy that he made an unprecedented public appeal for increased defense spending. In 1995 the MoD proposed a defense budget of 115 trillion rubles, which was countered by an MoF budget of only 60 trillion. The Duma eventually approved a budget of 55 trillion, to which an additional 10 trillion was later added. Deputy Prime Minister Oleg Soskovets ordered the MoF to pay its debts to the MoD, and Yeltsin said that the military budget would not be cut in the future. The 1996 budget was larger than the previous year's. This allotment of 76 trillion rubles, representing 20 percent of central government expenditures, was supplemented with an additional 12 trillion rubles. Still, neither Grachev nor First Deputy Minister of Defense Andrei Kokoshin was completely satisfied. Grachev's successors continue to be unhappy with this low level of funding.

While in general civilian preferences seem to have prevailed over those of the military in recent budgets, there are some reasons for thinking that things are not quite as bad as the military makes them out to be. First, it appears that the military is only loosely constrained by the defense budget in its actual expenditures. Second, defense budgets as a percentage of central government expenditures are still quite high—20 percent, or 40 percent if paramilitary forces are included. Third, the Russian government itself projects that it will increase defense spending from 3.7 to 5.5 percent of GDP (gross domestic product) by the year 2000. Fourth, military spending is sometimes hidden in other accounts. Finally, Yeltsin encouraged "off-budget" means, such as arms sales, to make up for reduced budgets. The bottom line is that the defense budget has been bad for the military, but perhaps not as bad as it first appeared.

The Draft

On conscription, the Russian military may have gotten something more than civilians were initially disposed to give. In August 1993, in the run-up to his confrontation with Parliament, Yeltsin promised that he would increase the number of contract troops in the Russian Army. But by November 1995, Grachev had changed his mind about such heavy reliance on contract troops because of their cost, and instead he began pushing for more conscripts. This has proved to be extremely controversial.

The Soviet/Russian military experienced some very lean draft years between 1989 and 1994. The main problem was that public enthusiasm for serving in the military evaporated. In 1978 more than 78 percent of draft-age males polled said that they "would be pleased to serve in the military." In 1995 only 12 percent responded positively. This lack of enthusiasm has been manifested in widespread draft dodging and a proliferation of categories of exemption from service. In December 1994 the Yeltsin administration increased the penalties for draft dodging from a few rubles to a multiyear jail term. But this was hardly sufficient to make up for the increasingly small cohorts of draft-age males, so the military pushed for two additional changes: a decrease in the number of deferments and an increase in the term of service, from eighteen to twenty-four months.

Reflecting public hostility to these changes, Prime Minister Viktor Chernomyrdin initially refused to consider them. When the Duma finally voted to decrease the number of deferments and increase the term of service, it did so in secret. Though the final outcome did not completely accord with the wishes of the military, it got most of what it wanted. The military continues to resist a transition to an all-volunteer army and insists upon continued conscription.

Chechnya

The conduct of the war in Chechnya is an issue that has divided the military against itself and against civilians. High-ranking military officers, such as deputy ministers of defense General Georgii Kondratyev and General Boris Gromov, and former commander of the Russian Fourteenth

Army Lieutenant General Aleksandr Lebed, sharply criticized the initial decision to escalate Russian involvement to direct military intervention in December 1994. On December 15 and 16, Major General Ivan Babichev, commander of one of the Russian columns moving on the Chechen capital of Grozny, refused to advance in the face of nonviolent opposition from civilians. In early January 1995 there were press reports from Ekaterinburg that an entire Ministry of Internal Affairs special-forces unit (OMON) refused to remain in Chechnya. In mid-January 1995 General Eduard Vorobyov refused to assume command of Russian forces in Chechnya. Altogether, more than five hundred Russian military officers refused to fight in the breakaway republic.

If Chechnya divided the Russian military, it nevertheless increased the personal influence of then–Defense Minister Grachev. Grachev took advantage of criticism of the war by military rivals, such as Generals Gromov and Kondratyev, to oust them. He also turned civilian criticism of the army's performance in Chechnya into a rationale for increased defense spending. Although civilian leaders such as Prime Minister Chernomyrdin and Yeltsin's envoy Arkadii Volskii pushed for a negotiated settlement, Grachev derailed these efforts and also managed to sidetrack a Duma bill withdrawing troops from Chechnya. And he got his way on the conduct of military operations there. For example, on January 4, 1995, Yeltsin ordered a halt to aerial bombing of Chechen civilians, but it continued unabated. Both the military and the Ministry of Internal Affairs (MVD) forces denied any involvement in the continued bombing, but investigation revealed that unauthorized bombings of the Chechen cities of Roshuichu, Dargo, and Beklgatoi were carried out by Russian Air Force units based in Tbilisi, Georgia, under the command of a close Grachev ally, General Fyodor Reut. Civilian leaders demanded that the perpetrators be punished, but they have not been. Moreover, President Yeltsin subsequently adopted the hard-line military strategy he had previously rejected.

In March 1996 Yeltsin tried to impose a cease-fire, but Grachev and other top military officials resisted. Even after Grachev's ouster by his rival Aleksandr Lebed in June 1996, military resistance to civilian efforts to achieve a cease-fire in Chechnya continued, and in fact intensified in the summer of 1996. In June of that year, the commander of Russian forces in Chechnya, Lieutenant General Vyacheslav Tikhomirov, openly challenged the government's policy of withdrawing from the area. Yeltsin had trouble securing Tikhomirov's resignation. In July, Russian forces in Chechnya launched an unauthorized offensive against Grozny. And even after the military officers agreed to a cease-fire, they continued to undermine it. On the conduct of the war in Chechnya, the military—or at least Grachev—seems to have prevailed over civilians.

Conventional Forces in Europe Treaty

Although the Conventional Forces in Europe (CFE) treaty enjoyed wide support within the Soviet and Russian civilian leaderships, the Russian military has never really been happy with it. The issue was not conventional arms control per se or the treaty itself. Rather, after the breakup of the Soviet Union, the Russian military increasingly argued that flank restrictions in the Leningrad and North Caucasus Military Districts, which made sense when there was a Soviet Union, now unfairly impinged on Russia's national security.

Civilian leaders in the Ministry of Foreign Affairs, after supporting the treaty for years, did a 180-degree turn in April 1995 and came around to the military's position that the treaty had to be amended. In the same month, the Russian military created the Fifty-Eighth Army, which was based in the North Caucasus Military District. By November 1995 it had become apparent that the Russian military was virtually ignoring CFE limits east of the Ural Mountains, and the Russian Army's top armor officer, General Aleksandr Galkin, publicly stated that former president Gorbachev's "political commitment" to CFE was no longer in Russia's national interest. Former defense minister Rodionov suggested linking adherence to CFE to NATO's not expanding.

Other Forces

One important obstacle to any serious military threat to civilian rule has been the division of the "security forces." The MoD controls approximately 1.7 million men and women in the Russian Army, Navy, Air Force, Air Defense, and Strategic Rocket Forces, while another 2.3 million are in paramilitary units controlled by the Ministry of Internal Affairs, the Border Troops, and other internal security agencies. Yeltsin and other civilian leaders, no doubt guided by the adage *divide et impera,* have been careful to keep these forces divided. For example, Yeltsin recently subordinated the Border Troops directly to his office. In September 1994 he set up a special unit to protect himself, and in January 1995 he proposed establishing a separate national guard to handle internal security missions.

In contrast, former defense minister Grachev continually pushed for the consolidation of all armed forces under the MoD. Despite Yeltsin's consistent opposition to this demand, there were press reports in July 1995 that Yeltsin was considering creating a "superagency" to control all the armed forces and placing Grachev at its head. Grachev's successor Rodionov also consistently pushed for control of all these other forces. If that comes to pass, it will represent not only another victory of military over civilian preferences, but also a potential threat to civilian rule.

NATO Expansion

The Russian position on proposed NATO expansion has been hotly contested, with the Russian military playing a key role in shaping the government's position. Initially, the top civilian leadership was inclined to take a fairly relaxed view of Western proposals to include Poland, the Czech Republic, Slovakia, and Hungary in NATO. During a trip to Eastern Europe in August 1993, Yeltsin stated that he would have no objection if Poland and the Czech Republic joined NATO. This was echoed by Prime Minister Chernomyrdin in November 1993 and by former foreign minister Kozyrev as late as June 1994. In general, the civilian leaders have been more flexible on this matter, as evidenced by their willingness to sign the "Founding Act" agreement in 1997.

The security services and especially the military have consistently registered vigorous opposition. In March 1994, while Chernomyrdin was pushing the NATO Partnership for Peace (PFP) program, First Deputy Minister of Defense Andrei Kokoshin argued that the issue warranted further study. In the same month, Grachev sought to link PFP to NATO recognition of Russian "peacekeeping" efforts in the CIS states. In 1995 the MoD's newspaper *Krasnaya Zvezda* chided Yeltsin for not linking NATO expansion to renegotiation of the CFE treaty. In early 1996 Grachev threatened to shift Russian nuclear deployments and form a countervailing alliance if NATO expanded.

Very quickly, Yeltsin's position on NATO expansion changed. There is much evidence that military opposition played an important role in the shift of civilian attitudes from acquiescence to opposition. By December 1994 Kozyrev was warning that NATO expansion jeopardized Russian participation in PFP. In June 1995 Duma Defense Committee chairman Sergei Yushenkov cautioned that the proposal to expand NATO was strengthening military hard-liners. By the middle of 1995 the MoD's hard-line position opposing NATO expansion had clearly prevailed over the more moderate position of the Ministry of Foreign Affairs. Under Rodionov and his successor Sergeyev, the military continued to vigorously voice its opposition to NATO expansion. The final outcome of this issue remains uncertain, but it seems likely that the Russian military will continue to have a say in the Russian government's position.

Moldova

Military preferences also prevailed with respect to the withdrawal of the Russian Fourteenth Army from the Trans-Dniester region of Moldova. In June 1994 the Ministry of Foreign Affairs position was that no Russian troops would remain in the region. General Lebed, the Fourteenth Army Commander, reacted by saying that he "spit on" the withdrawal agreement.[61] In November 1994 Ground Forces commander in chief General Vladimir Semenov backed Lebed. The Russian military generally ignored the troop withdrawal agreement. And after Lebed was relieved of command, Grachev openly proclaimed that the Russian Army should not withdraw. By June 1995 Yeltsin was siding with the military on this issue as well. By early 1996 Russia had basically repudiated the withdrawal agreement.

Military Bases

Without consulting the Ministry of Foreign Affairs, the MoD launched a major initiative to maintain military bases in the CIS and other countries. In June 1994 Grachev indicated that the Russian military wanted access to bases in Armenia, Azerbaijan, and Georgia. In September he added bases in Tajikistan and Abkhazia to the MoD's wish list. A June 1994 German government report cited this as evidence of growing military influence on Russian foreign policy. In November 1994, then–chief of the General Staff Mikhail Kolesnikov indicated that the Russian military also wanted to maintain access to the electronic intelligence facility in Lourdes, Cuba. Well-connected Russian military analyst Pavel Felgengauer even raised the possibility that deployment of NATO nuclear forces in Eastern Europe might result in the redeployment of Russian nuclear weapons in Cuba. In August 1995 Russia negotiated an agreement with Vietnam to retain access to the base at Cam Ranh Bay.

Black Sea Fleet

The Russian military was an important obstacle to efforts to settle the dispute between Russia and Ukraine over the status of the Soviet Black Sea fleet. In August 1992 Yeltsin and Ukrainian president Leonid Kravchuk agreed to divide the fleet. The Russian military opposed this move, and the fleet was reportedly in a state of near revolt. Civilian hard-liners joined the military in opposition. Yeltsin tried to fire Admiral Eduard Baltin, Russian commander of the Black Sea fleet at the time, but he ran into opposition in the Duma. Finally, in late January 1996, Yeltsin succeeding in ousting Baltin. The issue was resolved at last in 1997, but it was settled largely on the Russian military's terms, with Russia retaining control of 80 percent of the fleet and access to bases on the Crimean Peninsula for twenty years.

Kurile Islands

Russian policy-makers have been deeply divided over whether Russia should return the disputed Kurile Islands to Japan. Yeltsin and the Foreign Ministry have been flexible, while Chernomyrdin and other civilian leaders have been intransigent. In August 1992 the Yeltsin administration proposed withdrawing Russian forces from the islands as a first step toward softening political conflict with Japan. The immediate response of the General Staff was to reinforce the Russian garrison. Yeltsin subsequently adopted the military's position on this issue. In July 1993 he once again tried to assure the Japanese that he would reduce the Russian military presence, but he soon backpedaled from this promise. Moreover, there have been continued military incidents between Russia and Japan in the area, and there is no evidence that the Russian military garrison has been reduced. While it would be an exaggeration to say that the Russian military was completely responsible for Yeltsin's change of heart, its opposition did play an important role in undermining his initial accommodationist stance.

The Baltics

The Russian military has also had significant influence on the terms and pace of its withdrawal from the Baltic states. The position of the Russian civilian leadership was initially not to link withdrawals to social guarantees. In December 1993 Grachev promised that there would be a complete withdrawal in 1994. Soon afterward, however, the Russian military leaders started adding conditions.

First they wanted continued access to the ballistic missile defense radar in Skrunda, Latvia. Next they wanted more time to decommission the nuclear reactors at the naval training facility in Paldiski, Estonia. Then they wanted social guarantees for military pensioners residing in the Baltic states. They also wanted assurances about the rights of ethnic Russians living in these areas. Finally, the military argued that the Baltic states should pay for the construction of housing in Russia for the withdrawing Russian forces. In July 1994 Grachev halted the military withdrawal from Estonia to protest that these demands were not being met. By mid-1994 Yeltsin had embraced his defense minister's demands. Russia finally agreed to pull out of the Baltic states, but only after the military's conditions were met.

Military Doctrine

The Yeltsin administration adopted the final draft of the military doctrine of November 1993, which had been written by the military with very little civilian input, largely to reward the military for its support during the October crisis.[62] When Grachev was asked about whether the Duma might seek to amend the new Russian military doctrine, he is reported to have replied, "We shall amend the parliament."[63]

The Military in Politics

The increasing political role of the Russian military has also become the subject of intense civil-military conflict. One way the military asserted itself was by taking sides in the bitter power struggle between Yeltsin and Speaker of Parliament Ruslan Khasbulatov over control of the Russian government in the spring of 1993. Although some observers thought the Russian military did not play much of a role,[64] a great deal of evidence suggests that despite Defense Minister Grachev's protestations of neutrality, the military was active behind the scenes.

To begin with, high-ranking military officers were reported to have demanded that Yeltsin confront Parliament. During the March 1993 crisis, Yeltsin actively courted military support. Grachev and other senior officers appear to have supported him because they believed that strong presidential rule was in the interest of the military. Grachev and the other "security ministers" made a public display of support for Yeltsin by seeing him off at the airport as he left for the Vancouver summit, and they deliberately remained in Moscow to ensure that a coup did not take place during his absence. Since the results of the April 25, 1993, referendum on the performance of President Yeltsin and Parliament did not really resolve the political conflict in Russia, the military continued to be the key to future power struggles.

In September 1993 an MoD spokesman again said that the Russian military would remain neutral in the conflict between the president and Parliament. But Grachev and General Staff chief Kolesnikov simultaneously assured Yeltsin that the military would support him. Meanwhile, Grachev's close ally Air Force chief of staff General Pëtr Deinken kept in close touch with Parliament during the crisis, and Vice President Aleksandr Rutskoi courted other members of the military. This suggests that the military was initially divided over the issue. Why did the military eventually line up behind Yeltsin?

The Russian military viewed Parliament's actions, especially the attack on the CIS military headquarters, as an attack on itself. When parliamentary leaders appointed General Vladislav Achalov as their minister of defense, there were widespread fears that this might split the military. Moreover, the old parliament had not been all that attentive to military interests: it had, for instance, raised the number of draft exemptions to twenty-one and lowered the level of troops in the military to no more than 1 percent of the population. In the aftermath of the crisis, the former commander of Russian forces in Germany, General Matvei Burlakov, publicly asked what must have been on the minds of many Russian officers—what do we get in return for saving the Yeltsin government?[65]

Further evidence of increasing politicization of the military emerged in December 1993 when it became known that many military officers had cast protest votes in the new Duma elections in favor of ultranationalist Vladimir Zhirinovsky. Throughout 1994 and 1995, there was more evidence that the once-apolitical military was becoming deeply politicized. A 1994 survey sponsored by the Friedrich-Ebert Stiftung showed increasing support among military officers for authoritarian rule in Russia.[66] A 1995 poll by the newspaper *Izvestia* had similar findings.[67] While neither of these surveys revealed much interest on the part of the military in *directly* assuming power, both suggested that there was increasing military interest in playing an *indirect* role.

There have been three serious manifestations of the Russian military's involvement in politics. First, throughout 1995 there was a proliferation of military-political organizations dedicated to advancing various agendas on behalf of military officers. Second, political parties increasingly began actively courting the military vote, in part by including retired and even active-duty officers on their election slates. Finally, and most important, the military has become actively involved in Russian electoral politics. As former Black Sea fleet commander in chief Admiral Eduard Baltin put it, "Generals and officers are obligated to go into politics."[68] The MoD ran its own slate of 123 candidates in the December 1995 Duma elections and spent 500 million rubles to identify and support more than a thousand civilian candidates sympathetic to military interests. The MoD also sought to influence the 1996 presidential elections.

Civilian leaders strenuously objected to this military electioneering. Yeltsin aide Sergei Filatov argued that military involvement in the Duma campaign was illegal and destabilizing. It is indeed worrisome that the Russian military has gone from being apolitical to being thoroughly political. Once-potent norms of military subordination to civilian control have weakened considerably, as evidenced by retired general and current Duma member Lev Rokhlin's call in June 1997 for servicemen to become more politically assertive in order to protect their interests.

Grachev's Tenure

Troubling questions about civilian control were raised by the puzzling longevity of former minister of defense General Pavel Grachev. Any Western defense minister who had been involved in only a fraction of Grachev's scandals and blunders would have been dismissed immediately. But despite frequent calls for his resignation or firing, recurrent speculation about possible successors, and a widespread belief that he has little support within the rest of the officer corps, Grachev remained in office for four and a half years.

Yeltsin had reason to be unhappy with Grachev as early as October 1993. Despite Grachev's promises of support, army troops were slow to move against Parliament, and at the height of the crisis Grachev requested written orders from Yeltsin before he would move. This led Yeltsin's military advisor General Dmitri Volkogonov to predict that Grachev's ouster was imminent. Instead, Volkogonov was removed (although he was later reinstated in an unofficial position).

Throughout 1994, evidence mounted of widespread corruption among the Russian forces in Germany. Yet in August 1994 Yeltsin appointed General Burlakov, the former commander of those forces, to the position of deputy minister of defense. Duma Defense Committee chairman Sergei Yushenkov questioned this "hasty" appointment, but Grachev succeeded in installing his close friend and ally in the MoD. Burlakov and Grachev managed to weather an even more serious scandal in October 1994 when

Moskovsky Komsomolets reporter Dmitri Kholodov, who had been investigating corruption in Germany and the then-covert operation in Chechnya, was killed by a bomb. Suspicion was immediately directed toward the minister and deputy minister of defense. Grachev not only denied the charges but later successfully sued the editor in chief and another reporter from the paper. Despite an ongoing Duma investigation of the corruption charges, Yeltsin defended Grachev throughout this scandal.

In November 1994 Yeltsin tried to fire Burlakov. Grachev defended his protégé, and Burlakov remained in place. Eventually, Prosecutor General Aleksei Ilyushenko concluded that the corruption charges against Grachev and Burlakov were groundless. Despite Grachev's refusal to testify before Yushenkov's Duma committee hearings, the Duma refrained from censuring him. In fact, Grachev went on to criticize Yeltsin for not pushing for larger defense budgets and greater manpower for the army.

Grachev also managed to emerge from the Chechen debacle not only unscathed, but with his position actually strengthened. As noted earlier, he took advantage of opposition to the Chechen operation by some of his military rivals to secure their ouster. Next he attacked civilian opponents of the war, calling Yushenkov, for example, a "vile toad."[69] Grachev also managed to defuse potentially embarrassing revelations by former CIS minister of defense Marshal Yevgenii Shaposhnikov that he had authorized the transfer of weapons to the leader of the breakaway Chechen Republic.

But the most remarkable manifestation of Grachev's durability was his survival of the June 1995 Budennovsk hostage crisis in southern Russia. There are many reports that Yeltsin asked for Grachev's resignation at the time. In the aftermath, however, Grachev was the *only* "power minister" to remain in place. He reportedly survived despite Yeltsin's opposition because he was able to mobilize support within the military. Some have speculated that Grachev may have some other leverage over Yeltsin as well. In an interview, *Moskovskiye Novosti* national security editor Aleksandr Zhilin recounted stories he had heard that the source of Grachev's leverage over Yeltsin was some sort of compromising information and that Yeltsin openly acknowledged this.[70]

Finally, Grachev succeeded in ousting his main military rival, the widely popular General Aleksandr Lebed. In May 1995 Grachev called on Lebed to either step down as commander of the Russian Fourteenth Army in Moldova or resign. Duma deputies from across the political spectrum urged Yeltsin not to accept Lebed's resignation,[71] and the president's prolonged hesitation suggested that he was not eager to accommodate his defense minister. But by June Yeltsin had acceded to Grachev's wishes, and Lebed was out of the military.

Throughout much of 1995, Grachev was virtually running Russian foreign policy, clearly eclipsing Minister of Foreign Affairs Andrei Kozyrev. Though Yeltsin once again publicly expressed his dissatisfaction with the pace of military reform, Grachev remained in office through the June 1996 elections. Moreover, he was ousted only after Yeltsin made Lebed his national security advisor and chairman of the National Security Council. In other words, Yeltsin merely replaced one insubordinate general with another.

Lebed's Influence

Though he was eventually ousted from the army by his rival Grachev, retired Lieutenant General Aleksandr Lebed remains an important figure both in the Russian military and in Russian politics. Lebed has a long history of insubordination, not only toward Grachev but also toward Yeltsin himself. Moreover, he is extremely popular, not just in the military, but among civilians across the political spectrum. This is troubling because the ex-general is not a proponent of democracy. He is an admirer of former Chilean military dictator General Augusto Pinochet and an advocate of an authoritarian solution for Russia. "What's wrong with a military dictator?" he once remarked.[72]

Lebed is quite active in Russian politics: he won a Duma seat in December 1995 and throughout most of that year led the polls for the upcoming presidential race. And despite a poor showing by his party in the Duma elections, Lebed garnered nearly 15 percent of the vote in the June 1996 presidential elections, making him the "kingmaker" in the July runoff. Once Yeltsin appointed him to his administration, Lebed lost little time in wielding his influence. One important manifestation of this was his ultimately successful effort to get his former commander General Rodionov (the "butcher of Tbilisi") appointed minister of defense. Even after Yeltsin finally grew tired of Lebed's insubordination and fired him in October of 1996, Lebed remained by far the most popular Russian politician. For example, a 1997 poll found that 58 percent of Russians trusted Lebed, while only 23 percent trusted Yeltsin.[73] Something is obviously amiss with Russian democracy when one of the country's most influential figures is a rebellious and insubordinate general who admires Pinochet and thinks that Russia is not ready for democracy.

Reform of the Military

One of the long-standing objectives of Russian civilian politicians, including Duma members and Yeltsin himself, has been to reform the Russian military. This would involve reducing its size, rooting out corruption, depoliticizing it, modernizing it by putting it on a professional, volunteer basis, and employing high technology. The military has consistently resisted most of these reforms. Former minister of defense Rodionov argued that they would require more, rather than less, money and that the necessary manpower could only be secured through continued conscription. The issue of reform has not only divided civilians from military officers, it has also divided military officers among themselves. As a result, the pace of military reform will remain glacial.

Civilian Minister of Defense

One of the prerequisites for successful reform of the Russian military is the appointment of a civilian as minister of defense. Military analyst Stanislav Lunev argues that "it is the lack of civilian control which has hindered the process of rebuilding the armed forces."[74] Unfortunately, the likelihood of there being a civilian minister of defense in the near future—the sine qua non of reliable civilian control of the military—is small. The Russian military has so far successfully resisted all such efforts. Former defense minister Grachev once remarked that the military would not "understand" a civilian minister of defense. In 1996, Yeltsin took the symbolic step of "retiring" Defense Minister Rodionov from the military, but for all intents and purposes he was not a civilian minister of defense. Yeltsin dropped all pretense of this when he appointed Strategic Rocket Forces commander General Igor Sergeyev as Rodionov's successor in 1997.

Assessment of the Theory

With the end of the Cold War, civilian control of the Russian military has weakened, rather than strengthened. This clearly confounds the Lasswellian argument and provides support for Andreski's argument that a less challenging external threat environment is not as conducive to civilian control. To see why this is the case, we need to explore how the changing external threat environment affected individual, military organizational, civilian governmental, and societal factors.

TABLE 3
Outcomes of Russian Civil-Military Conflicts

Issue	Civilians	Unclear	Mixed	Military
Armed forces size	X			
Defense spending	X			
Draft			X	
Chechnya			X	
CFE				X
Other forces		X		
NATO expansion			X	
Moldova				X
Bases			X	
Black Sea fleet		X		
Kuriles			X	
Baltics		X		
Military doctrine				X
Military in politics				X
Grachev	?			
Lebed			X	
Reform of military			X	
Civilian minister of defense		X		

Since the mid-1980s, an increasing number of Russian politicians have come to power who are far less sympathetic to the military than their predecessors were. Russian president Boris Yeltsin's relationship with the military has been troubled; it was Yeltsin who, as head of the Moscow branch of the Communist Party, took the lead in June 1987 in castigating the Soviet military for negligence and incompetence in connection with the Mathias Rust affair. (Rust was a West German citizen who flew a light plane into the Soviet Union and landed it on Red Square in hopes of meeting Gorbachev.) A retired Soviet General Staff officer observed, "I know many marshals, generals, and colonel-generals, but apart from [Yeltsin advisor retired General Dmitri] Volkogonov, I don't know any supporters of Yeltsin at all."[75] There are even reports that threats by anonymous Soviet General Staff officers kept Yeltsin from declaring a state of emergency to prevent the convening of the Congress of People's Deputies in December 1992.[76] There has been at least one plot against Yeltsin's life by a military officer.[77] Aleksandr Zhilin reported, "Time and again I have heard officers, from lieutenant to colonel, saying: 'Just tell us who the enemy is, who is preventing us from living a normal life and we'll know what to do.'"[78] Beginning with the Gorbachev administration and continuing into the Yeltsin period, then, the civilian leadership has had tense relations with the military.

In addition, civilian authority and domestic politics in Russia have been anything but stable. The main institution of civilian rule in the Soviet Union—the Communist Party—has collapsed, and nothing comparable has yet replaced it.[79]

Moreover, since the late Gorbachev period, civilian leaders have increasingly come to rely on subjective control mechanisms and have begun to try to exert influence in a number of matters previously regarded as being within the exclusive purview of military professionals. The events of October 1993 are illustrative of this tendency inasmuch as both Yeltsin and the parliamentary opposition tried to cultivate military support.[80]

The unity and cohesiveness of the Russian military have declined precipitously with the end of the Cold War. Military officers are divided over substantive issues, such as reform, as well as over more personal issues, such as corruption.[81]

The orientation of the Russian military has also become uncertain. The external mission of the old Soviet army has become less central for the new Russian Army. The ambiguity of the Russian military's post–Cold War mission is particularly evident in the military doctrine adopted in late 1993. While the doctrine does deal with some traditional external warfighting missions, more than two-thirds of it deals with such nontraditional and internal missions as combating crime, terrorism, ethnic separatism, the narcotics trade, and tax evasion.[82]

Finally, as the Russian military becomes smaller and fewer Russians serve in it, military and civilian cultures are increasingly diverging.[83] For example, only about 16 percent of civilian leaders surveyed in 1993 thought Russia needed "strong authoritarian rule" to survive the "present critical situation," while 62 percent of military officers partially or fully agreed with the statement "Without authoritarian rule we will never come out of the existing chaos."[84]

Military Doctrine

In the less challenging external threat environment of the post–Cold War era, military doctrine has taken on a greater role in shaping the pattern of civil-military relations in Russia. According to Russia's 1993 military doctrine, "[the Russian Federation] regards no state as its enemy."[85] The key point here is not that there are no external threats, but rather that they are not as serious as during the Cold War and the Russian military regards them as only "potential" rather than actual.

On the other hand, a significant internal role for the Russian military has been formalized by this new military doctrine. It points to such internal threats as the rise of separatist and nationalist organizations; attempts to overthrow the constitutional system; attacks on Russian nuclear, chemical, and biological facilities; creation of armed formations; the growth of organized crime; attacks upon military installations in Russia; the distribution of weapons; narcotics; and the uncertain status of some border regions. The military has taken on an increasing role in such purely internal missions as law enforcement and tax collection.[86] More significantly, the new doctrine incorporates the Ministry of Internal Affairs and militia forces, as well as explicitly giving the army an internal security role. Finally, the new doctrine holds that the internal "sociopolitical" conditions of Russia are a matter of concern to the military.[87]

There is some reason to think the Russian military is adopting a broad definition of national security reminiscent of the internally oriented national security doctrines of the military dictatorships of South America. According to the Russian journal *Voennaya Mysl* (Military thought),

> *National Security (general national [obshchenatsionalnaya] security of the CIS)* [is] protection of the individual, society and state (Commonwealth of States) against external and *internal* threats, stability against unfavorable factors, and provision of those external and *internal* conditions of existence which guarantee the possibility of stable, comprehensive progress of society and its citizens.[88]

"In effect," said Zhilin, the new doctrine "sanctions the use of the army in internal political conflicts."[89] Another Russian analyst notes that "despite lengthy mantras against the army's involvement in political processes, despite the doctrine's stated inadmissibility of using the army in the interests of individual groups of people, parties, and public organizations, the army has effectively been given an indirect opportunity to influence the life of society."[90] This bodes ill for future civilian control of the Russian military.

All these changes in the intervening individual, military organizational, state, and societal variables were coincident with the end of the Cold War, and all of them have in different ways contributed to the weakening of civilian control of the Russian military. The Soviet/Russian case thus supports Andreski's argument, and undermines Lasswell's, about the effects of a less challenging international environment on civilian control of the military.

Before closing, let us briefly consider some possible objections to my argument that the Russian military is not under firm civilian control. Many maintain that the abrupt policy changes of the Yeltsin administration are due not to military pressure, but rather to Yeltsin's erratic character.[91] This is possible, but it seems unlikely given Yeltsin's consistent behavior on other issues, such as his strong opposition to the August 1991 coup attempt.

Some argue that the military remains too divided and corrupt to play much of a role in Russian politics. Stephen Meyer suggests that the politicization of the Soviet army divided it and made it a relatively impotent actor in pre-coup Soviet politics.[92] Others agree. "A military that has done so badly is no great danger politically," observes Anders Aslund.[93] Retired Soviet military officer Dmitri Trenin, now a program associate at the Carnegie Endowment's Moscow office, points to the "apparent powerfulness but real powerlessness" of the Russian military.[94] Yet all that is needed for the military to play a significant domestic role is that it be less divided than Russian society in general. Despite its very real loss of combat power, the Russian military is still an important domestic actor.[95] As Heinrich Tiller and Manfred Schroeder conclude, its political influence "is attributable not so much to [the military's] intrinsic importance as rather to the instability of the political system and the low level of competence on the part of the political elites."[96] Increasing domestic chaos and the weakening of civilian institutions could lead to even greater military influence.

Others acknowledge some early problems with civilian control but argue that with the failure of the August 1991 coup, a turning point in the domestic power of the Soviet military was reached.[97] Former defense minister Grachev repeatedly protested that the Russian military was under firm civilian control, a belief shared by some Western analysts.[98] But as I have shown, civilian control of the Russian military has been mixed compared with civilian control of the Soviet military.

Finally, some point out that many civilians also support hard-line policies, which may account for Yeltsin's about-face on various issues. The evidence offered in this chapter suggests, however, that the key reason for changes in government policy has been the extent to which the military has joined the hard-line coalition. Hard-line civilian opposition to liberal policies has been a constant; the variable has been military support.

Conclusions

What, then, can we say about the present state of civilian control of the Russian military? While the likelihood of a coup d'état is quite small given how deeply divided the military has become, there will undoubtedly be more manifestations of low-level military insubordination such as Grachev's outburst of "The President will do what I say."[99] The effectiveness of the Russian Army will also continue to decline without firm civilian control, as the Chechen debacle made crystal clear.[100] The military is likely to remain riddled with corruption. In short, it will be harder for Russian civilian leaders to get the Russian military to do what they want than it was for Soviet civilian leaders to prevail over the Soviet military. The growing internal focus of Russia's military doctrine makes it likely that this problem will continue. In short, compared with the firm civilian control over the Soviet military, civilian control of the Russian military is mixed.

Chapter 5

The Anger of the Legions

The Hindenburg-Ludendorff Dictatorship, the Algerian Crisis, and Interwar Japan

The Hindenburg-Ludendorff dictatorship in Germany (1916–18) and the French civil-military relations crisis over Algeria (1954–62) illustrate what civilian control of the military will be like in states facing both international and domestic threats. While there is some variation in both cases in the actors' perception of the external and internal threat environments, both cases clearly involve states that were facing external and internal threats.

Such a threat environment is structurally indeterminate. The civilian leadership may or may not have come to power possessing experience with, and interest in, military affairs; the strength and cohesiveness of civilian institutions is uncertain; it is unclear what method of control civilian leaders will favor. The level of the military's unity and its orientation are likely to be unclear. Finally, civilian and military ideas about the use of force and the nature of international politics may or may not be in sync.

Because of the structural indeterminacy of this threat environment, various aspects of a state's military doctrine can play a greater independent role than they otherwise would. Civilian control of the military will be firm if the primary focus is the external threat; it should weaken if the military focuses mainly on the state's internal problems. The military's perception of which threat is more pressing will be a function of its doctrine. The legacy of the past is important in explaining what sort of doctrine will be embraced in a structurally indeterminate threat environment.

Cases involving this type of threat environment also provide evidence about how different military orientations affect wartime performance. Internally oriented militaries perform badly in wartime. Externally oriented militaries not only will be more amenable to civilian control, but also are likely to be more successful on the battlefield.

The German and French cases each begin with an examination of the internal and external threat environments—the independent variables—facing the military. Since these situations are structurally indeterminate, there is also a need to examine closely the impact of changing military doctrines. These doctrines affected the intervening variables of the individual, the military, the state, and society. Then the dependent variable—civilian control of the military—is examined by looking at the outcomes of issues on which the civilian and military authorities had divergent preferences. Finally, a brief consideration of interwar Japan, the strongest case for Harold Lasswell's "garrison state" theory, shows that it in fact exhibits most of the patterns of civilian control predicted by the structural theory for a state facing both external and internal threats.

The Hindenburg-Ludendorff Dictatorship during World War I

The Hindenburg-Ludendorff dictatorship in Germany during World War I demonstrates how the presence of both internal and external threats complicates civilian control of the military. As the threat environment was indeterminate, an internally oriented military doctrine played a crucial role in weakening civilian control by pushing the German military ever deeper into domestic politics after 1916.

Threat Environment

A state at war is, by definition, always facing something of an external threat. But perceptions of that threat can vary over the course of the war. Such variations in threat perception directly affected civilian control of the German military during World War I. Civilian control of the military reached its lowest ebb at precisely the time when many military officers and some of the civilian leaders believed that the war was going well.[1] During the periods in which the external threat was perceived to be the most challenging (1914–16 and August 1918 through the end of the war), the German military was most responsive to civilian control.[2]

After the initial optimism of August 1914 had faded, the German mil-

External threats

		High	Low
Internal threats	High	Aug. 1914 to 1918 (Q3)	(Q4)
	Low	(Q1)	(Q2)

FIGURE 8 The German Threat Environment in World War I

itary remained pessimistic about how the war was going for the first two years. By 1916 the German military had become more optimistic about the external threat environment. In 1917 there was a widespread sense among Germans that the course of the war had shifted in their favor. This belief was not completely groundless: 1917 saw an improvement in the Austro-Hungarian military position; the thwarting of France's Neville offensive in March and April and the subsequent mutinies throughout the French Army; the defeat of the Russians' Brusilov offensive in July; the defeat of the Italian offensives in October; and the Bolshevik seizure of power in November. This led to Germany's receiving peace overtures from Russia. In addition, the Germans had unleashed unrestricted U-boat warfare, and the United States, despite having declared war, had not yet had much military impact in Europe. General Erich von Ludendorff, the First Quartermaster General of the German Army and its de facto commander in chief, thought that 1918 would be an even better year.[3] Although by May 1918 the Oberste Heeresleitung (the German High Command, or OHL) had an inkling that it would not win the war, it was not finally convinced until August.[4] Between early 1917 and the summer of 1918, then, the external threat environment seemed less challenging for Germany.

If the external threat environment seemed to improve for the Germans during this period, the domestic threat environment looked far less promising. While the Commander of the Field Army General Paul von Beneckendorff und Hindenburg and his nominal deputy Ludendorff were confident they could win the war, they feared that meddling by civilian politicians and an internal political collapse might rob them of this victory.[5] In his memoirs, Ludendorff recounted an instance of civil-military conflict and then explained, "I mention this incident only because it was characteristic of the feeling [among the civilian leaders] in Berlin. They were always ready to go against, instead of with, us."[6] Of the public, Ludendorff observed that "the spirit of the people at home rendered action imperative. We had the best prospects of winning the war, but it was not over, and what we had won had to be kept. The popular state of mind jeopardized everything."[7]

The main problems with the "popular state of mind" were war weariness and growing left-wing sentiment. Ludendorff later observed that "England gave China opium, our enemies gave us the revolution."[8] A tenuous truce had been struck between the Social Democrats and the government before the war. However, by 1916 the truce had begun to fall apart. Gerhard Ritter attributed this decreasing internal unity to the perception of a less challenging external threat environment: "The fall of reactionary czarism had disposed of one of the major party slogans of 1914. . . . In other words, the party truce of 1914, the national unity front, disintegrated."[9] This severely weakened the civilian institutions of the German government and set the stage for growing military assertiveness.

In view of all this, many military leaders—especially Hindenburg and Ludendorff—concluded that greater military involvement in civilian affairs was essential. They felt that the military needed to control all facets of war production, maintain adequate social conditions for the workers, and directly combat the spread of ideological subversion. In short, Hindenburg and Ludendorff had come to believe that some form of military dictatorship was essential for Germany.

Military Doctrine

The German military's growing internal focus cannot be explained solely by the structural threat environment because the presence of both external and internal threats meant that the environment was indeterminate. The structural theory anticipates that in such a situation, military doctrine should play a major role in shaping civil-military relations. Prior to World War I, ideas about war and international politics, such as the famous "cult of the offensive," were important in leading Germany to adopt an aggressive foreign policy and an offensive military doctrine.[10] But there was also an internal analogue to the "cult of the offensive": the doctrine of "total war."[11]

The origins of the idea of "total war" lie deep in Prussian history. The army's central importance in the formation and consolidation of the Prussian state and in the periodic suppression of internal unrest meant that the military traditionally had a significant domestic role. Ironically, even such liberal Prussian military reformers as Stein and Boyen advocated a major domestic role for the military, as the "school of the nation." The military viewed rebellion inspired by the left wing, especially, as a direct threat because the German Left consistently advocated an antimilitary agenda. Even in the absence of an actual internal threat, German military leaders saw domestic involvement as critical to the successful conduct of war. Writing in 1887, Lieutenant Colonel Colmar von der Goltz asserted that the "enigma to be solved in the present development of [war] is how to completely fuse the military life into the life of the people, so that the former may impede the latter as little as possible, and that, on the other hand, all the resources of the latter may find expression in the former."[12]

This strand of thought continued to influence important elements of the German military through World War I. According to Walter Goerlitz, "Ludendorff was the great advocate of war in its so-called 'true form.' Professing to complete Clausewitz, he evolved the theory according to which war was not an instrument of policy. On the contrary, politics were, according to this theory, a part of warfare."[13] In World War I, Ludendorff argued, "it was impossible to distinguish where the sphere of the army and the navy began and that of the people ended."[14] Doctrines such as these, which had been present in Germany for a long while, played a major part in the breakdown of civilian control of the military during the Hindenburg-Ludendorff dictatorship of 1916–18.

Civilian Control

Historically, periods of challenging external threat had led to increased, rather than decreased, civilian control of the German military. During the wars of German unification, Chancellor Otto von Bismarck was regularly able to overrule the military leadership. Similarly, Adolf Hitler had little difficulty in controlling his military from the 1930s through the end of World War II. It was primarily in less challenging external threat environments, such as the period between the wars of unification and World War I, that even such strong leaders as the "Iron Chancellor" Bismarck had difficulty controlling the military.[15]

Some believe that the German military called the shots from the very beginning of World War I. For example, many scholars argue that the military forced the war upon a reluctant civilian leadership.[16] Jack Snyder suggests that the military, largely for bureaucratic reasons, embraced an offensive military doctrine and presented it as a fait accompli to the civilian leadership during the "July crisis" of 1914.[17]

In contrast, the historian Fritz Fischer and his students have made a powerful case that World War I did not come about because of a lack of civilian control of the military. Fischer shows that since the late nineteenth century, civilian and military leaders had shared the same set of ideas about the conflictual nature of international politics and the need for German expansion. Moreover, once the war began, even such moderate civilian leaders as Chancellor Theobald von Bethmann-Hollweg shared the military's grandiose schemes of conquest.[18] Stephen Van Evera's analysis of the "cult of the offensive" in pre–World War I Germany makes clear that these ideas were widely embraced by both military and civilian leaders.[19] On the few occasions when civilian and military preferences did diverge early in the war, civilians prevailed. Marc Trachtenberg, for instance, demonstrates that in fact it was Chief of the General Staff Helmuth von Moltke, not the kaiser, who caved in during the July crisis.[20] In general, the first two years of the war saw relatively firm civilian control of the German military.

The erosion of civilian control would begin only in 1916. Even when Hindenburg and Ludendorff were still commander and chief of staff respectively of the German Eighth Army in the east, they were no strangers to controversy. In January 1915, wreathed in the laurels of their remarkable victory at the Battle of Tannenburg, the two leaders successfully flouted the authority of army chief of staff General Erich von Falkenhayn over the issue of German support for the Austrian offensives against Russia. In August 1916 Hindenburg and Ludendorff took control of the OHL despite the kaiser's reservations. This marked a clear watershed in German civil-military relations. As Gordon Craig notes, "the army became the controlling factor in German politics after the elevation of Hindenburg and Ludendorff to the High Command."[21]

> In the bitter political struggle that stretched from the end of 1916 until the middle of the following year, [Hindenburg and Ludendorff] created what has been called "a silent dictatorship," and in the subsequent period they were able to create and destroy chancellors at will, to force the dismissal of private servants of the emperor when their views did not coincide with their own, and to determine the objectives and tactics of the Foreign Office.[22]

The wide influence of the OHL did not become apparent, however, until July 1917. As John Wheeler-Bennett observes, "By the beginning of 1918 the position of the High Command in Germany was unique and supreme. They not only ruled but governed, and demanded a controlling voice in all internal and external affairs."[23] Ludendorff, rather than his nominal superior Hindenburg, was ultimately the most powerful military figure.

Some in the German military, such as Admiral Alfred von Tirpitz, advocated direct military rule, but Ludendorff resisted this because he felt it would be too difficult to run the war and the country simultaneously. He preferred to govern indirectly. To that end, Ludendorff established a "silent dictatorship" in which the military would have decisive influence on, but not direct responsibility for, domestic affairs. Ludendorff's main weapon was the threat that he and Hindenburg would resign if they did not get their way. He justified the military's extensive political role by arguing that the Allied leaders Lloyd George and Clemenceau were dictators because they controlled their parliaments.[24]

When the war seemed to be going Germany's way (roughly from early 1917 through mid-1918), the German military had great influence. But once it became clear that Germany would lose the war, the power of the OHL declined precipitously.[25] By October 1918 Ludendorff's power had diminished so much that it was he, rather than his civilian opponents, who had to resign.

The first instances of serious civil-military conflict in Germany did not emerge until 1916. In August a major dispute erupted among the German leadership over Poland. There were two facets to this debate. The first concerned the status of Poland: was it to be part of the Austro-Hungarian empire, as the kaiser initially desired; would it become part of Germany with the Baltics remaining independent, as Matthias Erzberger and Richard von Kühlmann advocated; or would Poland be divided to create a buffer around Prussia, with the Baltic states being annexed to the Reich and the rest of Poland becoming independent, as Hindenburg and Ludendorff wanted? The military represented a serious obstacle to German–Austro-Hungarian agreement on this issue and eventually forced the kaiser to come around.[26]

The second facet of the debate concerned whether Germany should raise an independent Polish army to fight the Russians. On this issue, too, Ludendorff overcame Bethmann-Hollweg's objections.[27] On all aspects of the Polish issue, the German military prevailed over civilian opposition.

The military and civilian leaderships also clashed repeatedly after 1916 about terms for ending the war. The first skirmish began over Bethmann-Hollweg's response to President Woodrow Wilson's peace note of December 1916. From late 1916 on, a number of issues were in dispute. The OHL balked at civilian proposals to give autonomy to Alsace-Lorraine. In mid-1917 Bethmann-Hollweg clashed directly with Hindenburg and Ludendorff over the German war aims to be laid out in the chancellor's peace resolution of July 1917. Bethmann-Hollweg advocated a return to the prewar status quo, but Hindenburg and Ludendorff succeeded in inserting far more ambitious territorial claims into the statement. Even as late as mid-1918, when virtually everyone in Germany realized that the country needed a quick end to the war, the military successfully pushed the government to adopt a hard line.

The postwar status of Belgium was a particularly nettlesome issue for the OHL. As Ritter notes,

> the German political leadership was certainly ready to forego Belgium and reach a negotiated peace—Kühlmann even more so than Michaelis, who kept looking for a compromise with the *OHL*—but the German generals and admirals were not; and the fall of Bethmann-Hollweg had but recently demonstrated that the military held the political whip hand. . . . they were even able to intimidate the Kaiser.[28]

It was not until October 1918 that civilians finally overcame the OHL's objections to Allied terms. From late 1916 until nearly the end of the war, then, the German military was able to impose its preferences on civilian leaders regarding war aims and peace terms.

The military was also largely responsible for the policy of unrestricted U-boat warfare. By March 1916 this issue had become the subject of a major political debate in Germany. In 1915 and 1916 Bethmann-Hollweg thwarted the navy's efforts to change German policy on the employment of submarines. But by late 1916 the military position had begun to prevail. In September of that year, the military forced Bethmann-Hollweg to take a much harder line on this issue in a note to Wilson. By December, the military had decided that if the chancellor would not endorse submarine warfare, he should be ousted. Things came to a head on January 9, 1917, at a meeting between the kaiser, Hindenburg, and Bethmann-Hollweg at which the military position was adopted. Bethmann-Hollweg later compared this clash to the "July crisis," and the historian Gerhard Ritter concluded that it "meant the formal capitulation of political authority to the military in the most crucial issue of the First World War by far."[29]

A fourth major arena of civil-military contention was Germany's eastern policy. Essentially, the OHL controlled this policy. The OHL and the civilian right wing advocated incorporating extensive annexations into the Treaty of Brest-Litovsk, while the Left and many other civilians were content to forgo them. By January 1918 the debate had become so intense that Ludendorff threatened to resign if the kaiser did not support annexations. Ludendorff and the OHL demanded territory in the east not only because they thought it was of value, but also because they believed annexation might forestall democratization in Germany. The military prevailed, and this led Ritter to conclude that "one immediate effect of the peace [of Brest-Litovsk] was to tell the world unequivocally who held the ultimate power of political decision in Germany—not the Reichstag, not the Kaiser, not the Chancellor, but Ludendorff."[30]

German involvement in the Russian civil war also became a contentious civil-military issue. The officers of the OHL advocated intervention and even launched a coup in Ukraine that installed their ally Hetman Paul Scoropadsky. Only when the war in the west worsened for Germany was the OHL forced to back down, and by August 1918 the Foreign Ministry succeeded in thwarting the military's even more ambitious plans for intervention.

A fifth major civil-military conflict concerned the domestic role of the German military. In his memoirs, Ludendorff repeatedly disclaimed any interest in domestic politics: "Neither the Emperor nor the Imperial Chancellor, von Bethmann, ever spoke to me about internal affairs. Nor was it my business to originate discussion on these subjects, as internal politics had nothing to do with me."[31] However, in these same memoirs, Ludendorff repeatedly complains about domestic developments in Germany. Under the influence of the "total war" doctrine, Ludendorff could not help being deeply concerned about internal affairs:

> The war called upon us to gather together and throw into the scale the last ounce of our strength, either in the fighting line or behind the lines, in munitions work at home or in government service. Each citizen could serve his country only in one post, but in some way his strength should be used to that end. Service to the State was the important thing.[32]

To that end, the OHL absorbed the Home Commands and, by imposing martial law, usurped a great deal of the authority of the Imperial government. Ludendorff was able to push through compulsory labor legislation despite Bethmann-Hollweg's opposition. In general, the OHL successfully opposed domestic reform in Germany until near the end of the war.

A final conflict involved the tenure of civilian personnel in the German government. The OHL succeeded in ousting a number of high-ranking civilian leaders who resisted its policy preferences.[33] In June 1917, after a long struggle with Bethmann-Hollweg, Hindenburg and Ludendorff finally obtained his resignation. They also handpicked his replacement, Georg Michaelis. When they became dissatisfied with Foreign Minister von Kühlmann's performance, Hindenburg and Ludendorff got the kaiser to replace him as well. The OHL's writ extended even to the kaiser's personal staff, as was demonstrated by the military officers' success in winning the dismissal of Chief of the Imperial Cabinet Graf Rudolph von Valenti in 1918. Military discontent with civilian leaders was so complete that Hindenburg and Ludendorff reportedly even wished secretly to be rid of the kaiser. Their wish was fulfilled at the end of the war, when General Wilhelm Groener informed the kaiser that "the army no longer stands behind your majesty," forcing him to abdicate and flee to Holland.[34]

Assessment of the Theory

The variation in strength of civilian control of the military in the case of World War I Germany seems to fit the general predictions of my theory. The structural threat environment was indeterminate, so the military doctrine of "total war" played an important role in shaping German civil-military relations. From August 1914 through mid-1916, when most Germans were preoccupied with the external threat, civilian control of the military was relatively firm. After mid-1916, when the doctrine of "total war" led the military to focus on the internal threat, civilian control of the German military weakened markedly.

The primary institution of civilian control of the German military was supposedly the kaiser. But given how weak the monarchy was by 1916, in part because of the growing assertiveness of the Reichstag, the kaiser could exercise little effective control over the demigods of the OHL.[35] Chancellor Bethmann-Hollweg was also a weak figure.[36] Moreover, social conflict, which had been submerged at the beginning of the war, resurfaced, and civilians in various political factions attempted to enlist military support against rivals.[37]

Because Germany was engaged in a major external war, the German Army remained, until near the end, a fairly unified and cohesive body—unlike the Russian and French armies, both of which suffered a serious loss of cohesion.[38] But because the specter of domestic social unrest posed a serious threat to the German war effort, the orientation of the military was unclear. This threat was certainly magnified by the doctrine of "total war," which had captured the minds of many members of the High Command.[39] The doctrine made the orientation of the German Army ambiguous and led to a growing assertiveness by German officers in domestic politics. Civilian and military ideas about war aims became very different as the war dragged on. In the face of both external and internal threats, and under the influence of ideas emphasizing the importance of a domes-

TABLE 4
Outcomes of World War I German Civil-Military Conflicts

Issue	Civilians	Unclear	Mixed	Military
July crisis	X			
Poland				X
War aims				X
U-boats				X
Eastern policy				X
Russian civil war				X
Domestic role of military				X
Civilian personnel				X

tic role for the army, civilian control was virtually nonexistent during the second half of the war.

What were the consequences of the military's predominance in Germany? In almost every instance in which the military successfully overruled civilian leaders, the result worked to Germany's disadvantage. The status of Poland, the unrestricted U-boat campaign, Bethmann-Hollweg's resignation, and the eastern and western annexations were all debacles.[40] The OHL's eastern annexations are a clear case in point. At the time of the spring 1918 German offensives in the west, in which the High Command had placed so much of its hope of winning the war, over a million German troops were engaged in the occupation of the annexed territories in the east. Historians have wondered whether even half these troops might have changed the outcome in the west.[41] A similarly negative assessment could be made of each of these other "victories" for the military in policy matters.

Altogether, the German case demonstrates that internally oriented military doctrines such as "total war" can have an independent role in structurally indeterminate threat environments. It also shows that a military deeply involved in domestic politics cannot successfully run the country and effectively prosecute a major external war at the same time.

Civilian Control of the French Military during the Algerian Crisis

The case of France during the Algerian crisis likewise supports my theory that military doctrine in a structurally indeterminate threat environment affects the strength of civilian control of the military. Like the case of World War I Germany, the French case involves a state that was facing both external and internal threats (fig. 9, Q3). The external threat was the Cold War. The internal threat was the Algerian conflict, which was waged in metropolitan France as well. Because of the indeterminacy of the structural threat environment, ideas embodied in successive French military doctrines played key roles in shaping different patterns of civilian control of the military.

This section begins with an assessment of changing perceptions of the internal and external threat environments in France from 1954 through 1962. It then considers the origins and consequences of the French military's internally oriented doctrine known as *guerre révolutionnaire*. Next it looks at variations in assertiveness by the French military as an indicator of the state of civilian control. Finally, it examines the strategies French president Charles de Gaulle employed to strengthen civilian control of the military.

Threat Environment

The international threat environment facing France during the Cold War period was obviously challenging. There was, however, some variation in the perception of that external threat: in particular, a definite sense of relaxation in tensions with two important adversaries coincided with this critical period in French civil-military relations.

France's traditional adversary since the late nineteenth century had been Germany. Despite its defeat in World War II, Germany remained a strategic concern to France until the mid-1950s. In the immediate postwar period, France sought to keep Germany at bay by occupying a buffer state east of Rhine, regularly intervening in German domestic affairs and isolating Germany in Europe.

The attitudes of the French toward Germany changed in part because their occupation experience made clear to them how weak their traditional adversary had become.[42] After the St. Petersburg Protocol of 1949, French strategy shifted to integrating Germany into a united Europe. By 1955 France had ended the occupation of the Saar and recognized German sovereignty. The French no longer viewed Germany as a threat.[43] In 1958 de Gaulle and Chancellor Konrad Adenauer of the Federal Republic of Germany met at a historic summit. After that meeting, de Gaulle observed that France "was unhampered by any threat from her immediate neighbors. Germany, dismembered, had ceased to be a formidable and

		External threats	
		High	Low
Internal threats	High	1954–62 (Q3)	(Q4)
	Low	(Q1)	(Q2)

FIGURE 9 The French Threat Environment during the Algerian Crisis

domineering power. . . . Thus we were relieved of the state of constant tension in which dangerous neighbors once held us and which gravely hampered our activities."[44] The perceived German threat eased dramatically between the mid- and late 1950s.

Similarly, the French perceived a significant reduction in the Soviet threat. De Gaulle and many of his countrymen believed that Nikita Khrushchev was a less dangerous adversary than Josef Stalin; they characterized Russia as a defensively expansionist power and in general had a much less alarmist view of the Soviet military threat than did the United States and some of the other European powers.[45] De Gaulle clearly expressed this more benign view: "In 1958, I considered that the world situation was very different from what it had been at the time of the creation of NATO. It now seemed fairly unlikely that the Soviets would set out to conquer the West."[46] The French president thought that the Soviet threat had diminished because of Western political and economic strength, the Soviet Union's increasing problems in controlling its East European empire, the emerging Chinese threat, and the West's robust nuclear arsenal. By 1959 France and the other powers of the West had embarked on a full-scale détente with the Soviet Union, which seemed to formalize the relaxation in tensions of the previous years.

If the international threat environment facing France seemed benign, the domestic threat environment appeared increasingly grave. The sources of this growing internal threat were twofold. First, the civilian institutions of the French government were weak. De Gaulle noted that "the Army, more than any other body, felt a growing resentment against a political system which was the embodiment of irresolution."[47] This was somewhat ironic, for de Gaulle himself had played a not-insignificant role in weakening these institutions.

The institutional degeneration of France began after May 1940.[48] The split between the collaborationist government of Marshal Henri Philippe Pétain at Vichy and the Free French under de Gaulle splintered the French military and undermined its loyalty to civilian authority. Though there can be no denying that de Gaulle made the best decision for France and the Allies in breaking with Pétain and opposing Nazi Germany, he did clearly establish a very bad precedent for future civil-military relations. Not surprisingly, one of the central figures in the later French military revolt against de Gaulle, Colonel Antoine Argoud, would cite this as a precedent: "On a certain day in June 1940, officers of France were called upon to choose between the way of honor and that of discipline. Some chose honor; others, much more numerous, discipline. One cannot say precisely that all were rewarded for their decision."[49]

The Fourth Republic was the legacy of this institutional collapse. Between 1946 and 1958 there were seventeen prime ministers and twenty-two cabinets. There is a broad consensus in the literature that this institutional weakness played a key role in the civil-military crisis in France between 1954 and 1962.[50] One problem was that the French military received conflicting signals from the civilian leadership about public support for the military's efforts in Indochina and Algeria.[51] Another was that the febrile Fourth Republic could not supply the material needs of the military in numerous respects, ranging from equipment to housing. The weakness of the Fourth Republic led many French military officers to regard it as the enemy.[52]

Many French military officers also saw the French Left, especially the Communist Party, as another threat to the military. Since the 1930s the Communist Party had been an important force in French politics. Because of the party's increasing postwar power, many in France saw the Cold War less in terms of a purely external threat from the Soviet Union and more in terms of an internal threat from an indigenous opposition aligned with international communism.[53] The combination of weak governments and a strong Left led many French military officers to believe that the domestic threat to their security was more serious than the international one.

Military Doctrine

The military's perception of an internal threat was largely the result of a military doctrine called *guerre révolutionnaire,* which after 1954 became increasingly influential. The sources of this doctrine included the French Revolution and France's colonial legacy, but the real stimulus to its development was the French military's defeat by the Vietminh.[54] "If Indo-China had turned its French pupils into superb warriors, it had also made them highly political animals," noted Alistair Horne, "a fact that was to have as potent an impact upon the French republic as it did on the Algerian war."[55] Guerre révolutionnaire led many officers to conclude that French civilian leaders were weak and unreliable and that Marxist theoreticians such as the Chinese Communist leader Mao Tse-tung had a better understanding of this new form of warfare than did most Western military thinkers. The pervasive influence of guerre révolutionnaire is evident in a wide variety of places, including such influential novels as Jean Lartéguy's *Les Centurions*.

The main tenets of guerre révolutionnaire included a belief that the development of nuclear weapons by the two superpowers had produced a nuclear stalemate in which unconventional conflicts could proliferate; that military operations would become secondary to political struggles; that these political struggles would become more frequent; and that in order to win, the West should adopt the enemy's methods and develop an attractive counter-ideology to communism. Psychological rather than strictly military operations would become the central mission of the French military. The doctrine of guerre révolutionnaire led many French officers to believe that there would be no direct conflict between France and the Soviet Union. Rather, the conflict would be waged indirectly by the Soviet Union's allies within France. These allies included most of the French Left, especially the Communist Party. Guerre révolutionnaire encouraged many in the French military to see the Algerian conflict as a war for "the spiritual and national future of France."[56]

The French Army flirted with the doctrine of guerre révolutionnaire between 1954 and 1956. The doctrine found its first home in the Bureaux Psychologiques in Algeria. From 1958 through 1960, guerre révolutionnaire was France's predominant military doctrine. It was attractive to many French officers because it seemed to cut against the exclusively nuclear focus of the British and Americans; it made sense of the many revolutionary wars that were going on in the world; and it provided a simple but coherent view of the modern world in a period of great uncertainty. Guerre révolutionnaire made the Algerian war the primary mission for the French military.[57]

The adoption of the doctrine of guerre révolutionnaire by significant parts of the French Army had important consequences. The growing influence of the doctrine among the French officer corps strained relations with other NATO military officers. Despite an attempt by French corps commander General Jacques Allard to persuade his colleagues that NATO's "ultimate line of defense is Algeria,"[58] most Allied military officers did not buy the argument that the real Cold War threat was internal subversion rather than external invasion, and that the most important theater was the Maghreb rather than the North German plain. Moreover, as John Steward Ambler notes, "Almost all the political colonels of 1958–62 were strongly committed theorists or practitioners of that doctrine."[59] The doctrine of guerre révolutionnaire not only focused the attention of many officers inward, setting the stage for a greater military role in politics, but also sowed the seeds of the eventual military withdrawal from politics by dividing the military along functional lines (counterrevolutionary warfare vs. conventional and nuclear warfare, and regular vs. elite units) and along political lines (Gaullist vs. anti-Gaullist).[60]

Civilian Control

Guerre révolutionnaire mandated a larger domestic role for the French military. If the key to victory was the will and character of the people, and if the main enemies were domestic allies of and sympathizers with international communism, then the military could hardly fail to take a deep and active interest in internal matters. A French military document entitled "Use of the Psychological Arm in the Armed Forces" clearly suggests that the army might be engaged in combating subversives in France itself.[61]

Guerre révolutionnaire provided the "software" that programmed the French military to become a major force in domestic politics. There is evidence that the French military was chafing under civilian control as early as 1954. In March of that year, many French officers, including Marshal Alphonse Juin, expressed opposition to France's participation in the European Defense Community.[62] When their views were ignored by civilian leaders, senior officers such as General Lionel-Max Chassin hinted that it was "time for the army to cease being deaf and dumb."[63] Additional early evidence that the military was starting to resist civilian control included its hijacking of a plane carrying Algerian rebel leader Ben Bella in October 1956 and the February 1958 raid by French forces on Algerian rebel forces in Sakiet, Tunisia.

However, the issue that would provide the focus of civil-military conflict was the ultimate status of Algeria. Should Algeria remain part of France, as most French military officers believed and almost all of the ethnic French living in Algeria (the *pieds noirs*) desired, or should it become independent, as most civilian leaders and much of the population of metropolitan France eventually concluded?

The roots of the French military's commitment to *Algérie française* were deep and twisted. Obviously, the humiliation of defeat in Southeast Asia and withdrawal on the brink of victory from Suez played a role in tying the honor of the French military to the defense of Algeria. But there were other factors as well. Military officers, like many other French people, distinguished Algeria from other colonies. Tunisia and Morocco could be given independence because they were merely colonies; but Algeria had a large native French population and even comprised two departments of the French state. Moreover, most French officers did not see their efforts on behalf of French Algeria as an act of reactionary colonialism. Rather, they saw their commitment to French Algeria as being inextricably linked to a sincere, progressive commitment to protect their Algerian allies and improve social conditions for the other Muslims.[64] As the Battle of Algiers (fought in early 1957) became more intense and the French Army relied more heavily on repression and even torture to combat the urban insurgents of the Front de Libération Nationale (FLN), the military's commitment to complete victory in Algeria became more unshakable, for only success could vindicate the questionable means it had employed.

Although there was a consensus among the military that Algeria should remain part of France and that the civilian government of the Fourth Republic was not up to the task of saving it, there was little agreement about what to do. Most officers wanted a change in policy, but few thought the military should assume power.[65] It was against this background that elements of the French Army began plotting to overthrow the Fourth Republic in early 1958.

In May the top military commanders in Algeria sent a thinly veiled ultimatum to the French prime minister Félix Gaillard:

> The army in Algeria is disturbed by the sense of its responsibility for the men who are fighting on behalf of the French population inland and who feel abandoned, and of the Muslim French who have renewed their trust in France. The army to a man, would regard any abandonment of this national heritage as an outrage. We could not predict its desperate reaction.[66]

This was no bluff. At precisely that moment, General Jacques Massu, commander of the Tenth Parachute Division, was preparing to initiate a plan code-named Resurrection, which would have overthrown the civilian government in Paris by force. Since most officers thought the military should not actually seize power but only change the state's policy, there was a frantic search for a new civilian leader. The army came together behind retired General Charles de Gaulle.

At the time, some claimed that the army was not responsible for de

Gaulle's taking power.[67] The evidence suggests otherwise. A delegation of military officers visited de Gaulle at his retirement house in Colombey and told him that if he did not assume power, the military would do so. De Gaulle himself subsequently acknowledged that the army had been the key to his return to power in May 1958, replying to critics that it was either him or the paratroops.[68] Many French politicians, including Pierre Mendès-France and François Mitterand, believed that de Gaulle rode to power on the military's caissons.[69]

The military played both an active and a passive role in the fall of the Fourth Republic. The details of Resurrection—the plan for an armored and airborne seizure of Paris—were widely known in France. Before Massu canceled the operation, army units actually seized power in Corsica. The bulk of the military played a passive though important role by not supporting the civilian government or opposing the rebel military units.

The primary reason the French military rallied behind de Gaulle was its belief that he was firmly committed to maintaining control of Algeria. De Gaulle himself gave the military some reasons for optimism on that score. Immediately after assuming power he stated, "I believe that the best thing to do—and even the only thing—would be to prevent Algeria from drawing away from France; Algeria must remain with us."[70] Despite the general's public rhetoric, however, there were indications that from the beginning de Gaulle had other plans for Algeria.

After he won a referendum ratifying his return to power in September 1958, de Gaulle began to approach the FLN. In July and September 1959, he started speaking publicly about the right of the Algerian Muslims to "self-determination." Not surprisingly, this *volte face* aroused the wrath of the pieds noirs. More ominously, Marshal Juin, the military's highest-ranking officer, gave a speech in October 1959 criticizing de Gaulle's policy of self-determination.[71] Military opposition manifested itself in four attempted coups against de Gaulle. The two most serious of these were the "revolt of the barricades" of January 1960 and the "generals' putsch" of April 1961.

The "revolt of the barricades" began when General Massu, the architect of Resurrection, gave an injudiciously candid interview to Hans Kempski, a reporter for the *Süddeutsche Zeitung* and a former German paratrooper. Massu openly criticized de Gaulle's policy of self-determination and intimated that he was cooperating with pied noir militants in Algeria. De Gaulle had no alternative but to transfer Massu out of Algeria. When the pieds noirs learned that the hero of the Battle of Algiers would be reassigned, they took up arms and occupied government buildings.

The army's response was ambivalent. On the one hand, Massu seemed to encourage the revolt in his subsequent statements, and the army in Algeria refused to suppress the revolt even after blood was shed. On the other hand, the military did not lend the pieds noirs active support. Furthermore, Massu accepted his transfer from Algiers and continued his distinguished military career, later playing a decisive role in supporting de Gaulle during the critical days of May 1968. This lack of military support ensured the failure of the "revolt of the barricades."

Why did the French military not join the pied noir militants? For one thing, deep divisions in the military, which had been papered over in May 1958, resurfaced. Though the military in Algeria favored the revolt, the army in France and Germany did not. Since most officers agreed that maintaining the unity of the army was essential, they decided not to act against de Gaulle.

Second, though many Algerian Muslims supported the revolt against the Fourth Republic in May 1958, few supported the "revolt of the barricades." This made clear to many members of the French military that they had not won the "hearts and minds" of the Muslims, and it led them to reassess whether keeping Algeria was worth the probable cost.

Finally, de Gaulle exercised decisive leadership during the crisis, demonstrating that the civilian institutions of the Fifth Republic, unlike those of the Fourth, were quite robust. De Gaulle gave an important speech on French television on January 29 in which he appeared in his uniform, emphasizing his role as commander in chief of the French military.[72]

Though the "revolt of the barricades" failed, French civil-military relations were hardly ideal. Had the military been under firm civilian control, the incident could not have occurred. Moreover, the army in Algeria refused civilian orders to suppress the revolt by force. The events of April 1961 would make clear just how close the military had come to playing an active role in the revolt.

The "generals' putsch" of April 1961 is regarded by some analysts as the most extreme breakdown of civil-military relations in French history and has led others to compare France at that time to such coup-plagued regions of the Third World as Latin America.[73] The immediate catalysts were de Gaulle's negotiations with the FLN and a particularly conciliatory speech he gave that month. There was a growing consensus among French military officers in Algeria that their ambivalence in January 1960 had been a mistake and that de Gaulle had to go, either by coup or by assassination. Unlike the "revolt of the barricades," the "generals' putsch" would be purely a military operation. Its titular leaders were Generals

Maurice Challe, Edmond Jouhaud, Raoul Salan, and André Zeller. The actual driving force was a "colonels' soviet" made up of junior officers, many of whom were associated with elite paratroop units such as the Foreign Legion's First Expeditionary Parachute Regiment and the Fifth Bureau (the psychological warfare branch).

Nonetheless, the "generals' putsch" did not succeed, for many of the same reasons as the earlier revolt. As in January 1960, many French officers recognized that the Algerian Muslims were irrevocably committed to independence. Moreover, divisions within the French military, based on regional focus, functional specialty, and elite versus regular status, also hindered the plotters. This was especially evident in the unwillingness of many conscript soldiers to support their rebellious officers. Even such prominent supporters of French Algeria as General Massu did not rally to the plotters. Finally, de Gaulle reacted energetically and took vigorous steps to suppress the coup.

Though the "generals' putsch" failed, it was further evidence that the French military was not yet completely under civilian control. The weak institutions of the Fourth Republic probably could not have withstood it. The coup failed in part for tactical reasons; more skillful plotters might have succeeded. Even though 95 percent of the French Army supported de Gaulle this time, over fourteen thousand French troops (including two hundred officers) were implicated in the revolt. Clearly, there was still much to be done to reestablish a stable civil-military equilibrium in France.

The activity of the Organization Armée Secrète (OAS) provided still more evidence that French civil-military relations were not yet completely healthy. The OAS, an underground organization made up of pieds noirs and soldiers committed to "direct action" against Muslims and pro-independence French civilian politicians, made its debut in January 1961 and gained substantial military support after the failure of the "generals' putsch" drove some of the plotters underground. The OAS presented the rest of the French Army in Algeria with a dilemma. Many officers sympathized with its goals and maintained connections with their former comrades who were active members. This led the pro–de Gaulle commander of French forces in Algeria, General Charles Ailleret, to estimate that only 10 percent of his officers would actively fight the OAS, another 10 percent would support it, and the rest would remain ambivalent.[74] However, as the OAS began to attack the army directly, military sympathy and support eroded. The massacre of seven conscripts in March 1962 led many officers to conclude that the OAS was a threat to the army itself.

De Gaulle's Doctrinal Revolution and Civilian Control

The evidence presented above shows that between 1958 and 1962, civilian control of the French military gradually improved. The reason is that de Gaulle formulated both a short-term and a long-term strategy for ending the civil-military crisis that resulted from the Algerian war.

The primary component of his short-term strategy was to appease the French military. As Jean Lacouture observed, "De Gaulle now knew that peace in Algeria would come about through peace with the army."[75] In March 1960 de Gaulle staged his famous *tournée des popotes* (tour of the mess halls) to court the military in Algeria. During this visit he praised the soldiers for their successes, subtly tried to persuade them that the Algerians must decide their own fate, and emphasized that the military must ultimately be subservient to civilian authority. De Gaulle employed this same strategy in visits to military units in France.

In addition to courting the military, de Gaulle also gave it a free hand tactically in the conduct of operations against the rebel Armée de Libération Nationale (ALN) in Algeria. This policy not only defused military opposition, but also achieved substantial battlefield results. The Battle of Algiers had already been won with the death of FLN leader Ali la Pointe in October 1957, even before de Gaulle came to power. The struggle against the rural and Tunisian-based ALN took longer, but by 1959 most experts agreed that the ALN was on the ropes. De Gaulle could credibly warn his army opponents that "you are surely heading toward ruin and at the same time you are running the risk of causing France to lose Algeria at the very moment when the decline of the rebellion is becoming evident."[76]

Furthermore, De Gaulle toned down his pro-self-determination rhetoric. As Alistair Horne described de Gaulle's thinking:

> If it was for the future salvation of the army that de Gaulle wanted to be disencumbered of Algeria, then it was for the sake of preserving it intact that he could not risk telling it the whole truth of his intention. Thus, to save it for a brilliant future that only he could see glimmering in the distance, de Gaulle had—from 1958 onwards—to speak carefully to the army in a special language; or, more crudely put, lie to it for its own good.[77]

De Gaulle also kept military concerns in mind during negotiations with the FLN: the final peace agreement gave France continued access to the naval base at Mers el-Kébir for fifteen years and to bases in the Sahara for five years.

While this short-term strategy undoubtedly helped de Gaulle's Fifth Republic avoid the fate of the Fourth, it was his long-term political and military strategies that really put an end to the civil-military crisis. The political strategy had two components. First, he attacked head-on the idea, widely held by many French civilians and military officers, that Algeria was not just a colony but an integral part of metropolitan France. It was not surprising that the pieds noirs and Algerian-based military units such as the Foreign Legion would regard Algeria as part of the homeland.[78] The problem was that many other French, even Socialists such as Pierre Mendès-France, agreed.[79] De Gaulle's strategy was to distinguish between the *métropole* and the *outre-mer* (overseas) and argue that Algeria was part of the latter. De Gaulle also advanced the moral argument that "self-determination is the only policy worthy of France."[80] But his most powerful argument was that the costs of keeping Algeria had come to exceed the benefits.[81] This political strategy undoubtedly played some role in ending the civil-military crisis.

Above all, however, it was de Gaulle's military strategy that made the difference. Almost immediately after taking power in 1958, he sought to effect far-reaching changes in the geographic deployment, equipment, organization, and mission of the French military.[82] He implemented these changes gradually, beginning with a purge of some fifteen hundred officers in Algeria. He disbanded the psychological warfare Fifth Bureau and relieved the military of political responsibilities in Algeria. De Gaulle believed that he needed a twentieth-century army rather than a nineteenth-century colonial constabulary, so one of his primary targets was the doctrine of guerre révolutionnaire.

The first step in this direction was to transfer the bulk of the French army from Algeria to Europe. As de Gaulle noted, "the gradual return of our military forces from Algeria is enabling us to acquire a modernized army . . . it is absolutely necessary morally and politically, for us to restation it, for the most part, on our soil; for us to give it once again direct responsibility in the *external* defense of the country."[83] The primary mission of the French military would once again be external defense rather than internal counterrevolutionary warfare.

Military modernization played a central part in this effort. In September 1959, de Gaulle laid out France's new national security strategy.[84] He argued that the military should assume three missions: the defense of France, the projection of power, and continental defense.[85] A 1959 ordinance reorganized the military: two divisions were assigned to NATO, four divisions were placed under French control but would support NATO, one division was configured for power projection, and each military region had reserve forces for internal defense. This process continued with the enactment of the "programme law relating to certain military equipment" of December 1960 and with the March 1961 reorganization of the Ministry of Defense and the High Command.

The watershed in de Gaulle's efforts to promote military reform was his speech in Strasbourg on December 23, 1961, to over two thousand active-duty officers. De Gaulle recounted that in that speech he

> pointed out how and why the deliberate disengagement of France and her armed forces for so long tied down in Algeria would enable us to build up a national defense system adapted to our age. . . . Thus, our basic interest in terms of military power in bringing the Algerian affair to an end was made clear, and the prospect of an immense new field of activity opened up for our Army.[86]

As Lacouture observed, de Gaulle "was there above all to demonstrate that the destiny of the army lay here, in Europe, on the Rhine, at the heart of the modern world, and that to bring ruin to the present State was to destroy national defence."[87]

Nuclear forces played a special role in de Gaulle's strategy for reestablishing civilian control and reclaiming France's place among the great powers. One indication of this was his appointment of Pierre Guillaumat, head of the French nuclear program, as minister of defense. The military's initial reaction to de Gaulle's nuclear program was lukewarm. However, de Gaulle's skepticism about the credibility of the American nuclear umbrella was contagious.[88]

De Gaulle's greatest success in his campaign to repair civil-military relations was persuading the bulk of the officer corps that the real threats facing France were external, above all the Soviet Union. Whereas in 1958 de Gaulle and many other French people thought the Soviet threat was abating, by August 1961 the Berlin crisis had shifted these threat assessments 180 degrees.[89] De Gaulle explicitly tied withdrawal from Algeria to an increased Soviet threat in the fall of 1961:

> We have to go about the transformation of the country and the complete change in our relations with Algeria in a period of *international* danger. Everything we do is very much complicated by this. Since we are France, a country that is essential to Europe and necessary to the free world, it is our duty to stand firm and erect in the face of demands from the totalitarian bloc and to urge our allies to do the same.[90]

Others also saw the Algerian withdrawal as a response to the more challenging external threat environment at the time of the Berlin crisis.[91]

In de Gaulle's estimation, the Soviet Union was the most serious but not the only potential external threat. The general, and an appreciable number of his compatriots, also viewed the United States as something of a threat to French security. The threat from the west, unlike that from the east, was not direct attack. Rather, de Gaulle feared a loss of influence in a world increasingly dominated by the United States. Growing French dependence on the United States since World War II, American pressure on France to shed its colonies, lack of support during the Suez crisis and in Algeria, and American "cultural imperialism" all led de Gaulle to identify the United States as a threat. At times he seemed to equate the Soviet and American threats: "Two world groups, the Anglo-Saxons and the Soviets, have for many years been making and stockpiling atomic weapons. At this very moment one or the other of these two groups is in a position to unleash in the world, in an instant, a gigantic cataclysm."[92]

Intimately linked with this desire to distance France from the United States was de Gaulle's disenchantment with the North Atlantic Treaty Organization (NATO). De Gaulle increasingly saw NATO as an instrument of U.S. domination of Europe, and he had a completely different view of NATO's proper role.[93] He also seemed to be more concerned about the German threat. Thus, his increased emphasis on conventional and nuclear forces and the reduction of counterrevolutionary warfare capability did not entail closer integration into NATO.

Assessment of the Theory

The indeterminate threat environment facing France during the Algerian war affected the individual, military, state, and societal variables in different ways. Individual French leaders during this period ran the gamut from the hesitant Gaillard to the decisive de Gaulle. Beginning with the fall of the Popular Front in the 1930s, continuing with the defeat of France in May 1940 and the establishment of the Vichy government at home and the Free French abroad, and concluding with the ill-starred Fourth Republic, the civilian governmental institutions of France had weakened dramatically and lost much of their popular legitimacy. The institutions of the Fifth Republic were far more robust than those of the Fourth. As de Gaulle noted in 1962, "it is because the new institutions enabled the state to act—whereas the old ones only hindered it—that Government can

TABLE 5
Outcomes of French Civil-Military Conflicts

Issue	Civilians	Unclear	Mixed	Military
Algeria (1954–61)				X
De Gaulle putsch				X
Revolt of barricades			X	
Generals' putsch			X	
OAS uprising			X	
Algeria (1962)	X			

make decisions instead of constantly equivocating and that it stands fast instead of forever tottering and stumbling."[94]

During World War II, General de Gaulle and Marshal Pétain vied for the allegiance and support of the French military. Partly as a consequence, French civilian leaders adopted subjective control mechanisms. This competition helped divide the military and drew it into domestic politics.[95] During the late 1950s, the French military became deeply divided along both functional lines (conventional vs. revolutionary warfare) and political lines (Gaullists vs. others). Part of de Gaulle's reform was a return to objective control of the military.

The orientation of the French military also wavered. The end of World War II and the beginning of the Cold War meant the end of a serious external threat from the traditional adversary, Germany. Whereas the United States and most of its European allies saw the threat as coming primarily from the 175 Warsaw Pact divisions apparently poised to strike at the heart of Western Europe, the French focused on the internal and nonmilitary aspects of the Communist challenge. The French Communist Party, one of the most pro-Soviet in Western Europe, had become a major irritant in French politics, and as wars of national liberation broke out in their colonial empire, many of the French came to see domestic leftists as agents of international communism. For many French military leaders, the Cold War was an internal and largely unconventional conflict.

Finally, for much of this period, civilian and military ideas about Algerian policy were widely at variance, and civilian and military cultures were, in general, divergent.[96] The key to de Gaulle's success was his ability to bring them back together.

It was no accident that the crisis in civil-military relations ripened during the Algerian conflict. The lesson the French military officers drew from their defeat by the Vietnamese Communists in 1959 was that their conventional military doctrine and tactics had been a grave liability. They also believed that the weakness of French political institutions and the treachery of the French Left had undermined their efforts. Brooding in the prison camps of the Vietminh after the defeat at Dien Bien Phu in 1954, members of the French officer corps formulated the doctrine of guerre révolutionnaire. As we have seen, the crux of this doctrine was the belief that the Cold War was not a conventional military conflict, to be fought against an external adversary using the traditional military means of infantry, armor, and artillery. It was a political, economic, and ideological conflict that would be fought in part with arms but also with propaganda, economic reform, and political persuasion. The doctrine of guerre révolutionnaire changed the military's mission from external war-fighting to internal counterrevolutionary warfare, which included a large number of nonmilitary activities. It was only through replacing this doctrine with a more traditional externally oriented one that de Gaulle reestablished firm civilian control over the French military.

The French case provides additional evidence that states facing both external and internal threats are likely to have a wide variety of patterns of civilian control of the military. In such an indeterminate threat environment, the orientation of the military's doctrine is also important. The internally oriented doctrine of guerre révolutionnaire weakened civilian control of the French military, while de Gaulle's externally oriented nuclear realism strengthened it. Finally, the French case suggests that inasmuch as the individual leader plays a role, it is through that leader's ability to recognize how the threat environment shapes civil-military relations.

The Case of Interwar Japan

At first glance, the case of interwar Japan seems an ideal illustration of Lasswell's "garrison state" hypothesis.[97] Military assertiveness apparently increased in response to growing international threats. The arrival of Commodore Matthew Perry in 1853 was the beginning of Japan's exposure to intense international security competition from the West. And many believe that since the establishment of the modern Japanese military, civilian control has been tenuous.[98] The height of Japanese military influence seemed to come on the eve of World War II, whereas the period of greatest civilian control was between the world wars (1922 through 1932).[99] During the latter, civilian leaders succeeded in reducing the army by four divisions and dramatically restricting the size of the navy through the

Washington Naval Arms Limitation Treaty.[100] It is not surprising, then, that many scholars accept Lasswell's characterization of this case.[101]

Closer examination, however, raises doubts. To begin with, the evidence suggests that far from increasing military influence, periods of greater international threat actually strengthened civilian control in Japan. The Western threat embodied in Perry's black ships played a central role in increasing the emperor's power and control over the Japanese military during the Tokugawa shogunate.[102]

During World War II, when Japan's external threat environment looked bleakest, civilian control was finally reestablished. According to Yale Maxon, "The succession of Japanese military defeats in the Pacific, together with the intimation of further ills to come which news of them conveyed to certain informed Japanese not then in positions of formal authority, were the underlying cause of the changes brought about in the Japanese government in 1944 and 1945."[103] In late 1944 and early 1945, it finally became clear to the Japanese leaders that their strategy for defending the homeland would not work.[104] At this point, Emperor Hirohito successfully reasserted his authority over the military and accepted Allied surrender terms.[105]

Moreover, the threat environment that Japan faced in the 1930s was more complicated than the Lasswellian view assumes. The interwar Japanese case would be best characterized not as quadrant 1 (high external/low internal threat) but as quadrant 3 (high external/high internal):[106] there were not only international threats, but serious domestic ones as well. Harries and Harries write: "As the Great Depression hit Japan, and *both* the domestic and international situation seemed to deteriorate daily, key elements in the officer corps began conspiring to end the policy of cooperation with the civilian government and instead take direct action to solve the problems facing Japan."[107] The Depression raised the likelihood of social unrest, and the growing power of communism was of particular concern. As Harries and Harries observe, "The fear shared by the more moderate renovationists and those on the extreme right was that the collapse of the present system would lead inevitably to communism. The reins of state must be taken firmly in hand before all control was lost."[108]

Political terrorism, especially the assassination of government officials, was widespread. Some of these acts were committed by right-wing civilian extremists, but others were carried out by military officers working through such extremist organizations as the Sakurakai (Cherry Blossom Society).[109] Whoever was responsible, the Japanese military saw domestic political violence as a threat to its ability to perform its missions.

Likewise, the international threat environment that interwar Japan faced was not as straightforward as it seems. The army thought that the key threat was a land war with the Soviet Union in Manchuria.[110] The navy was convinced that the main threat was a naval war with the United States in the western Pacific.[111] It was not as a result of some coherent grand strategy that Japan ended up engaging both powers. Rather, as Akira Fujiwara concludes, the Pacific war grew out of interservice strategic logrolling:

> Since there existed no governmental machinery to coordinate and establish priorities between the demands of the two services, the decision makers attempted to accommodate both, without, however coordinating their policies. Consequently, although in view of the limitations of Japan's naval power it was clearly irrational even to consider a policy based upon waging war simultaneously against a great land power, Russia, and a great naval power, the United States, such a policy was adopted.[112]

The threat environment confronting Japan was, it seems, more complicated than the "garrison state" theory suggests. The interwar Japanese case does not after all support the Lasswellian view, nor does it falsify Andreski's argument.

This case does, however, generally accord with the dynamics predicted by the structural theory for a state in quadrant 3 (high external/high internal threat). The 1920s and 1930s saw the rise of civilian politicians who were insensitive to how the reductions in defense spending and force posture during the 1920s would affect the Japanese military's view of its ability to execute its missions.[113] The institutions of civilian control of the military were divided between the cabinet and the emperor. Since 1900, there had been a requirement that the army minister be an active-duty general,[114] which meant that Japan relied on subjective rather than objective control mechanisms.

By the early 1930s, the military had become deeply divided. We have already noted the strategic split between the army and the navy. Each of the services was also deeply rent with internal fissures and factions. Internal army politics in the early 1930s were played out in the struggle between the Tosei-ha (Control Faction) and the Kodo-ha (Imperial Way Faction).[115] The failed coups of March and October 1931, the May 1932 coup attempt and assassination spree, and the successful uprising of 1936 were all legacies of this factional struggle. It was only after 1936, when some semblance of military unity was restored, that the military began to dominate the Japanese government.

		External threats	
		High	Low
Internal threats	High	1932–45 (Q3)	(Q4)
	Low	(Q1)	1922–32 (Q2)

FIGURE 10 The Interwar Japanese Threat Environment

The orientation of the Japanese military was also unclear. The German "total war" doctrine imported by Lieutenant Colonel Ishiwara Kanji and other Japanese theorists led the military to embrace both external and internal missions.[116] Samuel Huntington also notes the influence of "military socialism" on large sections of the officer corps.[117] The explicitly antirationalist content of Japanese military thought at the time further contributed to the lack of a coherent military strategy.[118]

Finally, civilian and military ideas about the international system and the role of the Japanese military were widely at variance in the interwar era. Pacifism was widespread among civilian leaders, especially in the 1920s, while the military was imbued with a radically different set of ideas based on power politics and calling for a greater domestic role for the military.[119] Given the predictions of the structural theory for a state in quadrant 3, it is not surprising that civilian control of the military was tenuous and Japan launched a catastrophic war.

Conclusions

The German and French cases suggest a number of important theoretical and practical lessons. First, Lasswell's hypothesis notwithstanding, in both cases the source of the difficulties for civilian control was not a challenging international threat environment, but rather preoccupation with domestic threats. The French case clearly supports Andreski's contention that a challenging external threat environment should have the opposite effect: de Gaulle's civil-military crisis was resolved only when he reoriented the military toward the external threat.

Second, when the structural threat environment is indeterminate, as it was in both cases, military doctrine takes on a more independent role in explaining the level of civilian control. Internally oriented doctrines, such as the German "total war" concept or the French notion of guerre révolutionnaire, can lead to political disaster; externally oriented doctrines, such as de Gaulle's nuclear and conventional realism, can actually improve civilian control of the military by focusing the military outward.

Third, the French and German cases shed light on the role of individual leaders in shaping civil-military relations. It was not de Gaulle's genius alone that solved the crisis precipitated by the Algerian war, but his recognition of how structure creates opportunities and constraints. The opposite was true of Ludendorff: his ineptitude gained even more scope in the complex threat environment of World War I. Finally, the German and Japanese cases confirm that internally oriented militaries are unlikely to be very effective in wartime.

Chapter 6

Twilight of the Generals?
Domestic Security and Civil-Military Relations in Southern Latin America

The military dictatorships of southern Latin America provide evidence that a challenging domestic threat environment, combined with few international threats (quadrant 4), dramatically weakens civilian control of the military. Argentina (1966–82), Brazil (1964–85), and Chile (1973–89) manifested many of the pathologies that the structural theory of civil-military relations would predict. All three countries witnessed the accession to power of civilian leaders who had problems dealing with the military. These civilian leaders were deeply divided, so the institutions of civilian rule were weak and ineffective. Civilians frequently sought to draw their militaries into domestic politics. All three militaries were relatively cohesive and unified, but they were also inwardly focused when they took power. Facing challenging domestic threat environments, they all embraced internally oriented military doctrines. Civilian and military cultures and ideas in these countries were widely divergent. Argentina, Brazil, and Chile all experienced the most extreme manifestation of loss of civilian control: military rule. Conversely, their transitions to democracy came about in the manner in which the structural theory would have predicted, due to changes in the internal and external threat environments.

These cases are important not only because they nicely illustrate my theory, but also because prospects for the consolidation of stable civilian democratic regimes in the developing world are critically dependent on the establishment of firm civilian control of the military. The role of the military in the transition from authoritarian to democratic rule ought to be a central concern for all scholars and policy-makers interested in the theory and practice of democratization in Latin America and elsewhere.

There are two competing views of the military's role in democratization in Latin America. Early analysts reflected the Lasswellian belief that militaries were invariably a threat to democracy.[1] A second wave of scholars argued that modernization and democracy would go hand in hand and that the key agent of modernization would be the military.[2] For the first group, a professional military was the main obstacle to democracy; for the second, it was one of its main props.

The argument of this chapter is that both positions are wrong. The effect of the military on democracy is indeterminate. It is the changing structural threat environment that plays a critical role in affecting civilian control of the military. The greater the domestic threat to the institutional interests of the military—defined here in ascending order of importance as protection of budget share, preservation of autonomy, maintenance of cohesion, and survival of the institution—the more difficulty civilians will have in controlling the military. The smaller the domestic threat to the military institution and its interests, the stronger civilian control will be.

This chapter also discusses an important paradox of military rule. While in the short run seizing political power may protect the interests of the military, the exercise of power often undermines the core values of the institution and threatens its cohesiveness, making eventual military withdrawal from power almost inevitable. This withdrawal is generally protracted, as it was in Brazil and Chile. However, the cases of Argentina and, to a lesser extent, Brazil suggest that the emergence of an external threat or mission can considerably hasten the military's withdrawal from power.

Transitions to Democracy, the Military, and Bureaucratic Authoritarianism

One of the most important conclusions to have emerged from the voluminous "transitions to democracy" literature is that the key to the maintenance of democracy is robust civilian control of the military. Unfortunately, the transitions literature has not produced a theory of the role of civil-military relations as a variable in the larger process of political change.[3] Is the military an independent agent, or is it merely reflective of other social forces?[4] The solution to this problem lies in finding a body of generalizable theory that explicitly incorporates the military in the larger process of political change.

One possibility is Guillermo O'Donnell's argument about the rise of the Bureaucratic-Authoritarian regime. This model has its roots in four distinct bodies of theory: dependency theory; Samuel Huntington's critique of modernization theory; organization theory; and Alexander Gerschenkron's and Albert Hirschman's theories about the political consequences of various stages of industrialization.[5] O'Donnell's most important observation was that, contrary to widespread expectations, modernization did not bring democracy in its wake. Rather, at least in southern Latin America, there seemed to be an "elective affinity" between high levels of modernization and authoritarian regimes.[6]

O'Donnell suggested that the exhaustion of the easy stages of import substitution industrialization—horizontal industrialization—forced the economic and military elites of the Southern Cone to establish a new sort of political regime to undertake the next stages of industrialization—vertical industrialization, or "deepening," which requires keeping up with changes in the global economy and in technology. Whereas previous regimes had relied on "activated" working classes mobilized through populist appeals, the new technocratic regimes needed to adopt fiscally orthodox economic policies, reducing wages and denying other working-class demands in order to attract foreign investment. These efforts to impose fiscal orthodoxy in the face of praetorian social mobilization produced a political and economic crisis. The political crisis, in combination with increased professionalism in the military, led that institution to become the senior partner in a "coup coalition." The economic crisis led technocratically oriented civilians to join with the military as the junior partner. The end result was the Bureaucratic-Authoritarian regime (BA).[7]

In some places, O'Donnell seemed to suggest that military variables had a major role in the process of political change. He argued that increased military professionalization facilitated greater internal cohesion.[8] This increased cohesion, a response to domestic threats to the military, resulted in the decision to seize power.[9] Military institutional variables had a measure of autonomy because "the evolution of military institutions (including the degree of penetration of technocratic roles) seems to be more independent of the social context . . . than other sectors are."[10] Thus, threats to military corporate interests were the main sources of military interventions.

O'Donnell's other formulations gave military institutional variables a far less significant role. In fact, the military nature of the BA seemed to be almost "typologically inconsequential";[11] the military was merely the executor of policies that served the interests of civilian economic elites. But as others have suggested,[12] and as I argue in the following sections, domestic threats to the military organization are crucial to understanding military seizures and withdrawals from power.

A Structural Theory of the Role of the Military in Political Change

There are three important reasons why the role of the military in political transitions should command special attention. First, in the case of the southern Latin American BAs, it was not the civilian technocrats who seized power; it was the military. The military was a central actor in political transitions because it was the core of the state's coercive apparatus, the major obstacle to the consolidation of a civilian regime, and the one social group that offered a seemingly viable alternative to democracy.[13] If the role of the military in transitions to democracy in the Southern Cone of Latin America is neglected, our grasp of what constitutes the prerequisites for civilian rule and political democracy will be weakened.

Second, decisions to seize or give up power are in large part explainable by the effect of structural changes on military institutional interests. Alain Rouquié has suggested that

> it is frequently the case that processes internal to the military apparatus shape the phases of demilitarization and open the way to eventual democratic alternation. . . . the return of the military to barracks is above all a military problem, and it would be some what paradoxical to study it without considering this decisive angle.[14]

Third, because of their functional similarities, militaries provide an important focus for comparative study.[15]

Civilian control of the military in southern Latin America has been problematic because of the structural threat environment in which modernization took place. The conventional wisdom, derived mostly from theorizing based on the Western European experience, is that a modernized military is more amenable to civilian control and ultimately enhances the prospects for democracy. If so, then why did the modernization of southern Latin American militaries produce just the opposite effect?

The answer is that modernization in Latin America occurred in a dramatically different structural threat environment than it did in Western Europe. European militaries modernized in an environment in which the threat was primarily international.[16] The opposite was true, for the most part, in the southern Latin American states. "Rather than the European models of national defense—the protection of frontiers and an orientation toward an external enemy," it was, Rouquié points out, "internal problems and domestic social and political dangers [that] were the object of the specifically military actions of the Latin American armies."[17] From the beginning, their orientation was almost exclusively domestic.

"Factionalism," José Garcia has argued, "is not only commonplace; its very presence may also be the key to understanding the dynamics of military intervention in Latin America countries."[18] The key factor in fostering military unity is a threat to the institution. As Alfred Stepan observed:

> Often, in fact, the threat to institutional self-interest or survival is the key factor in *finally* creating officer consensus, for whenever the traditional areas of military institutional authority are upset, such as its disciplinary and hierarchical structure, even non-activists and legalists within the officer corps are provoked into action.[19]

An institutional factor—military cohesiveness—is one crucial intervening variable between a threat to the military institution and the military's seizure of power. As Martin Needler has argued, "the military movement to seize power becomes effective only as it engages the military's concern for the defense of its own interests."[20]

The internal orientation of southern Latin American militaries was a threat to civilian rule, and ultimately democracy, because this orientation linked military institutional interests to the level of internal economic development and the course of domestic politics. This is clearly illustrated in Argentina, Brazil, and Chile by the development of so-called national security doctrines. The key characteristics of these doctrines are their domestic focus and their extremely broad definition of national security. These doctrines directly "contributed to an intensification of the belief that the old boundaries to military activism were no longer appropriate."[21] The structural origins of these doctrines are clear in that all three states developed them in response to domestic threats.

These national security doctrines had international and domestic sources. The external influence of U.S. and especially French counterinsurgency warfare doctrines played some role. A much more important, though frequently misunderstood, external source was foreign assistance aimed at increasing the level of military professionalization.[22] By making these militaries more cohesive, better organized, and more corporately focused, this aid also made them more of a threat to civilian control.

Too much, however, can be made of the importance of external sources of military doctrine. In fact, Rouquié notes, "rare are the armies that passively obey the commands of Washington, even in the protectorates of the Caribbean. As internal actors with specific corporate interests, the armies respond above all to a social dynamic in which external dependence is a conditioning, but not an explanatory element."[23] Internal factors, primarily domestic threats to the military institution, played a far greater role in the formation of national security doctrines.[24] These internally oriented doctrines provided a blueprint for how military rule could eliminate domestic threats to the military institution.

In addition to its effects on the military, the structural threat environment also affected individual, state, and societal variables. All three of the Latin American cases involved civilian leaders of a decidedly antimilitary bent. The cohesiveness of civilian governmental organizations was low. Civilian leaders frequently tried to bring the military into domestic civilian politics or to politicize the military in order to control it. Civilian and military ideas and cultures were widely at variance in these countries.

A structural explanation, focusing on how the location and intensity of a threat affect military doctrine and cohesiveness, provides an important tool for explaining military interventions, seizures, and withdrawals from power. The next sections will illustrate this theory by examining how the changing domestic threat environment influenced the most extreme military interventions in politics—seizures and withdrawals from power—in Argentina, Brazil, and Chile.

Argentina, 1955–1982

| | | External threats | |
		High	Low
Internal threats	High	(Q3)	1966–72 1976–82 (Q4)
	Low	1982– (Q1)	1955–66 (Q2)

FIGURE 11 The Changing Argentine Security Environment

The Argentine military was the central actor in Argentine political life from 1955 to 1983. As Aldo Vacs observed, "Even though all Argentine groups are extremely politicized, the most dangerous for the survival of a democratic regime is the military establishment. Other groups can destabilize a constitutional government, but the coup de grace has always been administered by the military."[25] It seems logical, then, to consider how military institutional interests were threatened by societal events. The two key variables are cohesion and doctrine.

Between 1955 and 1966, factionalism prevented the military from taking power.[26] Did the military actually want to take power during this period, or was it content merely to continue as kingmaker for civilian regimes? The 1962 coup attempt suggests that there was some interest in direct military rule. O'Donnell argues that this coup failed because of a low level of cohesiveness and lack of a suitable doctrine: "When in 1962, the *golpistas* tried to take over the government for an extended period of time, they failed because of their precarious control over a seriously divided military and the absence of a justifying ideology."[27] The absence of these two factors is attributable to the low level of domestic threat to the institution.

Between 1963 and 1966, the Argentine military underwent intensive professionalization.[28] This process had two important consequences. The military adopted an internally oriented military doctrine, whose sources included the Brazilian Escola Superior de Guerra (ESG), the French military mission, and the U.S. Army, though internal developments contributed in important ways.[29] And the Argentine military's potential for cohesion and unity was dramatically increased by changes in its organization and command structure.[30]

These two institutional changes made the difference between the failed 1962 coup and the successful 1966 coup, along with a societal crisis that threatened the military institution. O'Donnell succinctly summarizes the impact of these changes: "The conditions for a final systemic breakdown had reached a critical stage when, in 1965–66, the organizational evolution of the military gave it the internal cohesion and sense of its own ability that made intervention possible without apparent risk of failure and fractionalization."[31] The case of Argentina between 1962 and 1966 nicely illustrates the proposition that the nature of the threat environment influences organizational and doctrinal changes within the military and thereby its ability to intervene in politics or even assume direct control of the state.

Within the Argentine military, there was a fairly high level of consensus regarding the threat posed by Peronism. That, however, was as far as consensus went: once the Peronists were excluded from power, no such agreement ever materialized within the military on economic and political questions. In fact, the post-1966 Argentine military regime was characterized by two major factions: the Colorados, who advocated an economically liberal development program, and the Azules, who adopted a more nationalistic approach.[32] These factions grew increasingly estranged as a result of popular dissatisfaction with the regime's economic policies. Instead of uniting the military, the 1969 riots in Córdoba polarized the debate about economic and political questions.[33] It was not clear that these riots threatened military interests. And so, despite social unrest, military factionalization continued, culminating in the military's first withdrawal from power in 1973.

Unfortunately, this withdrawal was only temporary. More serious domestic threats to the Argentine military emerged in the early and mid-1970s that led the various military factions to reconcile their differences and take back power from civilians. The first threat was the nascent urban guerrilla movement. The less important component of this movement was the ultraleftist Ejército Revolucionario del Pueblo (ERP). The more serious threat, from the military's perspective, was the left-wing Peronist Montoneros. This rising insurgency was, of course, a symptom of the larger social crisis, which intensified after Juan Perón's return to power and sudden death in 1974. Perón's third wife (and his vice president), Isabel, took power after his death but could do little about the insurgency or the general climate of political chaos. The military viewed this situation as a serious threat to its corporate interests and quickly moved to depose Isabel Perón's government and retake power.

With this greater internal threat, the level of military unity was certainly higher in 1976 than it had been in 1966, so it is not surprising that the military established a more comprehensive regime the second time around. Nevertheless, this high level of consensus on the need to exterminate the guerrillas (and anyone even remotely connected with them) did not translate into a similar consensus on larger political and economic questions.[34] As the military destroyed the last remnants of the insurgency in 1978, fissures began to reappear in the regime. This time the military split into three groups: the old Azules, led by Admiral Emilio Massera, who pushed for a Peronist-type regime without the formal participation of the Peronist party or unions; the *gorílas*, such as Generals Suaréz Mason and Mario Menéndez, who continued to advocate a hard line against the Left; and the Liberals, such as Generals Jorge Videla and Roberto Viola, who supported a gradual political opening as the economy recovered.[35]

This factionalism was bound to lead to an eventual military withdrawal from power. "The contradictions between military government and the military institution are inescapable," argue Maria Susana Ricci and J. Samuel Fitch; "the armed forces cannot govern without subverting their essence."[36] The last-ditch attempt by General Leopoldo Galtieri to restore the military government's unity and prestige in April 1982 by forcibly reclaiming the Falklands/Malvinas Islands from the British actually further atomized the military by demonstrating the incompatibility between military rule and the successful conduct of an external war.[37] This defeat highlighted the fact that Argentina was vulnerable externally as long as the military governed the country. The severely divided military quickly withdrew from power in 1983.[38] This case provides clear evidence against Lasswell's claim that a challenging external threat environment should increase military influence.

Brazil, 1961–1985

		External threats	
		High	Low
Internal threats	High	(Q3)	1964–74 (Q4)
	Low	1982– (Q1)	1961–64 1974–82 (Q2)

FIGURE 12 The Changing Brazilian Security Environment

The Brazilian case offers further support for my argument. The reason there was a successful military coup against President João Goulart in 1964 but none in 1961 is best understood by considering the impact of a changed domestic threat environment on military doctrine and cohesion. There was no coup in 1961, despite anti-Goulart sentiments among some military officers, because there was no widespread agreement that he represented a threat to the institution.[39] The absence of a clear domestic threat contributed to the proliferation of military factions. The three most important of these were the so-called Sorbonne Group of anti-Goulart faculty and former students of the ESG; the pro-Goulart political appointees; and the largely apolitical field commanders.[40] The distribution of membership in these groups was roughly 10 percent anti-Goulart, 70–80 percent uncommitted legalists, and 10–20 percent Goulart partisans.[41] As long as these divisions persisted, the military could not take power for itself.

Scholars have identified five internal transformations in Brazil between 1961 and 1964 that changed the domestic threat environment. There was a serious economic crisis (not, however, the result of O'Donnell's exhaustion of import substitution industrialization) that hurt the Goulart government. The regional polarization that followed the Cuban revolution also poisoned Brazilian domestic politics. Goulart's populist policies heightened social tensions. There was widespread questioning of the effectiveness of Goulart's government. Most ominously, the stock of democracy declined precipitously among many sectors of Brazilian society. All these developments produced a marked weakening in the institutions of civilian rule in Brazil.

These changes began to arouse concerns within the Brazilian military. While they did not oppose the entire social agenda of the Left, many military officers were alarmed by its stridently antimilitary attitudes.[42] These officers also saw growing social chaos as undermining their long-term institutional unity. And as one Brazilian general made clear, unity was one of the military's core values: "Military unity is extremely important. Only if the military is split will there be a civil war. The optimum is if we stay unified and are on the right course. But the most fundamental thing is to stay unified."[43]

Yet these fears did not translate into support for a military seizure of power until several other factors emerged. One was the increasingly widespread call by civilians for a military coup against Goulart. Many civilians wanted the military to install a new civilian regime; this was essentially the role the military had played in the past. To play this "moderating" role, the military would have needed far less unity than it would have needed to rule on its own. But by 1964 the military had decided that it must go beyond its traditional role.

The main reason was a growing sense that Goulart's government presented a direct threat to the military institution. Many officers interpreted Goulart's speech of March 14, 1964, as a call for a popular uprising against the old order.[44] Many also came to believe that Goulart was advocating the creation of armed left-wing *grupos de onze* as a parallel military force.[45] Finally, and most decisively, Goulart's ambivalent response to a mutiny by enlisted men in the Brazilian navy between March 27 and 29 convinced the majority of officers that he actually condoned subversion in the ranks.[46] As Stepan observed,

> institutional self-preservation by means of control over the military was one area over which ideologically divided military officers had the highest

internal agreement. The naval mutiny caused a shift in position that hurt Goulart among all three major groups within the military—the active plotters, the legalist uncommitted officers, and the pro-Goulart officers.[47]

This domestic threat to the institution produced a high degree of consensus within the previously divided military on the need to do something more than it had done in the past. In addition, the availability of an internally oriented military doctrine of "national security" gave the military a blueprint for remaking society to ensure social peace, economic progress, and, ultimately, institutional security. The combination of these two factors produced a new type of military intervention into Brazilian politics: direct military rule.

As in the Argentine case, military unity was more apparent than real. Immediately after the coup, two military factions emerged. The soft-liners, or Blandos, led by General Arthur da Costa e Silva, advocated a regime with limited civilian participation. The hard-liners, or Duros, epitomized by General Alfonso Albuquerque Lima, demanded complete military rule.[48] After the coup, these two factions initially managed to reach a modus vivendi. "As semi-institutionalized rivals," Wilfred Bacchus explains, "the two groups remained united to each other out of fear of the chaos that might follow if they were unable to bridge their divisions and stand unified before both Brazilians and an observing world."[49] This highlights the two levels of discourse within the Brazilian military. The first, concerning whether there was a domestic threat to the institution, was virtually unanimous. The second, concerning economic and political issues, was vigorously contested.[50] So long as there was a domestic threat to the institution, military unity was relatively unproblematic. When that threat disappeared, however, maintaining military unity became extremely difficult.

This explains what happened in the early 1970s. By 1972 the domestic threat from the armed Left had been largely eliminated. Not surprisingly, serious tensions surfaced between the military-as-government and the military-as-institution. The regime's own apparent economic success undercut part of its justification for ruling. Debate about economic development strategy further polarized military politics. Some in the military government advocated an economically liberal strategy based on foreign investment; others took a more nationalistic, statist position.[51] Finally, the increasingly independent status of the Brazilian intelligence community directly impinged on other branches of the military.[52] Continued rule, in the absence of a clear threat to the institution, undermined military unity and cohesiveness, which is why General Ernesto Geisel started a gradual process of *apertura* (opening) in 1972. "Brazilian 'liberaliza-tion,'" argues Luciano Martins, "was originally triggered by the regime's difficulties in solving problems of its 'internal economy,' and did not orig-inate from any substantive change in the correlation of forces between the regime's protagonists and its opponents."[53]

The military did not make its final decision to withdraw from politics until 1982 (and did not ultimately relinquish power until 1985), but this decision was the culmination of the *apertura* begun ten years earlier. The reason it took so long was that despite the decreasing domestic threat, the paradox of military rule made itself felt only gradually. Moreover, it was not until the 1980s that perceptions of the external security environment changed. By 1982 the military had begun to reassess Brazil's external se-curity environment in light of the Falklands/Malvinas war. The military concluded not only that Argentina, Brazil's traditional external rival, was once again a potential threat, but also that internally oriented militaries were not capable of successfully waging external wars.[54] The Brazilian military's withdrawal from politics in 1985 was therefore the result of both internal and external developments.

Chile, 1970–1989

		External threats	
		High	Low
Internal threats	High	(Q3)	1973–78 (Q4)
	Low	(Q1)	1970–73 1978– (Q2)

FIGURE 13 The Changing Chilean Security Environment

The military's seizure of power in Chile in 1973 and its subsequent with-drawal, which began in 1978 but was not completed until 1989, also sup-port the general propositions of the structural theory about how the loca-tion and intensity of threats affect military doctrine and cohesiveness. The glacial pace of the Chilean military's withdrawal from power also high-lights the importance of other factors in explaining military disengage-ment. Unlike in Argentina, no serious external threat arose to hasten the military's withdrawal from power in the Chilean case. This suggests that there are important differences between withdrawing because of external threats and withdrawing because of the paradox of military rule.

By most indicators, Chile should have been one of the most stable civilian democracies in the Southern Cone. It had a long tradition of political democracy, truly national political parties, a high level of political participation, and a well-developed civil society—in other words, it had a strong democratic culture.[55] The inauguration of the Socialist president Salvador Allende Gossens in 1970, despite his election with barely a third of the votes cast, and his survival until 1973 in the face of severe domestic and foreign opposition are a tribute to the strength of Chilean democracy. One of the most important pillars of that democracy was the Chilean military's constitutionalist culture. Why did the military acquiesce in Unidad Popular rule until early 1973, then overthrow the regime on September 11 of that year?[56]

There are several answers. Until 1973 the Left, especially the Socialist Party, did not threaten the Chilean military. In fact, the Socialists had earned a measure of gratitude from military officers by supporting the military's position in a pay dispute with President Eduardo Frei in 1969.[57] It was initially the extreme Right—especially such groups as Patria y Libertad (Fatherland and Liberty)—that appeared to be the greatest threat to the military. It was this group, after all, that engineered the attempted kidnapping and assassination of army commander in chief General Rene Schneider in October 1970. Also, the force chiefly responsible for internal order in Chile was the Carabineros, a militarized national police force under civilian control. The army and the other branches of the military had little responsibility for internal security operations and little incentive to develop internally oriented military doctrines like those of the Argentine and Brazilian militaries. And there was little consensus among military officers that Chile needed a particular economic development policy. As long as Allende adhered to the constitution, there was no domestic threat that might bring the military factions to the level of cohesion necessary for the army to assume power.[58] Because of the low level of domestic threat, the Chilean military remained without an internally oriented military doctrine and was divided over Unidad Popular rule until early 1973.[59]

There were two main factions in the Chilean military during this period. The anti-Allende forces, the Golpistas, were led by General Roberto Viaux. Until early 1973 they were in the minority. The majority of the Chilean military was politically neutral regarding Allende but supported his right to remain in power as long as he respected the Chilean constitution. This faction, often referred to as the Constitucionalistas, was led by army commander in chief General Carlos Prats.[60] What shifted the balance of power between the military factions?

There is general agreement among scholars that the growing anti-Allende consensus within the Chilean military was largely reactive;[61] it did not endorse any positive social reordering, at least not to the same extent that the Argentine and Brazilian militaries did. A number of developments during the Allende regime triggered the military reaction. Allende himself adopted subjective control mechanisms, bringing military officers into his government. The weakness of the Unidad Popular coalition fostered increasing social chaos, which many officers saw as a domestic threat to the military institution.[62] This threat had two dimensions: a direct challenge to the army from the armed Left and an indirect threat through a breakdown of military hierarchy.[63] "It is significant," argues Frederick Nunn, "that the military executed the September 11 golpe in a unified fashion; it was an institutional golpe."[64] This double threat was the key unifying factor for the Chilean military and the stimulus for the development of a new, internally oriented military doctrine between March and July 1973. "For the majority of officers," noted Arturo Valenzuela, "it was no longer a matter of objecting to erroneous government policies but a matter of defending themselves and their institutions from the possibility of destruction."[65]

The principal author of this internally oriented military doctrine, General Augusto Pinochet, later summarized the situation: "This form of permanent aggression gives rise to an unconventional war, in which territorial invasion is replaced by the attempt to control countries from within."[66] Chilean analyst Genaro Arriagada has appropriately compared this view with the German theory of "total war" and the French doctrine of guerre révolutionnaire, both of which focused heavily on domestic crisis as a justification for military intervention into politics. In September 1973 the Chilean military ousted Allende and took power directly.

As in Argentina and Brazil, the Chilean military's experience with ruling had adverse consequences for the institution over the longer term. "Nothing is worse for military professional development," writes Nunn, "than political involvement."[67] This certainly proved true in the Chilean case. The main effect of political involvement on the military was the fostering of greater disunity.[68] In consequence, the military began gradually to withdraw from power in 1978. It is true that 1978 marked the point at which army commander in chief Pinochet gained ascendancy over his colleagues in the military junta, but subsequent factionalism ultimately eroded support for Pinochet. Once that happened, military rule became increasingly untenable and transition to civilian rule more likely.

How, then, did Pinochet manage to remain in power for eleven years after the beginning of the disintegration of the military junta in 1978? For one thing, he achieved a measure of legitimacy as a result of the 1981 constitutional referendum. He also evidenced remarkable personal determination to hold power. The Chilean Right's continued ambivalence about a return to democracy was a factor. The army also continued to support Pinochet's rule. Ironically, it was the high level of professionalism—especially norms of subordination to political authority and the command structure—that kept the Chilean military from openly challenging Pinochet's authority.[69] Most importantly, there is little evidence that the Chilean military learned the same lessons that the Argentine and Brazilian militaries did from the Malvinas War—about how high technology might be affecting the external threat environment.

Pinochet's manipulation of the culture of military professionalism, continued support from the army, and the lack of an external threat together explain the relatively long transition to civilian rule. This situation led one Chilean political scientist to argue before 1989 that "a decision by the armed forces to withdraw is needed."[70] The factors that led the military-as-institution to withdraw its support from Pinochet were internal to the regime and the military itself. According to Manuel Garreton, "The crisis confronting the regime since 1981 did not originate in the actions of the opposition. . . . Rather, the contradictions and problems created by the actions of the regime gave rise to the crisis."[71] The decreasing internal threat to the institution, combined with the increasing strains of actually ruling, played a large role in the military's gradual withdrawal from power in Chile.

The last stage in this process occurred in 1984 when the commander in chief of the Carabineros, General Rodolfo Stange, and the commander in chief of the air force, General Fernando Matthei, withdrew their support for Pinochet.[72] Despite Pinochet's continued position as commander in chief of the army, growing interservice rivalry weakened his grip on power. His withdrawal in 1989 was largely the result of his loss of solid military backing combined with Chilean traditions of constitutional legalism, which forced Pinochet to accept a referendum that ended his rule.

Assessment of the Theory

The military dictatorships of southern Latin America provide evidence that challenging internal threat environments, combined with few external threats, can seriously undermine civilian control of the military (figs. 11, 12, 13, Q4). Argentina (1966–82), Brazil (1964–85), and Chile (1973–89) all manifested many of the pathologies we would expect in states under prolonged military rule.

Each of these cases involved the accession of civilian leaders who had considerable problems dealing with the military. Juan Perón, although a former military officer himself, was the bane of military governments. João Goulart and Salvador Allende were both moderate leftists, but domestic developments during their administrations threatened the core interests of the Brazilian and Chilean militaries.

It is fair to say that the institutions of civilian rule in each of these states were quite weak. Between 1973 and 1976 Argentina witnessed the tumultuous return of Juan Perón, his death, the accession to power of his wife Isabel, and the emergence of a number of internal guerrilla movements, including the Montoneros.[73] In Brazil, the leftist regime of João Goulart appeared to be weak and ineffective.[74] The Chilean democratic socialist government of Salvador Allende was by 1973 under siege from both the Left and the Right.[75]

These regimes often sought to politicize the military. Various Argentine civilian politicians appealed to the army for support against other civilian factions throughout the 1960s and 1970s, and there is evidence that civilian opponents of the Goulart regime encouraged the military to play a more direct role in Brazilian domestic politics.[76] Allende himself encouraged the politicization of the Chilean military during the Unidad Popular period by bringing military officers into his government. Subjective control was rampant in southern Latin America immediately prior to military seizures of power in Argentina, Brazil, and Chile.

Moreover, the militaries of these countries, while divided over issues such as economic development strategy, were highly unified in terms of their opposition to leftist political currents.[77] The missions they embraced were primarily internal and frequently nonmilitary.

Finally, civilian and military ideas and cultures were widely at variance in Latin America during the 1960s and 1970s. Civilian leaders and military officers frequently differed over the nature of the internal threat (underdevelopment vs. communist subversion), and most Latin American militaries regarded civilian politics as deeply corrupt, with only the military embodying the highest virtues of the nation.[78]

All of these states had internally oriented military doctrines. Whereas the main influence on Latin American militaries had once been German geopoliticians, with their social Darwinist notions of interstate competition, by the 1960s the French theorists of guerre révolutionnaire had become the primary strategic influence.[79] In the 1950s, Brazilian military analysts at the ESG began thinking about strategic problems in terms different from those of the classical theories imported from Europe. The Argentines and the Chileans developed their own versions of guerre révolutionnaire, embodied in the so-called national security doctrines. Like their French predecessor, these doctrines recognized international communism as the key threat.

However, unlike the United States, the Latin American states thought that the main arena of the Cold War would be not the North German plain, but rather the streets and plazas of their own country. International communism would manifest itself through domestic leftist and communist movements and parties, rather than through external attack. These movements would exploit internal social, economic, and political problems in order to undermine the state, Western Christianity, and the military institution itself. Defense against this threat would have to go beyond traditional military weapons and tactics; military officers would also have to learn political and psychological warfare, economic development strategies, social welfare provision, and even national management. The link between these national security doctrines and the most extreme manifestation of a breakdown in civil-military relations—military seizures of power and even prolonged rule—is well-established. The key point is that in a structurally determinate situation such as that of quadrant 4, these doctrines are largely derivative of structure.

Conclusions

The southern Latin American military dictatorships demonstrate that challenging domestic threat environments produce internally oriented military doctrines, which inevitably lead to serious weaknesses in civilian control. These cases provide compelling evidence of the link between domestic threats, nontraditional military missions, and weak civilian control of the military. Finally, they also illustrate the paradox of military rule: seizure of power may protect the military institution in the short term but threaten it over the longer term.

Chapter 7

What the Future Holds

Let me recap the important and sometimes counterintuitive findings about civil-military relations presented so far. First, this is an extremely broad and multifaceted issue. Obviously, the ideal is to prevent coups, keep the military within its proper sphere, reduce the number of instances of civil-military conflict over issues of national importance, ensure that civilian and military leaders like and respect each other, and produce effective national policies. However, the most important issue of civil-military relations in developed democracies is civilian control: can civilian leaders reliably get the military to obey when civilian and military preferences diverge? There does not have to be any danger of a coup for there to be a problem with civilian control of the military, as the cases of post–Cold War America and Russia both make clear.

Second, despite its greater expertise in military matters, excessive influence by the military on national policy jeopardizes the successful conduct of war. This is illustrated by the German, Japanese, and Argentine cases. Far from making the effective prosecution of war more likely, lack of civilian control makes it less likely. Obviously, the American failure in Vietnam shows that civilian control does not always ensure good national policy, but the other cases studied in this book show that excessive military influence never does.

Third, not only is lack of civilian control bad for the country, it is also bad for the military itself. The experiences of the German, Brazilian, Argentine, and Chilean militaries clearly suggest that prolonged military rule undermines the cohesion and effectiveness of the organization. Thus, it is in the interest of the military itself to remain subordinate to civilian authority.

Finally, and perhaps most surprisingly, war—or at least challenging external threats—can, under certain conditions, enhance civilian control of the military and thereby strengthen, rather than weaken, democracy. This was Stanislaw Andreski's very important intuition. This was the case in the United States and France during the Cold War. While the Cold War Soviet Union was certainly not a democracy, it at least had firm civilian control of its military. Far from producing Lasswell's nightmare—the garrison state—the Cold War actually bolstered civilian control.

This chapter continues with an assessment of the four central predictions of the structural theory of civilian control of the military. It then offers some policy recommendations for civilian and military leaders in states facing a changing structural security environment. Finally, it moves to a more general discussion of what these findings tell us about the effects of a changing international security environment on domestic politics.

Assessment of the Predictions of the Structural Theory

Theories of civil-military relations that focus exclusively on domestic variables such as personalities of leaders, organizational characteristics of the military, the strength of governmental institutions, or the nature of civilian society are insufficient. What stands behind these variables are structural factors, such as the intensity of the domestic and international threat environments. A structural theory of civil-military relations is comprehensive yet parsimonious.

Quadrant 1

Contrary to Harold Lasswell's hypothesis, a state facing a clear external threat is likely to have firm civilian control of its military, as measured by the ability of the civilian leadership to impose its will. Such a state is more likely to have civilian leaders experienced in military affairs and operating through strong and cohesive institutions of civilian rule. The civilian leadership is more likely to rely on objective control mechanisms, and the military organization is likely to be highly unified but externally focused. Finally, civilian and military ideas and cultures are likely to be compatible.

External threats

		High	Low
Internal threats	High	Poor (Q3)	Worst (Q4)
	Low	Good (Q1)	Mixed (Q2)

FIGURE 14 Civilian Control of the Military as a Function of Location and Intensity of Threats

The cases of the United States and the Soviet Union—the two major antagonists of the Cold War period—support the proposition that challenging external threat environments lead to firm civilian control of the military. While these two countries were quite different with respect to political systems, cultures, and histories, they had two important things in common: both faced challenging external threat environments, and both were models of military subordination to civilian control.

During the Cold War, both states were governed by civilian leaderships with substantial experience and interest in military affairs. The civilian governmental institutions were strong and effective. Civilian leaders generally relied on objective control methods. The Soviet and American militaries were fairly unified during the Cold War, and both were externally oriented. Finally, in each country, civilian and military ideas about the use of force and the nature of the international system were largely the same. All of this made civilian control of the Cold War American and Soviet militaries fairly easy. Both of these cases contradict Lasswell and support Andreski.

Quadrant 2

The degree to which the structural environment is decisive can vary considerably. Where militaries face neither internal nor external threats (Q2), or both internal and external threats (Q3), other factors can play a greater role. In these cases, the key variable affecting civilian control of the military is military doctrine. Doctrinal factors such as the military's orientation, its organizational culture, and differing perceptions of the threat environment can divide civilian from military leaders. Structure certainly influences civilian control of the military, but it is not always the paramount influence.

The post–Cold War era has seen a weakening of civilian control in both the United States and Russia. This, as I have argued, is not a coincidence: the changed international security environment has reduced the external threat and undermined the old Cold War military missions.

As chapter 3 demonstrated, the record of civilian control in the post–Cold War United States has been mixed. Obviously, there is no real danger that the U.S. military will launch a coup and seize power. Nor is it realistic to expect that it would become openly insubordinate and disobey direct orders. Still, while talk of a "crisis" in U.S. civil-military relations is overdrawn, it is clear that civilian control is not as firm as it was during the Cold War.

Despite the accession to power of a cohort of civilian leaders with little experience with, or interest in, military affairs, and despite a weakening in U.S. civilian governmental institutions, these institutions remain much stronger than those of the coup-plagued states of the Third World. Even with the end of the Cold War, the U.S. military has not embraced nontraditional, internal missions, as the French Army did during the Algerian crisis or the "New Professional" military dictatorships did in the southern parts of Latin America. The real problem is that norms of subordination to civilian control have eroded, and civilian and military ideas about the use of force and the nature of the international system have diverged. Nothing illustrates this better than the debate over the U.S. military's Powell Doctrine.

Civilian control in post–Cold War Russia has weakened much further than it has in the United States. The Yeltsin administration is far less interested in military affairs than were most Soviet civilian leaders; the civilian governmental institutions of Russia are weak and divided; and civilian factions continue to try to draw the Russian military into politics. The deeply divided Russian military remains unreformed and corrupt. Its orientation is at best uncertain, although the 1993 military doctrine gives it a large internal role. Civilian and military ideas about military policy and foreign affairs have also diverged. All of this explains why civilian control of the Russian military is weak compared with civilian control during the Soviet era.

In sum, the end of the Cold War and the resulting loss of the traditional external missions that fostered military subordination to civilian authority in the United States and the Soviet Union have given rise to a deterioration of civilian control of the military in both countries. Civilian control in Russia is much weaker than it is in the United States because Russia faces greater potential internal threats and also seems to be embracing a more internally oriented military doctrine. However, I do not suggest that even the very serious domestic problems in contemporary Russia mean that the military is likely to launch a coup d'état, only that the military will be harder for civilians to control.

Quadrant 3

The "silent dictatorship" of Field Marshal von Hindenburg and his nominal deputy General Ludendorff in Germany during World War I suggests that military doctrine plays a greater independent role in a security environment consisting of serious threats on both the international and domestic fronts. In the face of a challenging external and internal threat environment, the effects of structure on most of the intervening variables is indeterminate. In the German case, the military doctrine of "total war"— the internal analogue to the famous "cult of the offensive"—eroded civilian control. As this case demonstrates, internally oriented military doctrines such as "total war" can decisively affect civilian control of the military in indeterminate threat environments.

This case also underscores how the wrong military doctrine can lead to disaster. The results of the breakdown in German civilian control of the military were catastrophic for both the army and the country. Every matter in which the military's preference prevailed turned out badly. The military's hard line on the Polish question alienated Germany's main ally, Austria-Hungary. The High Command's uncompromising position on maintaining territorial gains in response to Allied peace overtures prolonged the war. The military's dogged insistence on unrestricted U-boat warfare did little to interdict Allied supplies but ensured that a reluctant United States would be dragged into the war. The OHL's eastern policy diverted nearly a million troops from the western front at a crucial juncture. The ubiquitous domestic influence of the OHL, which extended to the top of the civilian government and the innermost reaches of the kaiser's court, could not solve Germany's domestic problems. This case also makes clear that a military deeply involved in domestic politics is not likely to succeed either in running the country or in prosecuting a major external war.

The Algerian crisis teaches similar lessons about the role of military doctrine in situations in which states face both external and internal threats. The period between 1954 and 1962, when the French army was animated by the doctrine of guerre révolutionnaire, witnessed a series of civil-military conflicts so grave that we may ask how de Gaulle managed to avert a complete breakdown in civil-military relations. The answer is that he succeeded in changing French military doctrine. De Gaulle reoriented military strategy, changing the principal mission from internal counterinsurgency back to external warfare. The French nuclear program would reestablish France as a major power in Europe and provide the military with a more traditional external role. De Gaulle's efforts to change French military doctrine from guerre révolutionnaire to nuclear realism played a central role in reestablishing firm civilian control of the military.

The French case, like the German one, shows how military doctrine takes on an independent role in structurally inconclusive threat environments. This case also provides evidence that internal, nonmilitary missions are a recipe for serious problems in civil-military relations. Furthermore, it suggests that to the extent an individual leader plays a role, it is by recognizing how structure shapes civil-military relations.

Quadrant 4

States facing primarily internal threats are likely to have inattentive civilian leaders working through weak and divided institutions. The civilian leadership is likely to adopt subjective control mechanisms, and the military is likely to be highly unified but internally focused. Civilian and military ideas and cultures are also apt to be at wide variance. A state whose military has an internal and nontraditional focus is likely to have the weakest civilian control of its military.

The military dictatorships of southern Latin America during the 1960s and 1970s illustrate how challenging internal threat environments, combined with few external threats, can seriously undermine civilian control of the military. These states were led by civilians who had little experience with, or interest in, military affairs. The institutions of civilian rule were weak and divided. Civilian leaders sought to control their militaries through subjective control. The militaries of these states were generally cohesive in the face of an internal threat, but their orientation was inward, rather than outward. Finally, civilian and military ideas about the use of force and the nature of international politics were widely divergent. Indeed, the cases of Argentina (1966–83), Brazil (1964–85), and Chile (1973–89) all manifested many of the pathologies we would expect in states with no civilian control of the military whatsoever.

The southern Latin American military dictatorships demonstrate that challenging internal threat environments invariably produce internally oriented military doctrines, which inevitably lead to serious weaknesses in civilian control. The fact that all three states developed similar military doctrines suggests that this threat environment was structurally determinate. Moreover, the state that faced the most challenging international threats (Argentina) had the most rapid military withdrawal from power, while the state that enjoyed the most benign international threat environment (Chile) had the slowest. Finally, these cases, like the ones previously discussed, confound Lasswell and bolster Andreski, because these states that faced few external threats experienced the most extreme breakdown of civilian control: military rule.

Policy Recommendations

Because the post–Cold War international security environment facing many states is structurally indeterminate (Q2 or Q3), civilian control of the military can vary widely. The challenge for civilian and military leaders is to find doctrines and missions for their militaries that are both appropriate for the changed international security environment and conducive to civilian control. Civilian control of the military has become a more pressing policy concern with the end of the Cold War; ironically, it is also now far more amenable to policy influence. The key mechanism is likely to be military doctrine. In particular, what matters is the doctrine's orientation, whether it encourages norms of military subordination to civilian authority, and the level of civilian support for the doctrine.

In structurally indeterminate threat environments, all of the intervening variables are subject to the effects of different sorts of military doctrines.

Civilian Attentiveness and Expertise

In high external/low internal threat situations (Q1), civilians are apt to be attentive and sensitive to national security affairs. In contrast, in low external/low internal threat environments (Q2), there will be few incentives for civilian leaders to educate themselves in, or pay attention to, national security matters. Nonetheless, it is important that there remain a solid core of civilian expertise in national security affairs to ensure that post–Cold War states do not embrace national security policies driven purely by inertia or military organizational interests. This is also important in high external/high internal threat situations (Q3).

In both quadrants 2 and 3, an externally oriented military doctrine should foster greater civilian interest in, and expertise with, national security affairs. Unfortunately, in low external/high internal environments (Q4), it will be extremely difficult to get civilians to attend to traditional national security issues and concerns.

Orientation of the Military

Quadrant 1 situations should conduce to an externally oriented military. In quadrants 2 and 3, orientation could go either way; in these cases, it makes sense for civilian leaders to emphasize traditional external military doctrines and missions. For example, the raison d'être of the U.S. military should remain traditional external military missions. Obviously, the domestic use of the military during natural or other disasters is appropriate.[1] But the regular assignment of military units to internal security, antiterrorism, law enforcement, or social welfare provision is undesirable in terms of both military readiness and maintaining good civil-military relations. Recent efforts by the Clinton administration to pull the American military into a larger internal security role after the bombing of the federal building in Oklahoma City are particularly ill-advised.[2] Plans to use the American military for domestic social welfare or infrastructure provision are likely to exacerbate rather than ameliorate U.S. civil-military tensions. American civilian leaders need to give fresh thought to formulating a new military doctrine for the post–Cold War security environment. This doctrine should not only be externally focused, but also emphasize professional norms of military subordination to civilian control. Civilian leaders also must come together to endorse a continuing external mission.

Even more important, the Russian military ought to be kept out of domestic politics and oriented externally but defensively. Its use in October 1993 to seize Parliament has made the Russian military a player in domestic politics. An externally oriented and defensively postured Russian military will be conducive not only to civilian control, but also to peaceful relations with the other former Soviet republics and with the West. A smaller and outward-looking, rather than a larger and inward-looking, military is better in a low threat environment.

Finally, civilian leaders in southern Latin America should pay close attention to the military doctrines adopted by their armed forces. Especially in structurally indeterminate threat environments such as that of the present, military doctrines can be the enabling conditions that allow militaries to deal successfully with threats. Here two concerns are paramount. First, the preferred focus of a state's military doctrine is external. Second, for international stability, the optimal type of external military doctrine is a defensive one. Civilian leaders in these newly democratizing states ought to encourage their militaries to adopt externally oriented, defensive doctrines. The Argentine government, in an effort to keep the country's once internally oriented military externally focused, has recently been having the military participate in international peacekeeping missions. This is a realistic and beneficial post–Cold War military mission.[3]

External powers such as the United States can also play a limited role in enhancing civilian control of the military in these newly democratic countries. To begin with, the United States could direct its military assistance toward building up the external defense capability of these states rather than encouraging them to focus internally on counterinsurgency, counternarcotics work, and domestic policing.[4] U.S. advisors might also include discussion of how civil-military relations are conducted in the developed countries of North America and Western Europe as part of standard training programs. Obviously, neither of these measures would be sufficient for avoiding future civil-military conflicts, but they would help.

Once again, in quadrant 4, it will be extremely hard for civilian leaders to reorient their military organizations outward, so civilian control is likely to be tenuous. The problem is that most Third World states will continue to face mainly internal threats, so it is unreasonable to think that they will devote the lion's share of their national security resources to less pressing external missions such as peacekeeping. The solution is for them to divide coercive power between the military and some internal security organization. In that way, one organization will not have a monopoly on the use of force in those countries.[5]

Mode of Civilian Control

In quadrant 1 cases (high external/low internal threat), it is likely that civilian leaders will embrace objective control mechanisms. In quadrants 2 (low external/low internal) and 3 (high external/high internal), the chosen mode of civilian control may be either objective or subjective. Unfortunately, civilian leaders in quadrant 4 (low external/high internal) situations are likely to face strong pressure to embrace subjective control mechanisms.

If civilian leaders in quadrant 2 or quadrant 3 situations use objective rather than subjective control mechanisms, civilian control of the military should be more robust. An externally oriented military doctrine should be more conducive to objective control; conversely, an internally oriented doctrine should push civilian leaders toward subjective control.

U.S. and Russian civilian leaders should eschew subjective control efforts such as politicizing the military or trying to make it look more like civilian society. In the Russian case, civilian leaders should resist drawing the military deeper into domestic politics. Its use in October 1993 to settle a political conflict has weakened civilian control. The situation in the United States is less fraught with peril, but it is still challenging. Social changes that civilian leaders wish to introduce into the military need to be justified in terms of military effectiveness rather than social progress.[6] Civilian leaders might also wait to implement them until the threat environment becomes more competitive, making it easier to justify these changes in terms of military efficiency. For example, the historical record suggests that the U.S. military has been far more tolerant of homosexuals during wartime than peacetime.[7] It would, in fact, have been easier for civilians to change the military's exclusionary policy on homosexuality in a higher external threat environment such as the Cold War.

Cohesion of Civilian and Military Institutions

Faced with a challenging external threat and few internal ones (Q1), both civilian and military institutions should be quite cohesive. In quadrants 2 (low external/low internal) and 3 (high external/high internal), there is more likely to be a problem. Weak and divided civilian institutions are not conducive to civilian control. Likewise, a deeply divided military will probably be a constant source of friction between the military and its civilian leaders, while a highly unified military, facing divided civilians, is likely to present a serious threat to civilian control.

At present, the Russians lack both the institutions and the civilian expertise in military affairs to oversee their military effectively. This is an area that would benefit from creative policy input from both Russian and Western civilian leaders. The efforts of the U.S. Army European Command's Marshall Center at Garmisch, Germany, to help Eastern European and former Soviet civilian leaders and military officers build strong civilian institutions for control of the military are especially laudable.[8]

Once again, an externally oriented military doctrine should strengthen civilian institutions that oversee the military. Unfortunately, in quadrant 4 there is not likely to be much that civilians can do to increase the cohesion of civilian institutions.

Convergence of Civilian and Military Ideas

A divergence of civilian and military ideas about the nature of the international system and the use of force is not likely to be a problem in quadrant 1 (high external/low internal threat environment). In quadrants 2 (low/low), 3 (high/high), and 4 (low/high), in contrast, it may well be. Since the clash of civilian liberalism and military realism has often been a source of civil-military conflict, it seems advisable to try to avoid this intellectual divergence in the future. Civilian leaders should resist the impulse to embrace the traditional liberal perspective on international relations and military affairs—particularly the "war to end all wars" rhetoric, which implies that there will never again be challenging external threats that would justify traditional external military doctrines and missions.[9]

The excessively optimistic rhetoric of Russian and American civilian leaders about how the end of the Cold War represented a dramatically new international security environment, in which military force might no longer be very relevant, may actually have contributed to current problems in civilian control of the military by calling traditional external military missions into question. It might be better for civilian leaders to use the inevitability of future conflicts as a way to buttress current civil-military relations by reemploying conventional external military doctrines. Despite the end of the Cold War, the realist perspective on international affairs and military policy—which largely dominated U.S. civilian thinking during the Cold War—will still serve this country well.[10] The realist worldview strengthens civilian control of the military because it emphasizes that there are always potential threats in the international system, because of its anarchical nature.

The main task for civilian leaders in the post–Cold War era is to find new doctrines and missions that will be as conducive to firm civilian control of the military as the old ones were. While this does not mean that post–Cold War militaries must remain wedded to fighting a major conventional or nuclear war, it does suggest that their primary mission ought to remain traditional external war-fighting rather than internal, nonmilitary activities. These doctrines should also emphasize professional norms of military subordination to civilian control. Finally, the civilian leaderships need to support these external missions for their militaries.

Other Cases to Watch

There are a number of other cases that will be interesting to monitor in light of the predictions of the structural theory. One such case is Israel, which for many years confounded the Lasswellian conventional wisdom that a state permanently at war would inevitably become a garrison state.[11] Despite the Arab-Israeli conflict, the Israeli Defense Forces (IDF) have since 1948 been a model of military subordination to civilian control (Q1). However, in recent years there have been important changes that may undermine this pattern of firm civilian control. First, the nature of the IDF has changed since the time when Israel was a revolutionary nation in arms; the IDF is now a more professional army. Second, Israeli society has undergone a marked polarization in recent years.[12] The key structural cause of these changes in military and civilian institutions has been changes in the external and internal security environments. The external threat environment has moderated over the past twenty years, beginning with the Camp David accords and continuing through the Oslo agreements. This reduced external threat environment (Q2) has clearly affected the relationship between the IDF and the rest of Israeli society.[13]

Since the beginning of the Palestinian *intifada,* the IDF has been forced to assume a larger internal and nonmilitary role. This has seriously divided the officer corps and politicized the IDF. With the decision to evacuate troops and settlers from parts of the West Bank and Gaza Strip, the IDF has been placed in the center of a bitter and deeply divisive national debate that threatens to pull it in opposite directions.[14]

One potential problem is that the IDF is increasingly plagued by the secular-religious cleavage that has divided Israeli civilian society. Whereas the IDF was once a bastion of secularism, ever-larger numbers of religious Jews are now serving. This could have profound implications for civilian control.[15] The participation by an active-duty IDF soldier from an elite unit in the assassination of Prime Minister Yitzhak Rabin is perhaps an extreme and unlikely portent of future problems.[16] More reasonable concerns revolve around how a largely secular civilian society is going to deal with an increasingly religious military on explosive issues such as the withdrawal from the occupied territories. In a rare incidence of insubordination to civilian authority in 1975, Chief of the General Staff Mordecai Gur refused Prime Minister Rabin's order to use force to disband an illegal Jewish settlement at Sabastia on the West Bank.[17] Imagine what would happen in the future if an Israeli prime minister tried to order a much less secular IDF to undertake a similarly controversial operation. The key to maintaining firm civilian control of the Israeli military is for it to continue to be guided by an externally oriented doctrine.

Another case to watch is the People's Republic of China. While the external threat environment remains challenging,[18] the domestic security environment has deteriorated (Q3). The most obvious manifestation of this was the pro-democracy movement of June 1989. There is evidence that the Chinese military sees an array of internal problems, from endemic corruption in the Communist Party to increasing regional and ethnic separatism, as a serious threat to itself.[19] Finally, even before Deng Xiaoping's death, the military was at the center of a power struggle to succeed him.[20]

Many analysts believe that the army's support was ultimately decisive in this power struggle, and that the lending of such support represents the single greatest source of the growing influence of the People's Liberation Army (PLA) in Chinese domestic politics.[21] Though there are reports that Chinese civilian leaders such as President Jiang Zemin fear a military coup d'état, most analysts think that military influence will be less overt and direct. "Overall," noted RAND analyst Michael Swaine in 1992, "the basic features of China's politico-military system suggest that the Chinese military will almost certainly play a decisive role in the transition to a post–Deng Xiaoping regime. [However], various forms of unified, overt intervention by the PLA will be less likely than various types of factional intervention."[22] The nearly 75 percent increase in defense spending in recent years and the growing military representation in the Central Committee and the Politburo may be evidence of the growing domestic influence of the PLA.[23]

The potential for greater PLA intervention into Chinese domestic politics also follows from the fact that the institutions of civilian political leadership—especially the Communist Party—are weak and divided. Various civilian factions have politicized the military by employing subjective control mechanisms and dragging the military into civilian politics. The rise to power of an increasing number of civilian leaders with little or no military experience suggests an estrangement between Chinese civilian and military cultures. Finally, military attitudes toward civilian leaders have deteriorated markedly.[24]

However, certain other factors may restrict Chinese military intervention in domestic politics. First, the Chinese military is itself deeply divided, and this undermines its potential for concerted, unified action in all but the most extreme circumstances. On the other hand, the case of interwar

Japan suggests that through logrolling, a deeply divided military might nevertheless embrace an aggressive external policy. Second, domestic involvement by the PLA, whether in internal security missions or simply making money through the large network of military enterprises, will further undercut its military effectiveness.[25] Finally, the Chinese military was deeply impressed by the role of high technology in the Gulf War, and it may learn lessons about the dangers of a greater role in domestic politics like those internalized by the Soviet, Argentine, and Brazilian militaries.

In short, the structural threat environment facing China has changed, making it likely that civilian control of the PLA will weaken. However, the threat environment has also become more complex, making it possible that the PLA will embrace a military doctrine that will foster continued subordination to civilian authority.

The U.S. government has made it clear that it would not be unhappy to see military coups in two other states: Iraq and Cuba.[26] There have been a number of unsuccessful coup attempts in Iraq since the Gulf War; and in June 1989 there was considerable evidence of military unrest in Cuba.[27] The structural theory expounded in this book should make clear why coups in these two countries are unlikely and how the confrontational policies of the United States have made them even more so.

A 1995 report commissioned by the Defense Department and directed by former CIA official Nestor Sanchez concluded that the likelihood of a Cuban military coup against Fidel Castro was low.[28] One reason is that hard-line policies toward Cuba stimulate a "rally 'round the flag" effect; Castro has used these policies to justify continued authoritarian rule, as well as to explain away the economic and social failures of his regime.[29] Similarly, U.S. efforts to use military exercises to provoke a military coup in Iraq have probably served to bolster rather than undermine Iraqi military support for Saddam Hussein.[30]

In both cases, if the United States wants to make it more likely that the military will move against these regimes, it needs to minimize rather than maximize external military threats to Cuba and Iraq. Rather than overtly threatening the Cuban and Iraqi militaries, as some have advocated,[31] the United States should contain these regimes from afar while doing its best to separate the Cuban and Iraqi militaries from the Castro and Hussein regimes. As the cases discussed in this book make clear, the situation most conducive to massive military involvement in domestic politics is a benign external threat environment combined with a challenging internal threat environment.

Finally, for post–Cold War Germany and Japan, the implications of the structural theory are mixed. Many analysts are optimistic about the future of civilian control of the military in those two countries. Their optimism is rooted in their belief—which is fully compatible with Lasswell's argument—that the key to firm civilian control in those countries during the Cold War was the fact that both these states had largely eschewed power politics and become trading states rather than warfare states.[32] But considering that the German Bundeswehr was one of the largest conventional components of NATO during the Cold War and that in recent years the Japanese have had the largest aggregate defense budget in Asia,[33] it is hard to sustain the claim that they were not fully involved in the Cold War international security competition. More likely, the reason for the relatively robust civilian control in these two states was the same as for the United States and the Soviet Union:[34] states facing challenging external threat environments and few internal threats usually have reliable civilian control of the military. If so, then the end of the Cold War may weaken civilian control in these two states in much the same way that it has in the United States and Russia. There is some disturbing evidence that control of the German military is becoming an issue of serious concern to civilian leaders.[35] At any rate, the end of the Cold War should not lead to undue optimism regarding the maintenance of firm civilian control of the German and Japanese militaries.

Globalization, the Revolution in Military Affairs, and Civilian Control of the Military

The post–Cold War international system is extremely complex. A number of important changes could affect civilian control of the military, especially economic globalization and a growing recognition that technological progress may be producing what is often called a revolution in military affairs (RMA). The implications of these developments for civilian control of the military have not yet been thoroughly explored, but an initial consideration suggests unexpected reasons for both caution and optimism.

The conventional wisdom is that globalization, or increasing economic integration, will be beneficial because it will lead to more efficient production and more harmonious relations among states.[36] But globalization may also have a downside if it causes a marked weakening of the nation-state. Although with the end of the Cold War the security rationale for the state has clearly diminished, one might argue that the state will continue to prosper for other reasons. In the past, the state has performed important equity functions, such as wealth transfers; and nationalism has proven to be a potent ideological force. Globalization could undermine both of these nonsecurity rationalizations for the state. The equity role of the state is threatened by the growing belief that states are economically inefficient actors. The state as the repository of nationalism is undermined by the fact that in a world of economic competition, economic interests tend to be not national but rather sectoral or even regional.[37] A weakening of the state could diminish civilian control of the military.

Brazil illustrates the point. Though the Brazilian military is not monolithic with regard to economic thought, it is fair to say that economic nationalism is widespread within it. But economic globalization is in conflict with many of the tenets of this military economic nationalism.[38] Globalization has clearly contributed to the decline of the arms industry in southern Latin America, for instance,[39] which in Brazil and the states of the Southern Cone was central to military nationalist desires to achieve greater autonomy in the international economy.[40]

The Brazilian military was deeply unhappy about several 1991 decisions by the civilian government concerning the Brazilian defense industry. Foreign investors were allowed to participate in the Brazilian arms companies EMBRAER (aircraft), AVIBRAS (missiles), and ENGESA (tanks). The Collor de Mello government also gave in to pressure from the United States to curb Brazilian arms exports,[41] a decision that seemed to many military officers to threaten Brazil's economy and social stability. Employment in the Brazilian defense industry had dropped rapidly since the mid-1980s. AVIBRAS went from 6,000 employees in 1986 to 900 in 1990, while ENGESA dropped from 3,300 to 1,100; only EMBRAER did not significantly downsize.[42] To the extent that the civilian government tries to adapt to changes in the global economy, it may find itself in conflict with the military.

A similar possibility exists with regard to growing global concern about the effects of Brazilian development efforts in the Amazon basin—efforts enthusiastically supported by many Brazilian military officers. Many in the military fear that world efforts to protect the ecological balance of the Amazon basin will result in its being "internationalized."[43] The military's concerns have clearly influenced the policies of the civilian government, and the issue could become a source of civil-military conflict.[44]

On the optimistic side, the widely recognized "revolution in military affairs" is likely to enhance rather than undermine civilian control of the military. This phrase refers to the application of new technologies into a significant number of military systems combine[d] with innovative operational concepts and organizational adaptation in a way that fundamentally alters the character and conduct of conflict. It does so by producing a dramatic increase—often an order of magnitude or greater—in the combat potential and military effectiveness of armed forces.[45]

There has been much discussion of the impact of the RMA on the nature and conduct of war, but little about its impact on domestic politics.[46] The RMA is likely to encourage firmer civilian control of the military because it tends to push militaries toward Western notions of military professionalism. It may also encourage civilian control because civilians may have equal or greater expertise in the emerging technologies that may change warfare.[47] Finally, the RMA will foster an external orientation for the military and discourage internal political intervention, because it will increase the perceived level of international threat. This was the case in the Soviet Union during perestroika, and I believe it has had a similar effect in Argentina and Brazil since the Falklands/Malvinas War.

The lesson that the Argentines took from the 1982 war was that they lost primarily because they were at a technological disadvantage.[48] The Argentine military decided to make two major changes: first, to shift its emphasis from quantity to quality; and second, to focus on increasing its level of professionalism.[49] The Argentines recognized that a modern, professional military force was not likely to be capable of running a country while prosecuting an external war with a serious adversary.[50] These conclusions bolstered the faction of the armed forces that was advocating high-technology-oriented modernization over the faction inclined toward domestic political involvement.[51] This emphasis contributed to stronger civilian control of the military in Argentina. There is some evidence that the Brazilian military learned similar lessons.[52]

In short, developments in the post–Cold War international system related to globalization and the RMA will have mixed, and sometimes surprising, effects on civilian control of the military in the future. Globalization may weaken civilian control, but a revolution in military affairs, if it is happening, may strengthen it.

Implications of International Change
for Domestic Politics

The primary aim of this book has been to investigate the relationship between the changing international security environment and one aspect of domestic politics: civilian control of the military. Civil-military relations is an ideal place to look for such a relationship. As Thomas Nichols notes, "the study of civil-military affairs provides one of the elusive links between the fields of international relations and comparative politics, because it is in the civil-military arena that the problems of domestic politics and foreign policy collide most directly."[53] Thus, my findings also speak to the larger question of what effects changes in international structure have on domestic politics. This is a perennial issue in international relations theory, and the end of the Cold War invites us to reconsider it.

For most of the twentieth century, international politics was dominated by World Wars I and II and the Cold War. These periods of intense international security competition had significant effects on the state and domestic politics. However, the end of the Cold War may represent a "threat trough"—a period of substantially reduced international security competition. This decline in the external threat environment may also affect the state and domestic politics.[54]

This issue is important for both theoretical and policy reasons. We need a better understanding of the impact of international change on domestic politics. Although there is a robust literature on this question in the subfield of international political economy (IPE), much less work has been done in the security studies subfield.[55] In security studies, there has been much speculation about how the end of the Cold War will affect international politics, but less discussion of its domestic impact.[56] There has been relatively little theoretical research in security studies across levels of analysis. This is because, as Kenneth Waltz argues, a theory of international politics should focus on the systemic determinants of international systemic outcomes.[57] While the use of a single level of analysis may be methodologically justifiable for some research questions, the apparent correlation between dramatic international changes and significant domestic developments is a compelling reason for exploring cross-level linkages in the realm of security affairs.

What these case studies of changing patterns of civilian control in a new security environment confirm is that structural realism, and second image reversed theories in general, are excellent starting points for such

(High/low and low/high) ↑Structure → ↓doctrine → civilian control [Q1 and Q4]
(Low/low and high/high) ↓Structure → ↑doctrine → civilian control [Q2 and Q3]

FIGURE 15 Determinacy of Different Threat Environments

an investigation. Jack Snyder makes a convincing case for why scholars should begin with structural variables.[58] Sometimes structure does not decide, and in that case we need to look to other factors, such as military doctrine. But these cases suggest caution toward the broad claims made by some scholars to the effect that international factors are rarely determinative.

The determinacy of international structural variables is a central issue that sharply divides scholars. Realists hold that structure is determinate in enough situations that it should be the explanatory variable of first resort. Conversely, other scholars think that structure is rarely, if ever, determinate, and that is why they believe that other factors ought to be the explanatory variables of first resort.[59] This issue is important inasmuch as realism is likely to accord much independent efficacy to other variables when structure is indeterminate. In a determinate material structural environment (states have only one or at most a few optimal choices), realism expects that other factors will serve as dependent, or perhaps intervening, variables that usually reflect the structural environment but at most might change slowly enough to cause a lag between structural change and changes in state behavior. In indeterminate structural environments (states have many optimal choices), realists would have little trouble according domestic ideational variables a greater independent role in explaining state behavior. Since in structurally indeterminate environments realism and its critics make similar predictions about state behavior and international outcomes, the main arena of competition between the two groups of theorists will be in structurally determinate environments. The most important debate will be on the question of how often structure is determinate.

Therefore, an important task for future research is to ascertain under what conditions structure becomes more or less determinate. In the cases explored here, I have argued that different combinations of domestic and international security threats produce more or less determinative structural environments. The challenge for other scholars interested in international relations and comparative politics is to determine when, under what conditions, and to what extent other structural environments—or other, nonstructural factors—affect outcomes.

Another question for future research is, what determines which ideas—such as those contained in particular military doctrines—prevail in structurally indeterminate threat environments? Do ideas float freely, or are they somehow constrained by previous ones? While these were not central questions in this book, the answers would seem to lie in the realm of path dependency and the legacy of the past.[60]

Finally, the cases in this book also speak to the normative debate between realists and their critics. There is a substantial body of opinion within the critical-theory approach to international relations that holds that conflict in the international system is not an inevitable consequence of the anarchical nature of that system, as realists believe. Many agree with Alexander Wendt that "anarchy is what states make of it," and that nonrealist ideas and discourses may be able to supplant realism and foster a more pacific international system.[61] According to Richard Ned Lebow, "contemporary realists' . . . theories and some of the policy recommendations based on them may now stand in the way of the better world we all seek."[62]

The cases discussed in this book suggest that realist thinking may in fact have some beneficial domestic consequences. There were many Cold War–related problems in the United States and the Soviet Union, but, contrary to Lasswell, civilian control of the military was not one of them. The end of the Cold War has in general been a welcome development. But it has not been without its own set of problems, including a weakening of civilian control in both the former Cold War antagonists. While we do not need a return to intense international security competition to solve this problem, a return to previous military doctrines that mandate a traditional external mission for the U.S. and Russian militaries would certainly help. The ideas that inform the realist view of international relations provide a compelling rationale for such a mission.

Appendix

Major U.S. Civil-Military Conflicts, 1938–1997

Date	Issue	Civilians	Unclear	Mixed	Military
World War II					
Nov. 1938	Increases in aircraft production (FDR=yes; JCS=no)	X			
July 1, 1939	Mil. Order No. 1 transferring mil. planning to White House (FDR=yes; JCS=no)	X			
1940	Nat'l. Guard activation (FDR=yes; JCS=no)	X			
June 1940	Aid short of war to U.K. (FDR=yes; JCS=no)	X			
June 1940	Transfer of B-17s to U.K. (FDR=yes; JCS=no)	X			
June 1940	Stationing of fleet at Pearl Harbor (FDR=yes; JCS=no)	X			
1941	Undeclared ASW vs. Germany (FDR=yes; JCS=no)	X			
May 1941	Lend-Lease to China (FDR=yes; JCS=no)	X			
May–June 1941	U.S. forces to bases in western Atlantic (FDR=yes; JCS=no)	X			
July 1941	Oil embargo on Japan (Acheson/FDR=yes; JCS=no)	X			
July–Aug. 1941	Reinforcement of Philippines (FDR=yes; mil.=no)	X			
Nov. 1941	"Ultimatum" to Japan (FDR/Hull=yes; mil.=no)	X			

Date	Issue	Civilians	Unclear	Mixed	Military
Mar. 1942	Full Lend-Lease to Soviet Union and new protocol signed (vs. mil.)	X			
May 1942	Molotov promised 2d front by 1942 (FDR=yes; mil.=no)	X			
May–June 1942	FDR's plan for reinforcing U.S. in Middle East (vs. mil.)	X			
June 1942	Pacific (Marshall/King) vs. Europe (FDR)	X			
July 1942	Torch (FDR=yes; JCS=no)	X			
Aug. 1942	Air force in the Caucasus	X			
Jan. 1943	Conditions on Lend-Lease (mil.=yes; FDR=no)	X			
Mar.–Apr. 1943	British import crisis	X			
May 1943	Scale of Roundup	X			
May 1943	FDR/Chennault vs. Stilwell/War Dept. on ANAKIM	X			
Aug. 1943	JCS vs. FDR on British Overlord priority	X			
Dec. 1943	FDR vs. JCS on Buccaneer	X			
Aug. 1944	FDR vs. Leahy/War Dept. on recalling Stilwell from China	X			
Early 1940s	Commission for Joseph Alsop (FDR/Chennault=yes; Marshall/Stilwell=no)	X			
Early 1940s	Promotion of Col. Philip Faymonville (FDR/Hopkins= yes; Marshall/Davies=no)	X			
Early 1940s	Promotion of FDR's son Elliot (FDR=yes; Marshall/ Arnold=no)	X			

Between World War II and the Cold War: 1945–1950

Date	Issue	Civilians	Unclear	Mixed	Military
1945–	Control of nuclear weapons	X			
1946–47	DoD reorganization and service unification (compromise)			X	
1948–49	Berlin blockade (Truman=hard line; mil.=accom.)	X			
1948–53	Integration of blacks in the mil. (Truman=yes; services=no)	X			
1949	Revolt of the admirals (B-36 vs. supercarrier)			X	

The Cold War: 1950–1989

Date	Issue	Civilians	Unclear	Mixed	Military
1948–52	Truman defense budgets	X			
1950	Korean War strategy (Truman/ JCS vs. MacArthur)	X			

Date	Issue	Civilians	Unclear	Mixed	Military
1952–60	New Look (Eisenhower/Air Force vs. Army)	X			
1952–60	Eisenhower defense budgets	X			
April 1954	Nuclear use around Dien Bien Phu (Radford/Twining=yes; Ike/Ridgway=no)	X			
May 1954	Nuclear use vs. PRC air force (JCS=yes; Ike=no)	X			
Feb. 1955	Nuclear use during Taiwan Straits crisis (JCS=yes; Ike=no)	X			
1959	B-70 decision (Air Force=yes; Ike=no)	X			
1960–68	Planning, Programming, and Budgeting System (Civ.=yes; mil.=no)	X			
1962	Cuban missile crisis (JFK vs. JCS)	X			
July 1962	JFK vs. Norstad on SACEUR	X			
1963	Tactical Fighter Experimental decision (Air Force and Navy=no; McNamara=yes)	X			
1965–68	Vietnam ground war strategy (civ.=limited; mil.=full mobilization)	X			
1965–67	Vietnam air war strategy (LBJ=gradual; JCS=all-out)	X			
1960s–70s	Limited nuclear options (civ.=yes; Air Force=no)	X			
1972	SALT I (civ.=yes; mil.=no)	X			
1973–	Increasing integration of women (civ.=yes; mil.=no)	X			
1973–76	Détente (civ.=yes; mil.=no)	X			
May 1977	Withdrawal of U.S. forces from Korea (Carter=yes; mil.=no)			X	
May 1977	"Revolt of the Navy" (Carter vs. carrier; Navy=pro)	X			
June 1977	Cancellation of B-1 (Carter=yes; Air Force=no)	X			
1978	SALT II (civ.=yes; JCS=no)	X			
1981	"Zero option" for U.S.-Soviet nuclear arms control (civ.=yes; JCS=no)	X			
Feb. 1982	Protracted nuclear war (Reagan=yes; JCS=no)				X
1982	Lebanon intervention (civ.=yes; mil.=no)	X			
Mid-1980s	Invasion of Central America (not considered)				?

Date	Issue	Civilians	Unclear	Mixed	Military
1983–86	JCS reform/Goldwater-Nichols (JCS/Cong./White House=yes; Weinberger=no)	?			
1986	SOLIC (civ.=yes; mil.=no)	X			
1986	0/0 at Reykjavik (Reagan=yes; JCS=no)	X			
1986	Stingers to Afghan rebels (civ.=yes; JCS=no)	X			

End of Cold War: 1989–Present

Date	Issue	Civilians	Unclear	Mixed	Military
1990	Gulf War strategy (Bush= offensive; JCS/CENTCOM= defensive)	X			
1992	Bosnia (Powell vs. civ.)				X
1992–94	Gays in the military (Clinton= yes; JCS/Nunn=no)				X
1993	FY 1994 defense budget (Clinton/Aspin vs. Powell)	X			
1993–94	Change in roles and missions (Clinton/Nunn=yes; JCS=no)				X
1993–94	"Win-hold-win" (Clinton/Aspin) vs. "win-win" (JCS)				X
1994	Haiti (Clinton/Talbot=invade; Perry/JCS=no)	X			
1994	No restrictions on women (Clinton/West=yes; JCS=no)			X	
1996–97	Bosnian war criminals (Clinton/Albright=yes; Cohen/JCS=no)				X
1997	Flinn honorable discharge (Widnall=yes; Fogelman no)				X
1997	Restrictions on land mines (Clinton/Gore=yes; JCS=no).				X
1997	Khobar Towers responsibility of Air Force C.O. (Cohen= yes; Fogelman=no)	X			

Sources: Kent Roberts Greenfield, *America's Strategy in World War II: A Reconsideration* (Baltimore: Johns Hopkins University Press, 1963), 49–84; Mark A Stoler, "U.S. Civil-Military Relations in World War II," *Parameters* 21, no. 3 (Autumn 1991): 60–73; Forrest C. Pogue, "George C. Marshall on Civil-Military Relationships in the United States," in Richard H. Kohn, ed., *The United States Military under the Constitution of the United States, 1789–1989* (New York: New York University Press, 1991), 193–222; Eric Larrabee, *Commander in Chief: Franklin Delano Roosevelt, His Lieutenants, and Their War* (New York: Harper & Row, 1987); David McCullough, "Truman Fires MacArthur," *Military History Quarterly* 5, no. 1 (Autumn 1992): 8–21; David McCullough, *Truman* (New York: Simon & Schuster, 1992); Lawrence J. Korb, *The Joint Chiefs of Staff: The First Twenty-five Years* (Bloomington: Indiana University Press, 1976); Stephen E. Ambrose, *Eisenhower: Soldier and President* (New York: Touchstone Books, 1990); Arthur Schlesinger, *A Thousand Days:*

John F. Kennedy in the White House (Boston: Houghton Mifflin, 1965); Lyndon Baines Johnson, *The Vantage Point: Perspectives of the Presidency, 1963–1969* (New York: Holt, Rinehart & Winston, 1971); Mark Perry, *Four Stars* (Boston: Houghton Mifflin, 1989); Richard Nixon, *RN: The Memoirs of Richard Nixon* (New York: Grosset & Dunlap, 1978); Gerald R. Ford, *A Time to Heal: The Autobiography of Gerald R. Ford* (New York: Harper & Row, 1979); Zbigniew Brzezinski, *Power and Principle: Memoirs of the National Security Advisor, 1977–81* (New York: Farrar, Straus, Giroux, 1983); Jimmy Carter, *Keeping Faith: Memoirs of a President* (Toronto: Bantam Books, 1982); Lou Cannon, *President Reagan: The Role of a Lifetime* (New York: Simon & Schuster, 1991); Bob Woodward, *The Commanders* (New York: Simon & Schuster, 1991); Rick Atkinson, *Crusade: The Untold Story of the Persian Gulf War* (New York: Houghton Mifflin, 1993); Elizabeth Drew, *On the Edge: The Clinton Presidency* (New York: Simon & Schuster, 1994); and recent issues of the *New York Times*.

Notes

Chapter 1. Introduction

1. Samuel Huntington, *Political Order and Changing Societies* (New Haven: Yale University Press, 1968), 194.

2. Mikhail Tsypkin, "Will the Military Rule Russia?" *Security Studies* 2, no. 1 (1992): 38–73; Stephen Foye, "Post-Soviet Russia: Politics and the New Russian Army," *Radio Free Europe/Radio Liberty* [hereafter *RFE/RL*] *Research Report* 1, no. 33 (1992): 5–12; Thomas M. Nichols, *The Sacred Cause: Civil-Military Conflict over Soviet National Security, 1917–1992* (Ithaca: Cornell University Press, 1993); Kimberly Martin Zisk, *Civil-Military Relations in the New Russia,* Occasional Paper (Columbus: Mershon Center, Ohio State University, Mar. 1993); Timothy L. Thomas, "Fault Lines and Factions in the Russian Army," *Orbis* 39, no. 4 (1995): 531–48; and Stephen Foye, "Civilian and Military Leaders in New Political Environment," *RFE/RL Research Bulletin,* 11, no. 5 (1994): 1, 2, 6.

3. Articles by the key proponents of the "crisis school" include Russell F. Weigley, "The American Military and the Principle of Civilian Control from McClellan to Powell," *Journal of Military History* 57, special issue (Oct. 1993): 27–58; Richard H. Kohn, "Out of Control: The Crisis in Civil-Military Relations," *National Interest,* no. 35 (Spring 1994): 3–17; Kohn, "Upstarts in Uniform," *New York Times,* Apr. 10, 1994, 19; Edward N. Luttwak, "Washington's Biggest Scandal," *Commentary* 97, no. 5 (1994): 29–33; and Charles Dunlap Jr., "Welcome to the Junta: The Erosion of Civilian Control of the U.S. Military," *Wake Forest Law Review* 29, no. 2 (1994): 341–92.

For less alarmist views, see Eliot Cohen, "Civil-Military Relations," *Orbis* 41, no. 2 (1997): 177–86 ; A. J. Bacevich, "Clinton's Military Problem—and Ours," *National Review,* Dec. 13, 1993, 36–40; Bacevich, "Civilian Control: A Useful Fiction?" *Joint Forces Quarterly,* no. 6 (Autumn/Winter 1994/95): 76–79; and Bacevich, "Tradition Abandoned," *National Interest,* no. 48 (Summer 1997): 16–25.

4. See Harold Lasswell, "The Garrison State," *American Journal of Sociology* 46, no. 4 (January 1941): 455–68. A more recent example of Lasswellian thinking is Jack Snyder, "Civil-Military Relations and the Cult of the Offensive, 1914 and 1984," in Steven E. Miller, ed., *Military Strategy and the Origins of the First World War* (Princeton: Princeton University Press, 1985), 108–46. Such Lasswellian thinking also pervades the "diversionary war" literature. See, for example, Michael Stohl, "The Nexus of Civil and International Conflict," in Ted Robert Gurr, ed., *Handbook of Political Conflict* (New York: Free Press, 1980); and Jack Levy, "The Diversionary Theory of War: A Critique," in Manus Midlarsky, ed., *The Handbook of War Studies* (Boston: Unwin & Hyman, 1989).

5. The seminal works on U.S. civil-military relations are Samuel P. Huntington, *The Soldier and the State: The Theory and Politics of Civil-Military Relations* (Cambridge: Harvard University Press, Belknap Press, 1957); Morris Janowitz, *The Professional Soldier: A Social and Political Portrait* (New York: Free Press, 1971); and Samuel E. Finer, *The Man on Horseback: The Role of the Military in Politics* (New York: Praeger, 1962).

6. The key works that emerged at this time were Richard K. Betts, *Soldiers, Statesmen, and Cold War Crises* (Cambridge: Harvard University Press, 1977); Amos Perlmutter, *The Military in Politics in Modern Times: On Professional, Praetorian, and Revolutionary Soldiers* (New Haven: Yale University Press, 1977); and Eric Nordlinger, *Soldiers in Politics: Military Coups and Governments* (Englewood Cliffs, N.J.: Prentice-Hall, 1977).

7. See Martin Edmonds, *Armed Services and Society* (Boulder, Colo.: Westview Press, 1988). In addition to my book and the articles cited in notes 2 and 3 above, important work is also being done on post–Cold War civil-military relations by younger scholars, including Peter Feaver, Brian Taylor, Kurt Dassel, Aaron Belkin, Eva Buza, Harold Trinkunas, Wendy Hunter, David Pion-Berlin, Laura Miller, and others.

8. R. W. Apple, Jr., "Clinton's Pentagon Blues Seem to Be Back Again," *New York Times*, June 6, 1997, 28.

9. Colin Powell and William Odom, "An Exchange on Civil-Military Relations," *National Interest*, no. 36 (Summer 1994): 23, 25–26.

10. These changed attitudes are apparent in recent books by former and current military officers. See Colin Powell with Joseph E. Persico, *My American Journey* (New York: Random House, 1995), 302–3; and H. R. McMaster, *Dereliction of Duty: Lyndon Johnson, Robert McNamara, the Joint Chiefs of Staff, and the Lies That Led to Vietnam* (New York: HarperCollins, 1997), 330–31.

11. Comments in a seminar held at the Diplomatic Academy of the Russian Foreign Ministry, Moscow, Dec. 13, 1995.

12. On the American public's post–Cold War indifference to military issues, see Alison Mitchell, "Running after the Cold War," *New York Times,* Mar. 10, 1996, "Week in Review," 4.

13. I thank Richard Betts for repeatedly bringing this point to my attention.

14. Article 2, section 2, clause 1 designates the president as commander in chief, while article 1, section 8, clauses 12–16 give Congress the authority to "raise and support Armies" and other powers relating to the military. What these distinctions mean in practice has been hotly debated since the Constitution was adopted. See Philip B.

Kurland and Ralph Lerner, eds., *The Founders' Constitution* (Chicago: University of Chicago Press, 1987), 3:93–216, 4:1–11.

15. This is one of the most important insights of Finer's *The Man on Horseback* (see p. 4), and why the provocative article by Col. Charles J. Dunlap Jr., "The Origins of the American Military Coup of 2012" (*Parameters* 22, no. 4 [1992/93]: 2–20), somewhat obscures the real difficulties in post–Cold War civil-military relations in the United States.

16. Huntington, *The Soldier and the State,* 20.

17. Janowitz, *The Professional Soldier,* 13.

18. Finer, *The Man on Horseback,* 147.

19. Huntington, *The Soldier and the State,* 329. Also see Demetrios Caraley, *The Politics of Military Unification: A Study of Conflict and the Policy Process* (New York: Columbia University Press, 1966), 279.

20. Both Col. David H. Hackworth ("Soldiers Know: Helms Got It Wrong," *Newsweek,* Nov. 29, 1994, 26) and Harry Summers ("Clinton and the Military," *Washington Times,* Dec. 2, 1994, 21) acknowledge that there is widespread contempt for Clinton in the American military. Despite this, Hackworth has "little doubt they'll follow his orders."

21. This is the implied definition in the "College of Naval Warfare and Naval Command College Course in Strategy and Policy, November 1994–March 1995" (U.S. Naval War College, 1994, mimeo), 3.

22. On this concern, see the discussion in Alexander Hamilton, "Federalist no. 8," in Hamilton, James Madison, and John Jay, *The Federalist Papers* (New York: Mentor Books, 1961), 66–71.

23. For a similar definition, see Kenneth W. Kemp and Charles Hudlin, "Civil Supremacy over the Military: Its Nature and Limits," *Armed Forces and Society* 19, no. 1 (1992): 9.

24. This method follows Robert Dahl, "A Critique of the Ruling Elite Model," *American Political Science Review* 52, no. 2 (1958): 366.

25. Robert Dahl, *Polyarchy: Participation and Opposition* (New Haven: Yale University Press, 1971), 51.

26. For similar arguments, see Stephen Van Evera, "The Causes of War" (Ph.D. diss., University of California at Berkeley, 1984), 206–398; Stephen M. Walt, "The Search for a Science of Strategy: A Review Essay on *Makers of Modern Strategy,*" *International Security* 12, no. 1 (1987): 140–65; and Bernard Brodie, *War and Politics* (New York: Macmillan, 1973), 433–96.

27. Carl von Clausewitz, *On War,* ed. Anatol Rapoport (Middlesex, England: Penguin Books, 1968), 405.

28. On the other hand, the military is subject to one powerful incentive not to fail: failure in wartime may cost soldiers their lives! This explains the well-documented caution of military officers about the actual use of force. See Betts, *Soldiers, Statesmen, and Cold War Crises.* In addition, the military does have greater technical expertise than the civilian leadership, and civilians are subject to certain biases. The bottom line is that while the civilian leaders should have the final word on most issues of national policy, they should not speak that final word until they are sure that they have fully utilized military expertise.

Chapter 2. Civilian Control of the Military in Different Threat Environments

1. Charles Moskos, oral presentation at the Olin Institute's "Strategy and National Security" conference, Wianno Club, Cape Cod, Massachusetts, June 1994. Also see Gregory D. Foster, "Raw Recruits vs. Old Troopers," *Wall Street Journal,* July 14, 1994, 11; Gary Wills, "Clinton's Troubles," *New York Review of Books,* Sept. 22, 1994, 7; James H. Meisel, *The Fall of the Republic: The Military Revolt in France* (Ann Arbor: University of Michigan Press, 1962), 108; Cyrus L. Sulzberger, *The Test: De Gaulle and Algeria* (New York: Harcourt, Brace & World, 1962), 162; and Walter Millis with Harvey C. Mansfield and Harold Stein, *Arms and the State: Civil-Military Elements in National Policy* (New York: Twentieth Century Fund, 1958), 259.

2. Morris Janowitz, *The Professional Soldier: A Social and Political Portrait* (New York: Free Press, 1971).

3. Richard H. Kohn, "Out of Control: The Crisis in Civil-Military Relations," *National Interest,* no. 35 (Spring 1994): 14–15; and Edward N. Luttwak, "Washington's Biggest Scandal," *Commentary* 97, no. 5 (1994): 30.

4. Samuel P. Huntington, *The Soldier and the State: The Theory and Politics of Civil-Military Relations* (Cambridge: Harvard University Press, Belknap Press, 1957), 74.

5. Ibid., 163–77, 414.

6. See Deborah Avant, "The Institutional Sources of Military Doctrine: Hegemons in Peripheral Wars," *International Studies Quarterly* 37, no. 4 (1993): 409–30; Avant, "U.S. Military Reluctance to Respond to Post–Cold War Low-Level Threats," *Security Studies* 6, no. 2 (1996/97): 51–90; and Peter D. Feaver, "Delegation, Monitoring, and Civilian Control of the Military: Agency Theory and American Civil-Military Relations," Project on U.S. Post–Cold War Civil-Military Relations Working Paper No. 4 (Cambridge: John M. Olin Institute for Strategic Studies, May 1996).

7. Samuel Huntington, *Political Order and Changing Societies* (New Haven: Yale University Press, 1968), 196. Guillermo O'Donnell's "Bureaucratic-Authoritarian" model has a similar logic. See his *Bureaucratic Authoritarianism: Argentina, 1966–1973, in Comparative Perspective* (Berkeley: University of California Press, 1988).

8. Huntington, *The Soldier and the State,* 80–85.

9. Ibid., 79, 144, 157, 457–66. Morris Janowitz agrees with Huntington that military officers tend to be more conservative than civilians. *The Professional Soldier,* 242–55.

10. Thomas E. Ricks, "On American Soil: The Widening Gap between the U.S. Military and U.S. Society," Project on U.S. Post–Cold War Civil-Military Relations Working Paper No. 3 (Cambridge: John M. Olin Institute for Strategic Studies, May 1996).

11. David S. Sorenson, "Soldiers, States, and Systems: Civil-Military Relations in the Post–Cold War World" (paper presented at the Mershon Center Conference on Civil-Military Relations, Ohio State University, Columbus, Dec. 4–5, 1992).

12. Stanislaw Andreski, *Military Organization and Society* (Berkeley: University of California Press, 1968), 202. Also see his "On the Peaceful Disposition of Military Dictatorships," *Journal of Strategic Studies* 3, no. 3 (1980): 3–10.

13. Harold D. Lasswell, "Sino-Japanese Crisis: The Garrison State versus the

Civilian State," *China Quarterly,* special no. (Fall 1937): 649. Also see Lasswell, "The Garrison State," *American Journal of Sociology* 46, no. 4 (1941): 455–68.

14. Compare the more Lasswellian Huntington—*The Common Defense: Strategic Programs in National Politics* (New York: Columbia University Press, 1961), 7, and , *The Soldier and the State,* 456—with his "The Soldier and the State in the 1970s," in Andrew J. Goodpaster and Samuel Huntington, eds., *Civil-Military Relations* (Washington, D.C.: American Enterprise Institute for Public Policy Research, 1977), 5–28, and his critical discussion of Lasswell in *The Soldier and the State,* 346–50.

15. Alfred Stepan, *The Military in Politics: Changing Patterns in Brazil* (Princeton: Princeton University Press, 1971), 55. Also see Henry Bienen, "Armed Forces and National Modernization: Continuing the Debate," *Comparative Politics* 16, no. 1 (1983): 2.

16. One partial exception, though lacking structured and focused case studies, is Martin Edmonds, *Armed Services and Society* (Boulder, Colo.: Westview Press, 1988), 113–35.

17. See Kenneth N. Waltz, *Theory of International Politics* (Reading, Mass.: Addison-Wesley, 1979), chap. 3. For a discussion of the limitations of structural theories, see Stephan Haggard, "Structuralism and Its Critics: Recent Progress in International Relations Theory," in Emmanuel Adler and Beverly Crawford, eds., *Progress in Postwar International Relations* (New York: Columbia University Press, 1991), 403–47.

18. Waltz, *Theory of International Politics,* 74, 124–28. For further discussion, see Colin Elman, "Horses for Courses: Why Not Neo-Realist Theories of Foreign Policy?" *Security Studies* 6, no. 1 (1996): 7–53.

19. Waltz, *Theory of International Politics,* 78.

20. Peter Gourevitch, "The International System and Regime Formation: A Critical Review of Anderson and Wallerstein," *Comparative Politics* 10, no. 2 (1978): 436.

21. I thank Henry Nau for pointing out the relevance of the "state/society" literature for threats. For a good overview of this literature, see Peter J. Katzenstein, "Introduction: Domestic and International Forces and Strategies of Foreign Economic Policy" in Katzenstein, ed., *Between Power and Plenty: Foreign Economic Policies of Advanced Industrial States* (Madison: University of Wisconsin Press, 1978), 3–22.

22. Lewis Coser, *The Functions of Social Conflict* (Glencoe, Ill.: Free Press, 1956), 107.

23. The classic statements of this idea remain Georg Simmel, *Conflict and the Web of Group Affiliation,* trans. Kurt Wolff and Reinhard Bendix (New York: Free Press, 1955), 96–123; and Coser, *Functions of Social Conflict.* An excellent analytical summary is Arthur A. Stein, "Conflict and Cohesion: A Review of the Literature," *Journal of Conflict Resolution* 20, no. 1 (1976): 143–72.

For the greatest increase in cohesion, the threat must be to the group as a whole and must be amenable only to a collective solution. See John T. Lanzetta et al., "Some Effects of Situational Threat on Group Behavior," *Journal of Abnormal and Social Psychology* 49, no. 3 (1954): 445–53; Robert T. Hamblin, "Group Integration during a Crisis," *Human Relations: Studies toward the Integration of the Social Sciences* 11, no. 1 (1958): 67–76; and Irving L. Janis, "Group Identification under Conditions of External Danger," *British Journal of Medical Psychology* 11, no. 3 (1963): 227–38.

24. Eric Nordlinger, *Soldiers in Politics: Military Coups and Governments* (Englewood Cliffs, N.J.: Prentice-Hall, 1977), 39–42.

25. Barry Posen, *The Sources of Military Doctrine: France, Britain, and Germany between the World Wars* (Ithaca: Cornell University Press, 1983), 74–78.

26. John E. Mueller, *War, Presidents, and Public Opinion* (Lanham, Md.: University Press of America, 1985), 58–59.

27. See Gerhard Ritter, *The Sword and the Scepter: The Problem of Militarism in Germany,* vol. 3, *The Tragedy of Statesmanship—Bethmann Hollweg as War Chancellor,* trans. Heinz Norden (Coral Gables, Fla.: University of Miami Press, 1972), 12.

28. Andreski, "Peaceful Disposition of Military Dictatorships," 4; Morris Janowitz, *Military Institutions and Coercion in the Developing Nations* (Chicago: University of Chicago Press, 1977), 156; and Michael Howard, *War in European History* (London: Oxford University Press, 1976), 94–115.

29. David H. Bayley, "The Police and Political Development in Europe," in Charles Tilly, ed., *The Formation of National States in Western Europe* (Princeton: Princeton University Press, 1975), 359.

30. For a related discussion, see Jeffrey Herbst, "War and the State in Africa," *International Security* 14, no. 4 (1990): 117–39; and Joel Migdal, *Strong Societies and Weak States: State-Society Relations and Capabilities in the Third World* (Princeton: Princeton University Press, 1988).

31. Samuel Huntington, "Patterns of Violence in World Politics," in Huntington, ed., *Changing Patterns of Military Politics* (Glencoe, Ill.: Free Press, 1962), 22.

32. J. Craig Jenkins and Augustine J. Kposowa, "The Political Origins of African Military Coups: Ethnic Competition, Military Centrality, and the Struggle over the Postcolonial State," *International Studies Quarterly* 36, no. 2 (1992): 271–92; and Stepan, *The Military in Politics,* 98.

33. On the differing threat environments facing Third World states, see Steven R. David, "Explaining Third World Alignment," *World Politics* 42, no. 2 (1991): 233–56.

34. Guillermo O'Donnell, "Modernization and Military Coups: Theory, Comparisons, and the Argentine Case," in Abraham Lowenthal, ed., *Armies and Politics in Latin America* (New York: Holmes & Meier, 1976), 230. For a general discussion of the literature on military withdrawals, see Claude E. Welch Jr., "Military Disengagement from Politics: Paradigms, Processes, or Random Events," *Armed Forces and Society* 18, no. 3 (1992): 323–42.

35. Stepan, *The Military in Politics,* 229.

36. Richard C. Rankin, "The Expanding Institutional Concerns of Latin American Military Establishments: A Review Article," *Latin American Research Review* 9, no. 1 (1974): 95.

37. Posen, *Sources,* 16–17; Jack Snyder, *The Ideology of the Offensive: Military Decision Making and the Disasters of 1914* (Ithaca: Cornell University Press, 1984), 10–11, 19–30; and Stephen Van Evera, "The Cult of the Offensive and the Origins of the First World War," in Steven E. Miller, ed., *Military Strategy and the Origins of the First World War* (Princeton: Princeton University Press, 1985), 58–107.

38. The best work on the internal consequences of military doctrines has been done by students of the military dictatorships of the Southern Cone of Latin America. Stepan's *The Military in Politics* and Alain Rouquié's *The Military and the State in Latin America,* trans. Paul E. Sigmund (Berkeley: University of California Press, 1987) are classics. In addition, an excellent recent work is David Pion-Berlin, *The Ideology*

of State Terror: Economic Doctrine and Political Repression in Argentina and Peru (Boulder, Colo.: Lynne Rienner Publishers, 1989).

39. Judith Goldstein and Robert O. Keohane, introduction to Goldstein and Keohane, eds., *Ideas and Foreign Policy: Beliefs, Institutions, and Political Change* (Ithaca: Cornell University Press, 1993), 12–13.

40. Andreski, "Peaceful Disposition of Military Dictatorships," 3–4. Also see Stephen P. Rosen, *Societies and Military Power: India and Its Armies* (Ithaca: Cornell University Press, 1996), 5.

41. Jeffrey Legro, *Cooperation under Fire: Anglo-German Restraint during World War II* (Ithaca: Cornell University Press, 1995), 19. Also see Elizabeth Kier, *Imagining War: French and British Military Doctrine between the Wars* (Princeton: Princeton University Press, 1997), 28.

42. Brian Taylor, "Culture and Coups: The Norm of Civilian Supremacy" (manuscript, Olin Institute, Feb. 1996).

43. Huntington, *The Soldier and the State,* 79, 144, 157.

44. Edward Luttwak, *Coup d'Etat: A Political Handbook* (New York: Knopf, 1968), 209. Luttwak's table 4 shows that 85 percent of coups from 1946 through 1964 worldwide occurred in the course of internal conflict, while only 15 percent took place during international conflict.

45. Gary King, Robert O. Keohane, and Sidney Verba, *Designing Social Inquiry: Scientific Inference in Qualitative Research* (Princeton: Princeton University Press, 1994), 155.

46. On process tracing, see Alexander L. George and Timothy J. McKeown, "Case Studies and Theories of Organizational Decisionmaking," in Robert Coulam and Richard Smith, eds., *Advances in Information Processing in Organizations* (Greenwich, Conn.: JAI Press, 1985), 2:21–58.

47. Harry Eckstein reminds us that "cases" are not countries but changes on the independent and dependent variables. "Case Study and Theory in Political Science," in Fred I. Greenstein and Nelson Polsby, eds., *Handbook of Political Science* (Reading, Mass.: Addison-Wesley, 1975), 7:85.

48. On the importance of selecting cases on the independent rather than the dependent variable, see Barbara Geddes, "How the Cases You Choose Affect the Answers You Get," *Political Analysis* 2 (1990): 131–50.

49. The cases are therefore "two-cornered fights" between my theory and the evidence. On this concept, see Imre Lakatos, "Falsification and the Methodology of Scientific Research Programmes," in Imre Lakatos and Alan Musgrave, eds., *Criticism and the Growth of Knowledge* (Cambridge: Cambridge University Press, 1970), 91–195.

Chapter 3. Losing Control?

1. Quoted in Allan Millett, *The American Political System and Civilian Control of the Military: A Historical Perspective* (Columbus: Mershon Center, Ohio State University, Apr. 1979), 1.

2. For discussion of these incidents, see Allan R. Millett and Peter Maslowski, *For the Common Defense: A Military History of the United States of America,* rev. ed.

(New York: Free Press, 1994), 88–90; and Arthur Ekrich, *The Civilian and the Military* (New York: Oxford University Press, 1956), 19–20, 22, 32.

3. See U.S. Senate, "Defense Organization: The Need for Change," Staff Report to the Committee on Armed Services, 99th Cong., 1st sess. (Washington, D.C.: GPO, Oct. 16, 1985), 32–35; and Russell F. Weigley, "The American Military and the Principle of Civilian Control from McClellan to Powell," *Journal of Military History* 57, special issue (Oct. 1993): 32–39.

4. Samuel P. Huntington, *The Soldier and the State: The Theory and Politics of Civil-Military Relations* (Cambridge: Harvard University Press, Belknap Press, 1957), chap. 9.

5. For a good discussion of this, see Stephen Skowronek, *Building a New American State: The Expansion of National Administrative Capacities, 1877–1920* (New York: Cambridge University Press, 1982), 89–90; and John B. Wilson, "Army Readiness Planning, 1899–1917," *Parameters* 64, no. 7 (1984): 61.

6. Walter Millis with Harvey C. Mansfield and Harold Stein, *Arms and the State: Civil-Military Elements in National Policy* (New York: Twentieth Century Fund, 1958), 139–40.

7. Ibid., 10.

8. This discussion is based primarily on Kent Roberts Greenfield, *America's Strategy in World War II: A Reconsideration* (Baltimore: Johns Hopkins Press, 1963), 49–84; Mark A. Stoler, "U.S. Civil-Military Relations in World War II," *Parameters* 21, no. 3 (1991): 60–73; and Forrest C. Pogue, "George C. Marshall on Civil-Military Relationships in the United States," in Richard H. Kohn, ed., *The United States Military under the Constitution of the United States, 1789–1989* (New York: New York University Press, 1991), 193–222.

9. Eric Larrabee, *Commander in Chief: Franklin Delano Roosevelt, His Lieutenants, and Their War* (New York: Harper & Row, 1987), 133, 639.

10. Quoted in Robert J. Donovan, *Conflict and Crisis: The Presidency of Harry S. Truman, 1945–1948* (New York: W. W. Norton, 1977), 265.

11. See Peter D. Feaver and Kurt M. Campbell, "Rethinking Key West: Service Roles and Missions after the Cold War," in Joseph Kruzel, ed., *American Defense Annual: 1993* (Columbus: Mershon Center, 1993), 158–59.

12. Russell F. Weigley, *The American Way of War: A History of United States Military Strategy and Policy* (Bloomington: Indiana University Press, 1973), 377–79.

13. The official history of the changing role of blacks in the military is Morris J. MacGregor Jr., *Integration of the Armed Forces, 1940–1965* (Washington, D.C.: U.S. Army Center for Military History, 1981). A comprehensive historical account is Bernard C. Nalty, *Strength for the Fight: A History of Black Americans in the Military* (New York: Free Press, 1986).

14. On the Truman-MacArthur conflict, see David McCullough, "Truman Fires MacArthur," *Military History Quarterly* 5, no. 1 (1992): 8–21; and Roy K. Flint, "The Truman-MacArthur Conflict: Dilemmas of Civil-Military Relations in the Nuclear Age," in Kohn, *United States Military,* 223–67.

15. David McCullough notes that according to a Gallup poll, 69 percent of the public supported MacArthur. *Truman* (New York: Simon & Schuster, 1992), 848.

16. Lawrence J. Korb, "The Budget Process in the Department of Defense, 1947–77: The Strengths and Weaknesses of Three Systems," *Public Administration Review,*

no. 4 (July/August 1977): 334–46; and Korb, *The Joint Chiefs of Staff: The First Twenty-Five Years* (Bloomington: Indiana University Press, 1976), 111.

17. See David H. Petraeus, "Korea, the Never-Again Club, and Indochina," *Parameters* 17, no. 4 (1987): 59–70.

18. For a detailed discussion of this, see H. R. McMaster, *Dereliction of Duty: Lyndon Johnson, Robert McNamara, the Joint Chiefs of Staff, and the Lies That Led to Vietnam* (New York: HarperCollins, 1997).

19. Johnson did eventually authorize the Air Force leaders to strike most of the targets they wanted to, but not as quickly as they would have preferred. See Robert A. Pape, "Coercive Air Power in the Vietnam War," *International Security* 15, no. 2 (1990): 103–46.

20. Mark Perry, *Four Stars* (Boston: Houghton Mifflin, 1989), 132–66.

21. See Samuel P. Huntington, "The Soldier and the State in the 1970s," in Andrew J. Goodpaster and Samuel Huntington, eds., *Civil-Military Relations* (Washington, D.C.: American Enterprise Institute for Public Policy Research, 1977), 13.

22. See Richard Nixon, *RN: The Memoirs of Richard Nixon* (New York: Grosset & Dunlap, 1978), 615.

23. Perry, *Four Stars*, 268, 304.

24. Ibid., 290–92.

25. See Richard K. Betts, *Soldiers, Statesmen, and Cold War Crises*, rev. ed. (New York: Columbia University Press, 1991), 216–17; and David H. Petraeus, "Military Influence and the Post-Vietnam Use of Force," *Armed Forces and Society* 15, no. 4 (1989): 491.

26. Lou Cannon, *President Reagan: The Role of a Lifetime* (New York: Simon & Schuster, 1991), 336n, 346.

27. Millett, *American Political System*, 38.

28. See Colin L. Powell, "Why Generals Get Nervous," *New York Times*, Oct. 8, 1992, 21; Michael R. Gordon, "Powell Delivers a Resounding No on Using Force in Bosnia," *New York Times*, Sept. 28, 1992, 1, 6; and Gordon, "U.S. Military Role in Bosnia Would Help Little, Aides Say," *New York Times*, Jan. 30, 1993, 4.

29. These remarks were made by Major General Harold Campbell at a banquet in the Netherlands in May 1993. See Eric Schmitt, "Clinton Facing More Unease about Military," *New York Times*, June 9, 1993, 7; Schmitt, "General to Be Disciplined for Disparaging President," *New York Times*, June 16, 1993, 10; and Michael R. Gordon, "General Ousted for Derisive Remarks about President," *New York Times*, June 19, 1993, 9. For evidence that Clinton is still held in contempt by many in the U.S. military, see Thomas E. Ricks and Jeffrey H. Birnbaum, "Clinton Aides Hope That D-Day Trip Will Establish a Beachhead with His Own Uneasy Military," *Wall Street Journal*, June 1, 1994, 14.

30. The officer involved was General Barry McCaffrey. See Thomas Friedman, "Clinton Mends Military Fences at West Point," *New York Times*, May 30, 1993, 1, 6.

31. Gwen Ifill, "It's a Tough Time to Take the Helm at the Pentagon," *New York Times*, Dec. 18, 1993, 8. For a fuller account, see Elizabeth Drew, *On the Edge: The Clinton Presidency* (New York: Simon & Schuster, 1994), chap. 26.

32. "Helms vs. Clinton," *Washington Times*, Nov. 23, 1994, 3.

33. Michael R. Gordon, "Joint Chiefs Warn Congress against More Military Cuts,"

New York Times, May 20, 1993, 8; and Gordon, "Cuts Force Review of War Strategies," *New York Times*, May 30, 1993, 6.

34. See Bob Woodward, *The Commanders* (New York: Simon & Schuster, 1991), 39–40, 247–62, 299–300, 303; and Rick Atkinson, *Crusade: The Untold Story of the Persian Gulf War* (New York: Houghton Mifflin, 1993), 110–11.

35. Atkinson, *Crusade,* 450.

36. Cheney later pointed specifically to this case as an example of his willingness to confront the military. Telephone discussion with the author, Jan. 3, 1996. Also see the discussion in Michael R. Gordon and General Bernard E. Trainor, *The Generals' War: The Inside Story of the Conflict in the Gulf* (Boston: Little, Brown, 1995), 100–101.

37. Patrick E. Tyler, "Schwarzkopf Says Truce Enabled Iraqis to Escape," *New York Times*, Mar. 27, 1991, 9; and Tyler, "General's Account of Gulf War's End Disputed by Bush," *New York Times*, Mar. 28, 1991, 1, 6.

38. Elaine Sciolino, "Top U.S. Officials Divided in Debate on Invading Haiti," *New York Times*, Aug. 4, 1994, 1, 10. The military's fear was not about getting in; it was about getting out. See Michael R. Gordon and Eric Schmitt, "Weighing Options: U.S. Aides Assess Invasion of Haiti," *New York Times*, May 30, 1994, 1, 4. After a series of leaks widely suspected to have originated with the JCS about the problems involved in the operation, the military eventually gave in. See, for example, "General Confident on Haiti," *Washington Times*, Aug. 16, 1994, 10.

39. John Kifner, "After Saudi Base Bombing, a Split over Blame Fixing," *New York Times*, Dec. 6, 1996, 1, 10.

40. See Eric Schmitt, "Army Will Allow Women in 32,000 Combat Posts," *New York Times*, July 28, 1994, 12; "Women Unfit for Combat, Marine Says," *Washington Post*, Aug. 14, 1995, 15; and Dana Priest, "Women Fill Few Jobs Tied to Combat," *Washington Post*, Oct. 21, 1997, 1.

41. Specifically, there were bitter recriminations over the death of Lieutenant Kara Hultgreen in October 1994. Initially the Navy argued that she was a highly qualified pilot and her F-14 crash was due to mechanical failure. Subsequent reports suggested that she was at best a mediocre pilot whom the Navy had advanced for affirmative action reasons, and that the cause of the crash was pilot error. See "A Gender Neutral Tragedy," *New York Times*, Mar. 2, 1995, 22; H. G. Reza, "Pilot Error Had Role in Fatal Crash," *Los Angeles Times*, Mar. 22, 1995, 1; and "The Death That Won't Die," *Newsweek*, Mar. 27, 1995, 6.

42. Lawrence Korb, "The Military and Social Change," Project on U.S. Post–Cold War Civil-Military Relations Working Paper No. 5 (Cambridge: John M. Olin Institute for Strategic Studies, July 1996).

43. This is discussed at length in Elaine Sciolino and Philip Shenon, "Air Force Officials Mirrored Pilot's Anguishing Decision," *New York Times*, May 25, 1997, 24.

44. Drew, *On the Edge,* 42–48.

45. The best discussion of this issue is National Defense Research Institute, *Sexual Orientation and U.S. Military Personnel Policy: Options and Assessment* [MR-323-OSD] (Santa Monica: RAND Corp., 1993).

46. Colin Powell with Joseph E. Persico, *My American Journey* (New York: Random House, 1995), 572–74. Elsewhere, Powell mentions that he worked for W. Graham Claytor, deputy secretary of defense during the Carter era, who was responsible

for tightening the DoD's regulations against homosexuality in the services. See Randy Shilts, *Conduct Unbecoming: Gays and Lesbians in the U.S. Military* (New York: St. Martin's Press, 1993), 375–80. Drew (*On the Edge*, 248–51) suggests that Clinton "compromised" not because he was convinced that the military's objections had merit, but rather because he would lose on this issue.

47. See Hanna Rosin, "The Ban Plays On," *New Republic*, May 2, 1994, 11–13; Eric Schmitt, "Gay Troops Say Revised Policy Is Often Misused," *New York Times*, May 9, 1994, 1, 14; Debbie Howlett, "For Homosexuals, '98% of the Old Policy,'" *USA Today*, July 28, 1994, 11; "'Don't Tell' Policy Applied to Counseling," *Washington Times*, Dec. 12, 1994, 7; Rowan Scarborough, "Coats Sticks by 'Don't Ask, Don't Tell,'" *Washington Times*, Dec. 29, 1994, 4; Lawrence Korb and C. Dixon Osburn, "Asked, Told, Pursued," *New York Times*, Mar. 19, 1995, 15; Philip Shenon, "Homosexuality Still Questioned by Military," *New York Times*, Feb. 27, 1996, 1, 20; and "When 'Don't Ask, Don't Tell' Means Do Ask and Do Tell," *New York Times*, Mar. 3, 1996, "Week in Review," 7.

48. For example, see Lawrence J. Korb, "An Overstuffed Military," *Foreign Affairs* 74, no. 6 (1995): 28.

49. James A. Baker III, *The Politics of Diplomacy: Revolution, War, and Peace, 1989–1992* (New York: G. P. Putnam's Sons, 1995), 649.

50. See Powell, "Why Generals Get Nervous"; and Gordon, "Powell Delivers a Resounding No." For a discussion of "military stalling" on Bosnia during the Clinton administration, see Drew, *On the Edge*, 145, 154, 274, 280; Thomas E. Ricks and Carla Anne Robbins, "Pentagon Officials Say Fewer Troops May Be Needed for U.S. Bosnia Pullout," *Wall Street Journal*, July 20, 1995, 1, 2. For evidence that the Dayton agreement met "virtually every condition the American military insisted on," see Eric Schmitt, "Commanders Say U.S. Plan for Bosnia Will Work," *New York Times*, Nov. 27, 1995, 1, 8. For evidence that the military is still resisting civilian efforts to direct the mission of NATO's Stabilization Force (SFOR) in Bosnia, see Philip Shenon, "G.I.'s in Bosnia Shun Hunt for War-Crime Suspects," *New York Times*, Mar. 2, 1996, 3.

51. Michael R. Gordon, "Report by Powell Challenges Calls to Revise Military," *New York Times*, Dec. 31, 1992, 1, 10; "Military's Plan to Cut Back Is Short of Clinton's Vision," *New York Times*, Feb. 13, 1993, 30; and Korb, "An Overstuffed Military," 32.

52. Patrick E. Tyler, "Top Congressman Seeks Deeper Cuts in Military Budget," *New York Times*, Feb. 23, 1992, 1, 11; and Michael R. Gordon, "Military Plan Would Cut Forces But Have Them Ready for 2 Wars," *New York Times*, Sept. 2, 1993, 1, 18.

53. Powell, *My American Journey*, 437.

54. Philip Shenon, "Pentagon's Plan on Shaping the Military Is under Fire," *New York Times*, May 15, 1997, 28; Lawrence J. Korb, "The Pentagon's War on Thrift," *New York Times*, May 22, 1997, 33; and "Timid Colossus," *Economist*, May 24, 1997, 25–26.

55. Tim Weiner, "U.S. Is Wary of Ban on Land Mines," *New York Times*, June 17, 1997, 10; and Steven Lee Myers, "Clinton Says That Ban on Mines Would Put U.S. Troops at Risk," *New York Times*, Dec. 18, 1997, 8.

56. Christopher P. Gibson and Don M. Snider, "Explaining Post–Cold War Civil-Military Relations: A New Institutionalist Approach," Project on U.S. Post–Cold War

Civil-Military Relations Working Paper No. 8 (Cambridge: John M. Olin Institute for Strategic Studies, Jan. 1997), 26–27.

57. See Alison Mitchell, "Running after the Cold War," *New York Times*, Mar. 10, 1996, "Week in Review," 4.

58. "Bill Cohen in the Labyrinth," *Economist*, Mar. 15, 1997, 34; and "Rep. Weldon Angrily Ends Hearing on Missile Defense," *Washington Post*, Nov. 6, 1997, 12.

59. Edward Luttwak, "Washington's Biggest Scandal," *Commentary* 97, no. 5 (1994): 30. Also see John Lehman, "An Exchange on Civil-Military Relations," *National Interest*, no. 36 (Summer 1994): 23–25.

60. Powell (*My American Journey*, 573) claims that Congress was mostly to blame for the flap over gays in the military.

61. Warren Christopher and William J. Perry, "Foreign Policy, Hamstrung," *New York Times*, Feb. 13, 1995, 19.

62. See Eric Schmitt, "Pentagon Chief Warns Clinton on Gay Policy," *New York Times*, Jan. 25, 1993, 1.

63. Philip Shenon, "Mandate That H.I.V. Troops Be Discharged Is Set for Repeal," *New York Times*, Apr. 25, 1996, 13.

64. For a comprehensive discussion, see Michael C. Desch, "War and Strong States, Peace and Weak States?" *International Organization* 50, no. 2 (1996): 237–68.

65. Deborah R. Lee, Assistant Secretary of Defense for Reserve Affairs, "Our Civil-Military Program Is Small, but It's Paying Big Dividends," *Washington Times*, May 24, 1995, 22; and Eric Schmitt, "Clinton Invites Retired Brass to Give Views," *New York Times*, Jan. 8, 1995, 14.

66. Michael R. Gordon, "Admiral with High-Tech Dreams Has Pentagon at War with Itself," *New York Times*, Dec. 12, 1994, 1; and Thomas E. Ricks, "Army at Odds," *Wall Street Journal*, Mar. 13, 1997, 1, 9.

67. See Eric Schmitt, "Civilian Mission Is Proposed for Post–Cold War Military," *New York Times*, June 24, 1992, 9; Charles Dunlap Jr., "Welcome to the Junta: The Erosion of Civilian Control of the U.S. Military," *Wake Forest Law Review* 29, no. 2 (1994): 359–61; Bradley Graham, "Responsibilities of U.S. Military Expanded," *Washington Post*, Mar. 9, 1995, 36; and Robert Kaplan, "Fort Leavenworth and the Eclipse of Nationhood," *Atlantic Monthly*, Sept. 1996, 75–90.

68. For anecdotal evidence of this, see Thomas E. Ricks, "The Widening Gap between the Military and Society," *Atlantic Monthly*, July 1997, 66–78. A more systematic study that confirms this thesis is Ole Holsti, "A Widening Gap between the Military and Civilian Society? Some Evidence, 1976–1996," Project on U.S. Post–Cold War Civil-Military Relations Working Paper No. 13 (Cambridge: John M. Olin Institute for Strategic Studies, Oct. 1997).

69. On the Powell Doctrine, see Powell, *My American Journey*, 302–3.

70. Kaplan, "Fort Leavenworth," 78.

71. Powell, *My American Journey*, 149.

72. See the sharp exchange between Madeleine Albright and Colin Powell recounted in "Albright Throws the Book at Powell," *New Yorker*, Oct. 2, 1995, 35.

73. John J. Mearsheimer, "Back to the Future: Instability in Europe after the Cold War," *International Security* 15, no. 1 (1990): 5–57.

74. See Tim Weiner, "U.S. Spy Agencies Find Scant Peril on Horizon," *New York Times*, Jan. 29, 1998, 3.

75. U.S. House, Armed Services Committee, "FY 1993 Defense Authorization Bill: Summary of Major Actions. Committee Mark-up" (May 13, 1992, mimeo), 1. Only 16 percent of U.S. leaders regarded Russian military power as a critical threat in 1994; in 1986, 59 percent thought it was. See John E. Reilly, ed., *American Public Opinion and U.S. Foreign Policy, 1995* (Chicago: Chicago Council on Foreign Relations, 1995), 24; and Reilly, ed., *American Public Opinion and U.S. Foreign Policy, 1987* (Chicago: Chicago Council on Foreign Relations, 1987), 12.

76. See Colin Powell and William Odom, "An Exchange on Civil-Military Relations," *National Interest,* no. 36 (Summer 1994): 23, 25–26.

77. See Steven Greenhouse, "Chairman of Joint Chiefs Defends Clinton against Attack by Helms," *New York Times,* Nov. 20, 1994, 24. Also see Bradley Graham and Dan Morgan, "Shalikashvili Rebuts Helms on Clinton's Ability as Commander," *Washington Post,* Nov. 20, 1994, 24.

78. Author's discussions with military officers at West Point (June 1994), Carlisle Barracks (Sept. 1994), Harvard University (Nov. 1994 and Apr. 1996), and the Naval War College (Dec. 1994). Also see Mackubin Thomas Owens, "Civilian Control: A National Crisis?" *Joint Forces Quarterly,* no. 6 (Autumn/Winter 1994/95): 80–83; and Brian McGrory, "U.S. Military, Clinton Achieve Wary Truce," *Boston Globe,* Feb. 24, 1998, 1.

Chapter 4. Controlling Chaos

1. Condoleeza Rice, "The Party, the Military, and Decision Authority in the Soviet Union," *World Politics* 60, no. 1 (1987): 80–81.

2. Stephen M. Meyer, "How the Threat (and the Coup) Collapsed: The Politicization of the Soviet Military," *International Security* 16, no. 3 (1991/92): 5–38; John W. R. Lepingwell, "Soviet Civil-Military Relations and the August Coup," *World Politics* 44, no. 4 (1992): 539–72; Bruce D. Porter, *Red Armies in Crisis* (Washington, D.C.: Center for Strategic and International Studies, 1991); David Holloway, "State, Society, and the Military under Gorbachev," *International Security* 14, no. 3 (1989/90): 5–24; and Brian Taylor, "Russian Civil-Military Relations after the October Uprising," *Survival* 36, no. 1 (1994): 3–29.

3. Paul Goble, "Between Poverty and Power: The Current State of the Russian Army," *Prism,* Aug. 25, 1995 [e-mail]. Also see the citations in chap. 1, n. 2.

4. See, for example, "Alexander Napoleonovich," *Economist,* Aug. 27, 1994, 45–46.

5. Penny Morvant, "Gaidar Says Yeltsin Risks Losing Control of the Military," *Open Media Research Institute—Daily Digest* [hereafter *OMRI—DD*], Jan. 13, 1995 [e-mail].

6. "Yushenkov Worried by Russian Militarism," *Jamestown Foundation Monitor* (hereafter *JFM*), May 25, 1995 [e-mail].

7. "Control of Military—A Priority of Women Legislators Agenda," *JFM,* Sept. 29, 1995 [e-mail].

8. Cited in Thomas M. Nichols, "An Electoral Mutiny? Zhirinovsky and the Russian Armed Forces," *Armed Forces and Society* 21, no. 3 (1995): 327–28.

9. Alexander Rahr, "Shakrai Warns of Army Take-Over," *Radio Free Europe/Radio Liberty—Daily Report* [hereafter *RFE/RL—DR*], Nov. 19, 1993 [e-mail]; Vladi-

mir Socor, "Lebed on Military Discontent, Pullout from Germany," *RFE/RL—DR,* Sept. 15, 1994 [e-mail]; Douglas Clarke, "Zhirinovsky Tells Americans of a Military Threat in Russia," *RFE/RL—DR,* Nov. 9, 1994 [e-mail]; "Duma Appeals to the Armed Forces," *JFM,* Mar. 25, 1996 [e-mail]; Scott Parrish, "Deputy Warns Military Is in 'Explosive' Situation," *OMRI—DD,* Aug. 20, 1996 [e-mail]; Parrish, "Lebed Warns of 'Armed Mutiny,'" *OMRI—DD,* Sept. 25, 1996 [e-mail]; Penny Morvant, "Tension Rising in Military," *OMRI—DD,* Oct. 1, 1996 [e-mail]; Morvant, "Think-Tank Sees Army as Threat to Russia," *OMRI—DD,* Feb. 17, 1997 [e-mail]; and Peter Rutland, "Is Military Coup in Preparation?" *OMRI—DD,* Feb. 19, 1997 [e-mail].

10. Aleksandr Zhilin, "Chechnya's Spreading Impact on Kremlin Politics," *Prism,* July 17, 1995 [e-mail].

11. "Militarization of Russian Politics Seen," *JFM,* Aug. 24, 1995 [e-mail]; and Michael R. Gordon, "Russian Army May Prove Unreliable, Official Says," *New York Times,* Oct. 2, 1996, 7.

12. See Stephen Meyer, "The Political Power of the Soviet Military Establishment" (paper presented at the sixth conference of the Japan-U.S. Joint Study on the Soviet Union, Sapporo, Japan, June 16–17, 1989), 5–6.

13. For a discussion of the importance of institutionalization for political stability in the Soviet Union, see Amos Perlmutter and William M. LeoGrande, "The Party in Uniform: Toward a Theory of Civil-Military Relations in Communist Political Systems," *American Political Science Review* 76, no. 4 (1982): 778–89, esp. 779.

14. For a discussion of the evolution of objective control mechanisms in the Soviet Union, see Kenneth Currie, "Soviet General Staff's New Role," *Problems of Communism* 33, no. 3 (1984): 32–33; and Timothy Colton, "The Party-Military Connection," in Dale Herspring and Ivan Volgyes, eds., *Civil-Military Relations in Communist Systems* (Boulder, Colo.: Westview Press, 1978), 71.

15. For a discussion of the role that Zhukov played in Khrushchev's struggle with the "anti-party group," see Carl Linden, *Khrushchev and the Soviet Leadership: 1957–1964* (Baltimore: Johns Hopkins Press, 1966), 43–44, 52–53. On the limited internal role of the Soviet military, see Alexander R. Alexiev and Robert C. Nurick, *The Soviet Military under Gorbachev: Report on a RAND Workshop* [R-3907-RC] (Santa Monica: RAND Corp., Feb. 1990), 23. On the primarily external mission of the Soviet military, see Timothy Colton, "Perspectives on Civil-Military Relations in the Soviet Union," in Timothy Colton and Thane Gustafson, eds., *Soldiers and the Soviet State: Civil-Military Relations from Brezhnev to Gorbachev* (Princeton: Princeton University Press, 1990), 21; and Harry Gelman, *The Soviet Turn toward Conventional Force Reductions: The Internal Variables at Play* [R-3876-AF] (Santa Monica: RAND Corp., Dec. 1989), 61.

16. Lepingwell, "Soviet Civil-Military Relations," 547.

17. Gelman, *The Soviet Turn,* 6–7; and Harry Gelman, "Gorbachev and the Future of the Soviet Military Institution," Adelphi Paper No. 258 (London: International Institute for Strategic Studies, Spring 1991), 27.

18. F. Stephen Larabee, "Gorbachev and the Soviet Military," *Foreign Affairs* 66, no. 5 (1988): 1003; and Abraham S. Becker, *Ogarkov's Complaint and Gorbachev's Dilemma: The Soviet Defense Budget and Party-Military Conflict* [R-3541-AF] (Santa Monica: RAND Corp., Dec. 1987), v. Both report that growth rates in Soviet military spending went from 4 percent to 2 percent per year during the period of perestroika.

19. Meyer, "How the Threat (and the Coup) Collapsed," 17; Alexiev and Nurick, *The Soviet Military under Gorbachev,* v–vi; and Gelman, "Soviet Military Institution," 33–36.

20. Jeremy R. Azreal, *The Soviet Civilian Leadership and the Military High Command, 1976–1986* [R-3521-AF] (Santa Monica: RAND Corp., June 1987), 40–41.

21. See Andrey Vladimirovich Kozyrev, "Confidence and the Balance of Interests," *Mezhdunarodnaya Zhizn,* no. 10 (Oct. 1988), in *Foreign Broadcast Information Service—Soviet Report,* Oct. 25, 1988, 1–7.

22. Stephen M. Meyer, "Sources and Prospects of Gorbachev's New Political Thinking on Security," *International Security* 13, no. 2 (1988): 129.

23. For specific references to Soviet military officers who made this argument, see Harry Gelman, *The Soviet Military Leadership and the Question of Deployment Retreats* (Santa Monica: RAND Corp., 1982), 4; Dale Herspring, *The Soviet High Command, 1967–1989: Personalities and Politics* (Princeton: Princeton University Press, 1990), 250; Rose E. Gottemoeller, *Conflict and Consensus in the Soviet Armed Forces* [R-3759-AF] (Santa Monica: RAND Corp., Oct. 1989), 41; and Alexiev and Nurick, *The Soviet Military under Gorbachev,* 45.

24. Erik Hoffmann, "Soviet Views of the 'Scientific-Technological Revolution,'" *World Politics* 30, no. 4 (1978): 615; Mary C. FitzGerald, "Marshal Ogarkov on Modern War: 1977–1985," CNA Professional Paper 443.10 (Alexandria, Va.: Center for Naval Analyses, Nov. 1986), 2–3; and William E. Odom, "Soviet Force Posture: Dilemmas and Directions," *Problems of Communism* 34, no. 4 (1985): 11.

25. Col. S. Barentov, "On the Level of Economic, Scientific, and Technical Progress," *Kommunist Vooruzhennykh Sil,* no. 5 (Mar. 1983), in Joint Publications Research Service [microfiche 83924], 6.

26. See John M. Collins, *U.S./Soviet Military Balance: Assessments and Statistics, 1980–1985* (Washington, D.C.: Congressional Research Service, Spring 1985), 78–82.

27. Gottemoeller, *Conflict and Consensus,* v; and Benjamin S. Lambeth, *Moscow's Lessons from the 1982 Lebanon Air War* [RF-3000-AF] (Santa Monica: RAND Corp., Sept. 1984). The final score of the June 1982 Israeli-Syrian air engagements was 86–0.

28. See Douglas L. Clarke, "What the Soviet General Staff Might Learn from the Gulf War," *RFE/RL Report on the USSR* 3, no. 5 (Feb. 1, 1991): 3–5; and Mary FitzGerald, "Soviet Military Doctrine—Implications of the Gulf War," *International Defense Review* 8 (1991): 809–10. A useful overview of Soviet sources is Benjamin S. Lambeth, *Desert Storm and Its Meaning: The View from Moscow* [R-4164] (Santa Monica: RAND Corp., 1992).

29. Thane Gustafson, "The Response to Technological Change," in Colton and Gustafson, *Soldiers and the Soviet State,* 194.

30. On Soviet efforts to steal high technology from the West, see *Soviet Acquisition of Militarily Significant Technology—An Update* (Washington, D.C.: GPO, Sept. 1985).

31. Interview with Brigadier General John Reppert, U.S. military attaché, Moscow, Dec. 6, 1995.

32. Valerie Bunce, "The Empire Strikes Back: The Evolution of the Eastern Bloc from a Soviet Asset to a Soviet Liability," *International Organization* 39, no. 1 (1985): 21–23. There were, however, a few strictly military objections as well; see 19–20.

33. Serge Schmemann, "Soviet Rightists See Nation Run Amok," *New York Times*, June 28, 1991, 6.

34. Two prominent examples are Generals Ivan Tretyak and Mikhail Moiseyev. Gelman, "Soviet Military Institution," 15.

35. Serge Schmemann, "Soviets, Citing Rise in Crime, Send Troops to Patrol Cities with Police," *New York Times*, Jan. 26, 1991, 1, 3; Francis X. Clines, "Soviets Increase Patrols by Army, Extending Crackdown to 86 Cities," *New York Times*, Feb. 6, 1991, 1, 3; and Schmemann, "Soviet Troops Join the Police on Patrol," *New York Times*, Feb. 2, 1991, 3.

36. Viktor Alksnis, "A Once Great Country Is on Its Knees," *Los Angeles Times*, Aug. 2, 1991, B11.

37. Mikhail Gorbachev, *The August Coup: The Truth and the Lessons* (New York: HarperCollins, 1991), 15–16. Also see Peter Rutland, "Gorbachev on August 1991 Coup Attempt," *OMRI—DD*, Aug. 16, 1996 [e-mail].

38. Francis X. Clines, "Troops Moving into Moscow, Russian Leader Urges a Strike," *New York Times*, Aug. 20, 1991, 1.

39. "K.G.B. Organized Coup, Yeltsin Says," *New York Times*, Sept. 8, 1991, 11.

40. Porter, *Red Armies in Crisis*, 57.

41. Gorbachev, *The August Coup*, 19.

42. Clifford Krauss, "Sergei Akhromeyev: Complete Soviet Soldier, Well-Liked in the West," *New York Times*, Aug. 26, 1991, 7.

43. Gorbachev, *The August Coup*, 42–44.

44. Porter, *Red Armies in Crisis*, 57–58.

45. Lilia Shevtsova, "The August Coup and the Soviet Collapse," *Survival* 34, no. 1 (1992): 6–7.

46. James Billington, "The True Heroes of the Soviet Union," *New York Times*, Aug. 30, 1991, 19.

47. Jerry Hough, "Assessing the Coup," *Current History* 90, no. 558 (1991): 306.

48. Gorbachev, *The August Coup*, 11, 31.

49. Meyer, "How the Threat (and the Coup) Collapsed," 11 n. 13; and Porter, *Red Armies in Crisis*, 58–59.

50. Gorbachev, *The August Coup*, 34–36; "Yeltsin's Army," *Economist*, Aug. 24–30, 1991, 12; and Lepingwell, "Soviet Civil-Military Relations," 559.

51. Quoted in Bill Keller, "The 3–Day Fiasco: Anatomy of a Failed Strike at the State," *New York Times*, Aug. 25, 1991, 10.

52. Keller, "Sporadic Mutinies Rack Soviet Army," *New York Times*, Aug. 21, 1991, 1.

53. Celestine Bohlen, "Gorbachev Vying for Army Backing over Yeltsin's Bid," *New York Times*, Dec. 11, 1991, 8.

54. "An Interview with General Kirshin," *Perspective* 2, no. 2 (1991): 3.

55. Obvious candidates include China, Ukraine, and Japan. But so far these potential threats have not received much attention in Russian military writings. And at least in the Chinese case, military cooperation has been growing rather than declining. See Patrick E. Tyler, "Russia and China Plan Pact to Avoid Conflict," *New York Times*, Dec. 5, 1993, 8; and Tyler, "Russia and China Sign a Military Agreement," *New York Times*, Oct. 11, 1993, 15. The inability of the Main Directorate of Intelligence of the Russian General Staff to determine either a likely external adversary or even from

which direction a potential threat might come is evident in "Report on Parliamentary Hearings," *Krasnaya Zvezda*, May 14, 1992, cited in Roy Allison, "Military Forces in the Soviet Successor States," Adelphi Paper No. 280 (London: International Institute for Strategic Studies, Oct. 1993), 22 n. 11.

56. Steven Erlanger, "Yeltsin Expresses Russian Impatience over Ethnic Wars," *New York Times,* June 22, 1992, 1, 7.

57. Celestine Bohlen, "A Russian Seeks 'Glorious' Borders," *New York Times,* Jan. 31, 1992, 6.

58. Scott Parrish, "Grachev Says Army Will Not Allow Russia to Disintegrate," *OMRI—DD,* Feb. 23, 1996 [e-mail].

59. Aleksandr Zhilin, "Russia's National Security Prospects," *Prism,* Jan. 12, 1996 [e-mail]; Valery Manilov, *The National Security of Russia,* trans. and ed. Richard Weitz (Cambridge, Mass.: Belfer Center for Science and International Affairs, June 1997), 16–18; and Stuart Goldman, *Russian Conventional Armed Forces: On the Verge of Collapse?* [CRS-97-820F] (Washington, D.C.: Congressional Research Service, Sept. 4, 1997), 2.

60. The following discussion is based on the *Radio Free Europe/Radio Liberty—Daily Report,* the *Open Media Research Institute—Daily Digest,* and the *Jamestown Foundation Monitor.* I am happy to provide specific citations upon request.

61. Quoted in Vladimir Socor, "Lebed, 'Dniester' Leaders Dismiss Troop Withdrawal Agreement," *RFE/RL—DR,* Oct. 27, 1994 [e-mail]. Also see Socor, "New Demand for Basing Rights in Moldova," *RFE/RL—DR,* Aug. 24, 1994 [e-mail].

62. Personal discussions with Russian National Security Council staff member, Moscow, Dec. 5, 1995; and interview with Duma Defense Committee member Alexei Arbatov, Moscow, Jan. 19, 1995.

63. Aleksandr Zhilin, "War Policy and the War of Politicians," *Moskovskiye Novosti,* no. 47 (Nov. 16, 1993), in "Experts See Hawks' Win on Military Doctrine," *Foreign Broadcast Information Service—Central Europe* (hereafter *FBIS—CE*), Nov. 18 1993, 40; and Aleksandr Mnatsakyan, "Again from the Taiga to the Baltic Seas . . ." *Rossiya,* no. 48 (Nov. 24–30, 1993), in "Military Doctrine Seen Increasing Army's Clout," *FBIS—CE,* Nov. 26, 1993, 44.

64. See, for example, "What Red Army?" *New York Times,* Mar. 30, 1993, 14.

65. See Stephen Foye, "Army Feels It Deserves Special Treatment," *RFE/RL—DR,* Oct. 6, 1993 [e-mail].

66. Vladimir Socor, "Military Opinion Survey," *RFE/RL—DR,* Sept. 9, 1994 [e-mail].

67. Robert Orttung, "Izvestiya Examines Political Tendencies in the Military," *OMRI—DD,* Apr. 21, 1995 [e-mail].

68. "Baltin Sets Sail," *JFM,* Oct. 26, 1995 [e-mail].

69. Julia Wishnevsky, "Grachev Attacks Yushenkov, Kovalev Lambastes Yeltsin," *OMRI—DD,* Jan. 23, 1995 [e-mail]; and Wishnevsky, "Ruehe's Criticism of Grachev Creates Stir in Russia," *OMRI—DD,* Jan. 24, 1995 [e-mail].

70. Interview with Aleksandr Zhilin, Moscow, Dec. 5, 1995.

71. "Duma Deputies Oppose Removal of Lebed," *JFM,* May 18, 1995 [e-mail].

72. Vladimir Socor, "Lebed 'Military Idol,'" *RFE/RL—DR,* Sept. 21, 1994 [e-mail]. Also see Stephen Foye, "Lebed Praises Pinochet, Calls for Strong Army," *RFE/RL—DR,* July 21, 1994 [e-mail]; "Lebed Advocates Authoritarian Path to Democracy," *JFM,*

Nov. 14, 1995 [e-mail]; and Peter Rutland, "Lebed: 'I Am Not a Full Democrat,'" *OMRI-DD*, July 20, 1996 [e-mail].

73. Penny Morvant, "Lebed Is Russia's Most Popular Politician," *OMRI—DD*, Jan. 17, 1997 [e-mail].

74. Stanislav Lunev, "The Myth of Reform in the Russian Army," *Prism*, Dec. 2, 1995 [e-mail].

75. "Interview with General Kirshin," 4.

76. See Peter Reddaway, "Russia on the Brink?" *New York Review of Books*, Jan. 28, 1993, 33–34, citing an article in the Russian journal *Den*, no. 47 (Nov. 22–28, 1992), 1.

77. See Serge Schmemann, "Russian Army Major Caught While Seeking to Kill Yeltsin," *New York Times*, Jan. 31, 1993, 10.

78. Quoted in "Hidden Enemy," *Economist*, Mar. 27, 1993, 21.

79. "Split Decisions," *Wall Street Journal*, June 4, 1996, 1, 6.

80. Boris Yeltsin, *The Struggle for Russia*, trans. Catherine A. Fitzpatrick (New York: Random House, 1995), 243, 266.

81. Scott Parrish, "Splits in Military Leadership over Reform Plans?" *OMRI—DD*, Jan. 7, 1997 [e-mail]; and Parrish, "Ground Forces Commander Still Refuses to Resign," *OMRI—DD*, Mar. 7, 1997 [e-mail].

82. See "The Main Provisions of the Russian Federation Military Doctrine," in *Voennaya Mysl*, Nov. 1993, 2–16; and, more recently, Liz Fuller, "Rybkin Calls for New Russian National Security Concept," *RFE/RL—DR*, Apr. 30, 1997 [e-mail].

83. Sarah Brown, "Modern Tales of the Russian Army," *World Policy Journal* 14, no. 1 (1997): 61–70.

84. On these and other attitudes, see *Russian Foreign Policy, 1993, Assessed by Experts* (Moscow: SINUS, July 1993); and *Military Elites in Russia, 1994* (Moscow and Munich: SINUS, Aug. 1994).

85. "The Basic Provisions of the Military Doctrine of the Russian Federation: Russia's Military Doctrine," *Rossiskiye Vesti*, Nov. 18, 1993, in "'Detailed Account' of Military Doctrine," *FBIS—CE* (suppl.), Nov. 19, 1993, 1.

86. Stephen Foye, "Yeltsin Proposes That Army Aid in Crime Fighting," *RFE/RL—DR*, Apr. 27, 1993, 1–2 [e-mail]; and John W. R. Lepingwell, "Paratroops Help to Collect Taxes," *RFE/RL—DR*, June 3, 1993 [e-mail].

87. See "Basic Provisions," 3–7. For a related discussion, see Igor Saltykov, "Confidential: Doctrine or Dictatorship," *Pravda*, Nov. 16, 1993, in "Aspects of New Military Doctrine Questioned," *FBIS—CE*, Nov. 17, 1993, 58–59.

88. "Articles from *Voennaya Mysl* regarding the New Russian Military Doctrine [May 1992]," in *Joint Publications Research Service* [UMT-92-008-L], June 16, 1992, 6. Emphasis on "internal" added.

89. Zhilin, "War Policy," 40.

90. Mnatsakyan, "Again from the Taiga," 45.

91. Stanislaw Kondrashev, "Military Doctrine in Political Context," *Izvestia*, Nov. 24, 1993, in "Further on Doctrine," *FBIS—CE*, Nov. 26, 1993, 45–46.

92. Stephen Meyer, "The Army Isn't Running Gorbachev," *New York Times*, May 8, 1990, 29; Meyer, "Troopers," *New Republic*, Oct. 25, 1993, 10; and Meyer, "The Devolution of Russian Military Power," *Current History*, Oct. 1995, 322–28.

93. Quoted in Claudia Rosett, "Fighting in Chechnya Is Isolating Yeltsin, Jeopardizing Reform," *Wall Street Journal,* Jan. 9, 1995, 19.

94. Interview with Dmitri Trenin, Moscow, Dec. 5, 1995.

95. Sonni Efron, "Army in Tatters May Pose Threat to New Russia," *Los Angeles Times,* Feb. 27, 1995, 1.

96. Heinrich Tiller and Manfred Schroeder, *Machtkrise und Militär: Die russischen Streikrafte während des Machtkampfes zwischen Präsident und Parlament im Herbst 1993* (Wiesbaden: Hessische Landeszentrale für politische Bildung, 1994), 46. Also see "The Military Mess in Russia," *Economist,* Dec. 17, 1994, 50. This was also a point emphasized in my interviews with Alexei Arbatov.

97. See "Excerpts from an Interview with Shevardnadze: Threat of Dictatorship 'Has Been Removed,'" *New York Times,* Aug. 29, 1991, 9; and Michael Scammell, "The Disaster That Didn't Happen," *New York Times,* Aug. 19, 1992, 19.

98. Stephen Foye, "Grachev Addresses Duma Committee on Budget, Civilian Control," *RFE/RL—DR,* July 12, 1994 [e-mail].

In addition to the Western analysts cited in note 2 of this chapter, the U.S. government and its embassy in Moscow seem to share this optimistic position, as I discovered in my interview with Brigadier General John Reppert, the U.S. military attaché in Moscow, on Dec. 6, 1995. Aleksandr Goltz, the political commentator for the Defense Ministry's organ *Krasnaya Zvezda,* sought to convince me (in an interview in Moscow on Dec. 6, 1995) of Grachev's subordination to Yeltsin by recounting how during his 1995 trips to Belgium and Israel, Grachev had made a point of calling Yeltsin to discuss even minor issues that arose. I asked Goltz whether it was not strange that Grachev would make such a public and ostentatious show of loyalty if his loyalty were not in doubt. Goltz shrugged, smiled, and conceded that I was "not the only one who has speculated on this."

99. Aleksandr Zhilin, "Corruption Keeps Generals in Line," *Prism,* Sept. 25, 1995 [e-mail]. Also see "Officer: Commands More Important Than Constitution," *JFM,* June 29, 1995 [e-mail].

100. Scott Parrish, "Chief of General Staff: Officer Corps Decaying," *OMRI—DD,* Mar. 17, 1997 [e-mail].

Chapter 5. The Anger of the Legions

1. See Gerhard Ritter, *The Sword and the Scepter: The Problem of Militarism in Germany,* vol. 3, *The Tragedy of Statesmanship—Bethmann Hollweg as War Chancellor,* trans. Heinz Norden (Coral Gables, Fla.: University of Miami Press, 1972), 486; and Herbert Rosinski, *The German Army* (Washington, D.C.: Infantry Journal, 1944), 94.

2. Gordon Craig, *The Politics of the Prussian Army, 1640–1945* (New York: Oxford University Press, 1956), 299; and Karl Tschuppik, *Ludendorff: The Tragedy of a Military Mind,* trans. W. H. Johnson (Boston: Houghton Mifflin, 1932), 303.

3. Ritter, *The Sword and the Scepter,* vol. 4, *The Reign of the German Military and the Disaster of 1918,* trans. Heinz Norden (Coral Gables, Fla.: University of Miami Press, 1973), 158.

4. Ibid., 287, 317; and Erich Ludendorff, *Ludendorff's Own Story: August 1914–November 1918* (New York: Harper & Bros., 1919), 2:332.

5. *Ludendorff's Own Story,* 2:43, 52; Ritter, *Reign of the German Military;* and John Wheeler-Bennett, *Hindenburg: The Wooden Titan* (London: Macmillan, 1936), 102.

6. *Ludendorff's Own Story,* 2:261.

7. Ibid., 67.

8. Ibid., 1:432.

9. Ritter, *Tragedy of Statesmanship,* 445.

10. On the "cult of the offensive," see Stephen Van Evera, "The Cult of the Offensive and the Origins of the First World War"; and Jack Snyder, "Civil-Military Relations and the Cult of the Offensive, 1914 and 1984," both in Steven E. Miller, ed., *Military Strategy and the Origins of the First World War* (Princeton: Princeton University Press, 1985), 58–107, 108–46.

11. Martin Kitchen, *The Silent Dictatorship: The Politics of the German High Command under Hindenburg and Ludendorff, 1916–1918* (New York: Holmes & Meier, 1976), 16.

12. Lieut.-Col. [Colmar] von der Goltz, *The Nation in Arms,* trans. Philip A. Ashworth (London: W. H. Allen & Co., 1887), 7.

13. Walter Goerlitz, *History of the German General Staff, 1657–1945,* trans. Brian Battershaw (New York: Praeger, 1953), 148.

14. *Ludendorff's Own Story,* 1:2.

15. Craig, *Politics of the Prussian Army,* xvi, xix, 167, 170, 181, 262.

16. The main culprit was the Schlieffen Plan. For an extended discussion, see Gerhard Ritter, *The Schlieffen Plan: Critique of a Myth* (Westport, Conn.: Greenwood Press, 1979).

17. Snyder, "Civil-Military Relations," 109, 115, 146. Also see Craig, *Politics of the Prussian Army,* 294–95; Richard Ned Lebow, *Between Peace and War: The Nature of International Crises* (Baltimore: Johns Hopkins University Press, 1981), 236; and Barbara Tuchman's classic *The Guns of August* (Toronto: Bantam Books, 1976), 99–103.

18. See Fritz Fischer, *Germany's Aims in the First World War* (New York: W. W. Norton, 1961), 6–49; Immanuel Geiss, "The Outbreak of the First World War and German War Aims," *Journal of Contemporary History* 1, no. 3 (1966): 80–81; and John J. C. Rohl, *The Kaiser and His Court: Wilhelm II and the Government of Germany* (Cambridge: Cambridge University Press, 1987).

19. Van Evera, "Cult of the Offensive," 58–107.

20. See Marc Trachtenberg, *History and Strategy* (Princeton: Princeton University Press, 1991), 57–64.

21. Craig, *Politics of the Prussian Army,* 310. Also see Rosinski, *The German Army,* 93.

22. Craig, *Politics of the Prussian Army,* 299.

23. Wheeler-Bennett, *Hindenburg,* 136.

24. *Ludendorff's Own Story,* 2:359.

25. Ritter, *Reign of the German Military,* 276, 340–45, 367.

26. Ibid., 143–71; and Wheeler-Bennett, *Hindenburg,* 130.

27. Ritter, *Tragedy of Statesmanship,* 216.

28. Ritter, *Reign of the German Military,* 55.

29. Ritter, *Tragedy of Statesmanship,* 318, 315.

30. Ritter, *Reign of the German Military,* 116.

31. *Ludendorff's Own Story,* 2:52.

32. Ibid., 1:388.

33. John Wheeler-Bennett, *Nemesis of Power: The German Army in Politics, 1918–1945* (New York: Macmillan & Co., 1954), 14–15.

34. Kitchen, *The Silent Dictatorship,* 262.

35. Ibid., 45–46.

36. Klaus Epstein, "German War Aims in the First World War," *World Politics* 15, no. 1 (1962): 177.

37. Kitchen, *The Silent Dictatorship,* 39.

38. Ibid., 45, 267.

39. Ibid., 249.

40. Goerlitz, *German General Staff,* 185.

41. Wheeler-Bennett, *Hindenburg,* 133–35.

42. Paul-Marie de la Gorce, *The French Army: A Military-Political History,* trans. Kenneth Douglas (New York: George Braziller, 1963), 366.

43. See Simon Serfaty, *France, de Gaulle, and Europe: The Policy of the Fourth and Fifth Republics toward the Continent* (Baltimore: Johns Hopkins Press, 1968), 3–4, 11, 25.

44. Charles de Gaulle, *Memoirs of Hope: Renewal and Endeavor,* trans. Terence Kilmartin (New York: Simon & Schuster, 1971), 164.

45. Jean Lacouture, *De Gaulle: The Ruler, 1945–1970* (London: Harvill, 1991), 388.

46. De Gaulle, *Memoirs,* 200.

47. Ibid., 15.

48. John Steward Ambler, *The French Army in Politics: 1945–1962* (Columbus: Ohio State University Press, 1966), 56, 81.

49. Quoted in ibid., 282.

50. Serfaty, *France, de Gaulle, and Europe,* 71, 115; George Armstrong Kelly, *Lost Soldiers: The French Army and Empire in Crisis, 1947–1962* (Cambridge: MIT Press, 1965), 369; and Ambler, *The French Army in Politics,* 327.

51. De la Gorce, *The French Army,* 390; and Alistair Horne, *A Savage War of Peace: Algeria, 1954–1962* (Harmondsworth: Penguin Books, 1985), 234.

52. De la Gorce, *The French Army,* 353–54.

53. Serfaty, *France, de Gaulle, and Europe,* 32.

54. Peter Paret, "The French Army and *la Guerre Révolutionnaire,*" *Survival* 1, no. 1 (1959): 29; and Paret, *French Revolutionary Warfare Doctrine from Indochina to Algeria* (New York: Praeger, 1964), 7, 100, 103.

55. Horne, *Savage War of Peace,* 167.

56. Paret, *French Revolutionary Warfare Doctrine,* 28.

57. Edgar Furniss, *De Gaulle and the French Army: A Crisis in Civil-Military Relations* (New York: Twentieth Century Fund, 1964), 50.

58. Quoted in Paret, *French Revolutionary Warfare Doctrine,* 25.

59. Ambler, *The French Army in Politics,* 309.

60. Douglas Porch, *The French Foreign Legion: A Complete History of the Legendary Fighting Force* (New York: HarperPerennial, 1991), 583, 604.

61. Paret, *French Revolutionary Warfare Doctrine,* 132; also see 56–57, 77.

62. Ambler, *The French Army in Politics*, 269–80; and de la Gorce, *The French Army*, 371–72.

63. Cyrus L. Sulzberger, *The Test: De Gaulle and Algeria* (New York: Harcourt, Brace & World, 1962), 132.

64. Lacouture, *De Gaulle*, 242.

65. De Gaulle, *Memoirs*, 20.

66. Quoted in Lacouture, *De Gaulle*, 166.

67. Sulzberger, *The Test*, 101.

68. De Gaulle, *Memoirs*, 18, 23, 26–27.

69. Lacouture, *De Gaulle*, 178.

70. "Press Conference of General de Gaulle Held in Paris at the Palais d'Orsay on the Conditions of His Return to Power on May 19, 1958," in French Embassy, *Major Addresses and Press Conferences of General Charles de Gaulle, May 19, 1958–January 31, 1964* (New York: Press and Information Division, 1964), 4.

71. Horne, *A Savage War of Peace*, 353.

72. "Address by President Charles de Gaulle on Algerian Policy Broadcast over French Radio and Television on January 29, 1960," in French Embassy, *Major Addresses*, 71. Also see the accounts in de Gaulle, *Memoirs*, 259–60; and Horne, *A Savage War of Peace*, 368.

73. Kelly, *Lost Soldiers*, 309; and Ambler, *The French Army in Politics*, vii.

74. Horne, *A Savage War of Peace*, 490.

75. Lacouture, *De Gaulle*, 261. Also see 188–89.

76. "Address by President Charles de Gaulle on Algerian Policy," Jan. 29, 1960, 73.

77. Horne, *A Savage War of Peace*, 381.

78. Roy C. Anderson, *Devils Not Men: The History of the French Foreign Legion* (London: Robert Hale, 1987), 110.

79. De Gaulle, *Memoirs*, 41.

80. "Address by President Charles de Gaulle on Algerian Policy," Jan. 29, 1960, 71.

81. De Gaulle, *Memoirs*, 37; and "Sixth Press Conference Held by General de Gaulle as President of the French Republic in Paris at the Elysée Palace on May 15, 1962," in French Embassy, *Major Addresses*, 172.

82. Furniss, *De Gaulle and the French Army*, 290.

83. De Gaulle, "Sixth Press Conference," May 15, 1962, 180–81. Emphasis added.

84. De Gaulle, *Memoirs*, 203.

85. Furniss, *De Gaulle and the French Army*, 45.

86. De Gaulle, *Memoirs*, 124. The full text of this speech is in Charles de Gaulle, *Discours et messages*, vol. 1, *Avec le Renouveau, mai 1958–juillet 1962* (Paris: Omnibus/Plon, 1993), 767–71. I thank Charles Cogan and R. Scott Lerner for help with translation.

87. Lacouture, *De Gaulle*, 297.

88. Alfred Grosser, *French Foreign Policy under De Gaulle*, trans. Lois Ames Pattison (Boston: Little, Brown & Co., 1965), 103.

89. Lacouture, *De Gaulle*, 391; de Gaulle, "Address Delivered by President Charles de Gaulle on Internal Affairs, Africa, East-West Relations, Broadcast over French Radio and Television on July 12, 1961," in French Embassy, *Major Addresses*, 138; and de Gaulle, "Address by President Charles de Gaulle on the Economy, Atomic Force, Euro-

pean Policy, Algeria, Broadcast over French Radio and Television on February 5, 1962," in French Embassy, *Major Addresses,* 160.

90. "Address by President Charles de Gaulle on the Future of France and Algeria Broadcast over French Radio and Television on October 2, 1961," in French Embassy, *Major Addresses,* 152. Emphasis added.

91. Sulzberger, *The Test,* 180.

92. "Press Conference of Premier Charles de Gaulle held in Paris at the Hotel Matignon on October 23, 1958," in French Embassy, *Major Addresses,* 27. This theme also recurs in his *Memoirs,* 64, 91, 164, 231.

93. Theodore Robert Posner, *Current French Security Policy: The Gaullist Legacy* (New York: Greenwood Press, 1991), 19; and de Gaulle, *Memoirs,* 11.

94. "Address by President Charles de Gaulle Prior to the Signature of the Evian Agreements, Broadcast over French Radio and Television on June 8, 1962," in French Embassy, *Major Addresses,* 186.

95. Ambler, *The French Army in Politics,* 64–65.

96. On the latter issue, see the frequent references to the differences between French civilian and military cultures in Jean Lartéguy's *Les Centurions,* trans. Xan Fielding (New York: Dutton, 1962).

97. See Harold D. Lasswell, "Sino-Japanese Crisis: The Garrison State versus the Civilian State," *China Quarterly,* special no. (Fall 1937): 643–49.

98. Meirion and Susie Harries, *Soldiers of the Sun: The Rise and Fall of the Imperial Japanese Army* (New York: Random House, 1991), 37.

99. Yale Condee Maxon, *Control of Japanese Foreign Policy: A Study of Civil-Military Rivalry* (Westport, Conn.: Greenwood Press, 1957), 72; and James D. Crowley, "Japan's Military Foreign Policies," in Crowley, ed., *Japan's Foreign Policy, 1868–1941: A Research Guide* (New York: Columbia University Press, 1974), 42.

100. F. C. Jones, "Japan: The Military Domination of Japanese Policy, 1931–1945," in Michael Howard, ed., *Soldiers and Governments: Nine Studies in Civil-Military Relations* (Westport, Conn.: Greenwood Press, 1978), 122.

101. Even Samuel Huntington seems to accept this interpretation. See *The Soldier and the State: The Theory and Politics of Civil-Military Relations* (Cambridge: Harvard University Press, Belknap Press, 1957), 134.

102. Jones, "Japan," 118.

103. Maxon, *Control of Japanese Foreign Policy,* 189.

104. This is discussed in detail in Robert A. Pape, *Bombing to Win: Air Power and Coercion in War* (Ithaca: Cornell University Press, 1996), 89.

105. Maxon, *Control of Japanese Foreign Policy,* 204–5, 206, 211, 212.

106. Jones, "Japan," 129.

107. Harries and Harries, *Soldiers of the Sun,* 146. Emphasis added.

108. Ibid., 168.

109. See Asada Sadao, "The Japanese Navy and the United States," and Misawa Shigeo and Ninomiya Saburo, "The Role of the Diet and Political Parties," both in Dorothy Borg and Sumpei Okamoto, eds., *Pearl Harbor as History: Japanese American Relations, 1931–1941* (New York: Columbia University Press, 1973), 242, 325.

110. Fujiwara Akira, "The Role of the Japanese Army," in Borg and Okamoto, *Pearl Harbor as History,* 189; and Harries and Harries, *Soldiers of the Sun,* 284, 377.

111. Asada, "The Japanese Navy," 225–59.

112. Fujiwara, "Role of the Japanese Army," 191.

113. Harries and Harries, *Soldiers of the Sun,* 177.

114. Ibid., 65.

115. W. G. Beasely, *Japanese Imperialism: 1894–1945* (New York: Clarendon, 1987), 180–81.

116. Ibid., 182; and Akira Iriye, *After Imperialism: The Search for a New Order in the Far East, 1921–1931* (Cambridge: Harvard University Press, 1965), 206.

117. Huntington, *The Soldier and the State,* 134.

118. Harries and Harries, *Soldiers of the Sun,* 451; and Asada, "The Japanese Navy," 254.

119. Harries and Harries, *Soldiers of the Sun,* 177.

Chapter 6. Twilight of the Generals?

1. See, for example, Edwin Lieuwen, *Generals vs. Presidents: Neomilitarism in Latin America* (New York: Praeger, 1964).

2. See John J. Johnson, *The Military and Society in Latin America* (Stanford: Stanford University Press, 1964).

3. Jorge Nef, "The Trend toward Democratization in Latin America: Shadow and Substance," *Latin American Research Review* 23, no. 3 (1988): 150.

4. Alain Rouquié's work is suggestive, but he has not produced a generalizable conceptual framework. For this criticism, see George Philip, *The Military in South American Politics* (London: Croom Helm, 1985), 388; and Barry Ames, "Military and Society in Latin America," *Latin American Research Review* 23, no. 2 (1988): 160.

5. Guillermo O'Donnell, "Reflection on the Patterns of Change in the Bureaucratic-Authoritarian State," *Latin American Research Review* 13, no. 1 (1978): 60; and O'Donnell, *Modernization and Bureaucratic Authoritarianism: Studies in South American Politics* (Berkeley: University of California Press, 1973), 73 n. 42.

6. O'Donnell, *Modernization,* xiii; and David Collier, introduction to Collier, ed., *The New Authoritarianism in Latin America* (Princeton: Princeton University Press, 1979), 3–4.

7. David Collier, "Overview of the Bureaucratic-Authoritarian Model," in Collier, *New Authoritarianism,* 28.

8. Guillermo O'Donnell, "Modernization and Military Coups: Theory, Comparisons, and the Argentine Case," in Abraham Lowenthal, ed., *Armies and Politics in Latin America* (New York: Holmes and Meier, 1976), 207.

9. John Markoff and Silvio Duncan Baretta, "What We Don't Know about Coups: Observations on Recent South American Politics," *Armed Forces and Society* 12, no. 2 (1986): 215; and O'Donnell, *Modernization,* 159–60.

10. O'Donnell, *Modernization,* 80 n. 51.

11. Karen L. Remmer and Gilbert W. Merkx, "Bureaucratic-Authoritarianism Revisited," *Latin American Research Review* 17, no. 2 (1982): 5; and Guillermo O'Donnell, "Tensions in the Bureaucratic-Authoritarian State and the Question of Democracy," in Collier, *New Authoritarianism,* 298. Also see Philip, *The Military in South American Politics,* 39.

12. Juan J. Linz, "Transitions to Democracy," *Washington Quarterly* 13, no. 3 (1990): 154–55.

13. Alfred Stepan, *Rethinking Military Politics: Brazil and the Southern Cone* (Princeton: Princeton University Press, 1988), x–xi.

14. Alain Rouquié, "Demilitarization and the Institutionalization of Military Dominated Politics in Latin America," in Guillermo O'Donnell, Philippe C. Schmitter, and Laurence Whitehead, eds., *Transitions from Authoritarian Rule: Comparative Perspectives* (Baltimore: Johns Hopkins University Press, 1988), 129.

15. Frederick M. Nunn, *The Military in Chilean History: Essays on Civil-Military Relations, 1810–1973* (Albuquerque: University of New Mexico Press, 1976), 193.

16. Samuel P. Huntington, *The Soldier and the State: The Theory and Politics of Civil-Military Relations* (Cambridge: Harvard University Press, Belknap Press, 1957), 33.

17. Alain Rouquié, *The Military and the State in Latin America*, trans. Paul E. Sigmund (Berkeley: University of California Press, 1987), 98–99.

18. José Z. Garcia, "Military Factions and Military Intervention in Latin America," in Sheldon W. Simon, ed., *The Military and Security in the Third World: Domestic and International Impacts* (Boulder, Colo.: Westview Press, 1978), 52–53.

19. Alfred Stepan, *The Military in Politics: Changing Patterns in Brazil* (Princeton: Princeton University Press, 1971), 98.

20. Martin C. Needler, "Military Motivations in the Seizure of Power," *Latin American Research Review* 10, no. 3 (1975): 68.

21. Stepan, *The Military in Politics*, 168. Also see David Pion-Berlin, "The National Security Doctrine, Military Threat Perception, and the 'Dirty War' in Argentina," *Comparative Political Studies* 21, no. 3 (1988): 283–407; and Pion-Berlin, "Latin American National Security Doctrines: Hard-and Softline Themes," *Armed Forces and Society* 15, no. 3 (1989): 411–30.

22. John S. Fitch, "The Political Impact of U.S. Military Aid to Latin America: Institutional and Individual Effects," *Armed Forces and Society* 5, no. 3 (1979): 368.

23. Rouquié, *The Military and the State*, 150.

24. Stepan, *The Military in Politics*, 174.

25. Aldo Vacs, "Authoritarian Breakdown and Redemocratization in Argentina," in James M. Malloy and Mitchell A. Seligson, eds., *Authoritarians and Democrats: Regime Transition in Latin America* (Pittsburgh: University of Pittsburgh Press, 1987), 13.

26. Philip, *The Military in South American Politics*, 160.

27. O'Donnell, "Modernization and Military Coups," 217. Also see Guillermo O'Donnell, "Permanent Crisis and the Failure to Create a Democratic Regime: Argentina, 1955–66," in Juan J. Linz and Alfred Stepan, eds., *The Breakdown of Democratic Regimes* (Baltimore: Johns Hopkins University Press, 1978), 170.

28. Marcelo Cavarozzi, "Political Cycles in Argentina since 1955," in Guillermo O'Donnell, Philippe C. Schmitter, and Laurence Whitehead, eds., *Transitions from Authoritarian Rule: Latin America* (Baltimore: Johns Hopkins University Press, 1986), 32.

29. Edward Gibson, "Nine Cases of the Breakdown of Democracy," in Robert A. Pastor, ed., *Democracy in the Americas: Stopping the Pendulum* (New York: Holmes & Meier, 1989), 177; and O'Donnell, "Modernization and Military Coups," 208–9.

30. O'Donnell, "Modernization and Military Coups," 207.

31. O'Donnell, "Permanent Crisis," 169.

32. Philip, *The Military in South American Politics,* 161; and Cavarozzi, "Political Cycles," 35.

33. David Rock, *Argentina, 1516–1982: From Spanish Colonization to the Falklands War* (Berkeley: University of California Press, 1985), 349.

34. David Rock, "The Military in Politics in Argentina, 1973–83," in Brian Loveman and Thomas M. Davies Jr., eds., *The Politics of Antipolitics: The Military in Latin America,* 2d ed. (Lincoln: University of Nebraska Press, 1989), 329.

35. Rock, *Argentina,* 369; and Virgilio Beltran, "Political Transition in Argentina: 1982 to 1985," *Armed Forces and Society* 13, no. 2 (1987): 215.

36. Maria Susana Ricci and J. Samuel Fitch, "Ending Military Regimes in Argentina, 1966–73 and 1976–83," in Louis W. Goodman, Johanna S. R. Mendelson, and Juan Rial, eds., *The Military and Democracy: The Future of Civil-Military Relations in Latin America* (Lexington, Mass.: D. C. Heath & Co., 1990), 68. Also see Rock, *Argentina,* 374–75.

37. Rock, "The Military in Politics in Argentina," 333; and Beltran, "Political Transition in Argentina," 217.

38. While there have been coup attempts since 1983 and civil-military relations have not been as stable as they could be, so far civilian democracy seems viable in Argentina. See Shirley Christian, "Banana Republic Image Worries the Argentines," *New York Times,* Dec. 5, 1990, 6.

39. Stepan, *The Military in Politics,* 92.

40. Wilfred A. Bacchus, "Development under Military Rule: Factionalism in Brazil," *Armed Forces and Society* 12, no. 3 (1986): 409–10.

41. Alfred Stepan, "Political Leadership and Regime Breakdown: Brazil," in Linz and Stepan, *Breakdown of Democratic Regimes,* 122.

42. Stepan, *The Military in Politics,* 155.

43. Quoted in ibid., 97.

44. Stepan, "Political Leadership," 128.

45. Stepan, *The Military in Politics,* 202.

46. Gibson, "Nine Cases," 180–82.

47. Stepan, "Political Leadership," 131.

48. Riordan Roett, "The Post-1964 Military Republic in Brazil," in Loveman and Davies, *The Politics of Antipolitics,* 387; Bacchus, "Development under Military Rule," 401; Scott Mainwaring, "The Transition to Democracy in Brazil," in Loveman and Davies, *The Politics of Antipolitics,* 418–19; and Stanley E. Hilton, "The Brazilian Military: Changing Strategic Perceptions and the Question of Mission," *Armed Forces and Society* 13, no. 3 (1987): 331.

49. Bacchus, "Development under Military Rule," 406.

50. John Markoff and Silvio R. Duncan Baretta, "Professional Ideology and Military Activism in Brazil: Critique of a Thesis of Alfred Stepan," *Comparative Politics* 17, no. 2 (1985): 185.

51. Bacchus, "Development under Military Rule," 415–16.

52. Stepan, *Rethinking Military Politics,* 59.

53. Luciano Martins, "The 'Liberalization' of Authoritarian Rule in Brazil," in O'Donnell, Schmitter, and Whitehead, *Transitions from Authoritarian Rule: Latin America,* 82.

54. Hilton, "The Brazilian Military," 346.

55. Manuel Antonio Garreton, "The Political Evolution of the Chilean Military Regime and Problems in the Transition to Democracy," in O'Donnell, Schmitter, and Whitehead, *Transitions from Authoritarian Rule: Latin America,* 95.

56. In the immediate aftermath of the coup in the mid-1970s, there was a heated debate about the role of the United States in Allende's downfall. Allende supporters tended to attribute the whole affair to the United States. Nixon administration officials such as Secretary of State Henry Kissinger minimized U.S. participation. In fact, the current scholarly consensus is that although the United States did impose an economic embargo on Chile, and while the Central Intelligence Agency did encourage dissident military officers early in the Allende period, neither of these really caused Allende's downfall. See Paul Sigmund, *The Overthrow of Allende and the Politics of Chile, 1964–1976* (Pittsburgh: University of Pittsburgh Press, 1977); and Nathanial Davis, *The Last Two Years of Salvador Allende* (London: I. B. Taurus & Co., 1985).

57. Nunn, *The Military in Chilean History,* 226.

58. Arturo Valenzuela, "The Breakdown of Democratic Regimes: Chile," in Linz and Stepan, *Breakdown of Democratic Regimes,* 108.

59. Ibid., 87; and Liisa North, "The Military in Chilean Politics," in Lowenthal, *Armies and Politics,* 172.

60. Nunn, *The Military in Chilean History,* 272–73; and Valenzuela, "The Breakdown of Democratic Regimes," 20.

61. Garreton, "Political Evolution," 99.

62. Gibson, "Nine Cases," 185.

63. Valenzuela, "The Breakdown of Democratic Regimes," 100–102; and North, "The Military in Chilean Politics," 186.

64. Nunn, *The Military in Chilean History,* 293.

65. Valenzuela, "The Breakdown of Democratic Regimes," 103. This question of the threat to the military from the Left still plays a role in contemporary Chilean politics. See Shirley Christian, "Chilean Military Defends Killings," *New York Times,* July 10, 1990, 2.

66. Quoted in Genaro Arriagada, *Pinochet: The Politics of Power* (Boulder, Colo.: Westview Press, 1991), 22. Also see 97–98.

67. Nunn, *The Military in Chilean History,* 186.

68. Silvia Borzutsky, "The Pinochet Regime: Crisis and Consolidation," in Malloy and Seligson, *Authoritarians and Democrats,* 70.

69. See Arriagada, *Pinochet,* 123–77.

70. Garreton, "Political Evolution," 122. Also see Brian Loveman, "Antipolitics in Chile, 1973–87," in Loveman and Davies, *The Politics of Antipolitics,* 451.

71. Garreton, "Political Evolution," 115.

72. Borzutsky, "The Pinochet Regime," 84–85. Also see Mark W. Falcoff, "Chile: Autumn of the Patriarch," *National Interest,* no. 14 (Winter 1988/89): 56.

73. Rock, *Argentina,* 352.

74. Stepan, *The Military in Politics,* 135.

75. Sigmund, *The Overthrow of Allende.*

76. Stepan, *The Military in Politics,* 210–20.

77. Bacchus, "Development under Military Rule," 406.

78. Rouquié, *The Military and the State,* 32–35.

79. A recent article that discusses the French influence in Latin American national

security doctrines is Carina Perelli, "From Counterrevolutionary Warfare to Political Awakening: The Uruguayan and Argentine Armed Forces," *Armed Forces and Society* 20, no. 1 (1993): 25–49.

Chapter 7. What the Future Holds

1. Samuel Huntington, "New Contingencies, Old Roles," *Joint Forces Quarterly,* no. 2 (Autumn 1993): 38–43.

2. "White House Looks to Military for Help in Anti-terrorism Effort; Congress Is Leery," *Baltimore Sun,* May 1, 1995, 7; and Judi Hasson, "Clinton Plan Will Expand Military Role," *USA Today,* May 4, 1995, 6.

3. For further discussion, see Deborah Norden, "Keeping the Peace, Outside and In: Argentina's United Nations Missions," *International Peacekeeping* 2, no. 3 (1995): 330–49.

4. For that reason, I am less concerned about the sale of high-technology conventional armaments to Latin America than are many others. For the contrary view, see "The Pentagon and Latin Armies," *New York Times,* Apr. 4, 1997, 28.

5. Alfred Stepan, *Rethinking Military Politics: Brazil and the Southern Cone* (Princeton: Princeton University Press, 1988), 136–37.

6. One possible approach to the problem of gays in the military would be to point out the cost of the military's exclusionary policy, which the General Accounting Office estimates to be $27 million a year in direct and indirect costs. See Eric Schmitt, "Challenging the Military," *New York Times,* Nov. 12, 1993, 22.

7. See Alan Berubé, *Coming Out under Fire: The History of Gay Men and Women in World War Two* (New York: Free Press, 1990); and Randy Shilts, *Conduct Unbecoming: Gays and Lesbians in the U.S. Military* (New York: St. Martin's Press, 1993).

8. Christopher Donnelly, "Evolving Problems in the Former Soviet Armed Forces," *Survival* 37, no. 3 (1992): 48.

9. Liberalism is, unfortunately, very attractive to civilian policy-makers, for reasons that John Mearsheimer enumerates in the conclusion to his "The False Promise of International Institutions," *International Security* 19, no. 3 (1994/95): 47–49.

10. I have made the argument about the superiority of realism in some detail in my contribution to "Is There a Logic of the West?" *World Policy Journal* 11, no. 1 (1994): 120–22.

11. For a discussion of how the Israeli case undermines Lasswell's argument, see Edward Luttwak and Dan Horowitz, *The Israeli Army* (London: Allen Lane, 1975), xiii; and Yehuda Ben Meir, *Civil-Military Relations in Israel* (New York: Columbia University Press, 1995), xi.

12. Ben Meir, *Civil-Military Relations,* xvii; and Thomas L. Friedman, "The War Within," *New York Times,* May 15, 1997, 37.

13. Clyde Haberman, "Israelis Deglamorize the Military," *New York Times,* May 31, 1995, 10.

14. Joel Greenberg, "Settlers' Evictions Put Israeli Army in the Middle," *New York Times,* Aug. 4, 1995, 2; and Greenberg, "Hand Over Israeli Bases? No Way, Rabbis Tell Troops," *New York Times,* July 13, 1995, 1, 3.

15. Yossi Klien Halevi, "Soldiers of Zion," *New York Times,* Nov. 15, 1995, 23.

16. Serge Schmemann, "Israeli Soldier Reported Held in Rabin Killing," *New York Times,* Nov. 12, 1995, 12.

17. This incident is discussed in Ben Meir, *Civil-Military Relations,* 174.

18. The United States is increasingly identified as a serious external threat by high-ranking officers of the People's Liberation Army (PLA), replacing the Soviet Union as the main external threat. See Patrick E. Tyler, "Chinese Military Sees U.S. as Foe," *New York Times,* Nov. 16, 1993, 16. There is little evidence that the Chinese military regards Russia as a threat of the same magnitude or that it believes the prospects for a major war with any country are very high at present. Ellis Joffe, "The PLA and the Chinese Economy: The Effect of Involvement," *Survival* 37, no. 2 (1995): 26.

19. Greg Austin, "The Strategic Implications of China's Public Order Crisis," *Survival* 37, no. 2 (1995): 7–23; and Nicholas D. Kristof, "As China Looks at World Order, It Detects New Struggles Emerging," *New York Times,* Apr. 21, 1992, 4.

20. Patrick E. Tyler, "Signs of Power Struggle Come to Light in China," *New York Times,* Mar. 29, 1995, 3; and Tyler, "Control of Army Is Crucial Issue for China Rulers," *New York Times,* Feb. 23, 1997, 1, 10.

21. Patrick E. Tyler, "Never Far from Power, China's Military Is Back," *New York Times,* Dec. 4, 1994, 24; and Nicholas D. Kristof, "The Army Gets into Position as China Awaits Change," *New York Times,* Oct. 25, 1993, "Week in Review," 5.

22. Michael Swaine, *The Military and Political Succession in China: Leadership, Institutions, Beliefs* [R-4254–AF] (Santa Monica: RAND Corp., 1992), 11.

23. Austin, "Strategic Implications," 14.

24. Swaine, *Military and Political Succession,* 9–10.

25. Patrick E. Tyler, "Chinese Military's Business Profits Being Put Back into Business, Not Arms," *New York Times,* May 24, 1994, 6; and Joffe, "The PLA and the Chinese Economy," 36–39.

26. On U.S. interest in fomenting a coup in Iraq, see Patrick E. Tyler, "U.S. Plans for a Possible Coup in Iraq," *New York Times,* Dec. 11, 1991, 6; and Tyler, "Gates, in Mideast, Is Said to Discuss Ouster of Hussein," *New York Times,* Feb. 7, 1992, 1, 5. On Cuba, see the op-ed piece by former head of Radio Martí Ernesto F. Betancourt, "The Castro Alternative," *New York Times,* Sept. 9, 1994, 27.

27. See Patrick E. Tyler, "U.S. and Iraqis Tell of a Coup Attempt Against Baghdad," *New York Times,* July 3, 1992; "U.S. Tells of Abortive Troop Mutiny against Iraq's Leader," *New York Times,* June 16, 1995, 9; Youseff M. Ibrahim, "Iraqi Defector Says He Will Work to Topple Saddam," *New York Times,* Aug. 13, 1995, 3; and Robert Pear, "Cuba Seizes 6 More Officers amid Signs of Big Shakeup," *New York Times,* June 17, 1989, 3.

28. Tom Carter, "Military Support for Economic Reforms Seen As Protecting Castro from Revolt," *Washington Times,* June 23, 1995, 17; and Peter Kornbluh, "From Here to Cuba," *New York Times,* May 17, 1995, 19.

29. Elizardo Sanchez Santacruz, "Cuba Can't Change on Its Own," *New York Times,* Apr. 22, 1997, 23.

30. Eric Schmitt, "U.S. Action in Persian Gulf Is Said to Seek Iraqi's Ouster," *New York Times,* Aug. 19, 1995, 6.

31. Gregory Grant ("A Situation Tailor-Made for Saddam Hussein," *Los Angeles Times,* Jan. 17, 1993, M1, M6) advocated direct attacks on the Iraqi military as an

incentive for it to topple Hussein. But if such attacks did not work during the Gulf War, why should we expect them to work now?

32. For examples of optimism based on Lasswellian arguments, see Peter J. Katzenstein and Noburo Okawara, "Japan's National Security: Structures, Norms, and Policies," *International Security* 17, no. 4 (1993): 84–118; and Thomas U. Berger, "From Sword to Chrysanthemum: Japan's Culture of Anti-militarism," *International Security* 17, no. 4 (1993): 119–50. On Japan's and Germany's transition to trading states, see Richard Rosecrance, *The Rise of the Trading State: Commerce and Conquest in the Modern World* (New York: Basic Books, 1986).

33. Germany had the third-largest number of personnel in the armed forces in NATO, after the United States and Turkey. On both Germany and Japan, see International Institute for Strategic Studies, *Military Balance: 1984/85* (London: IISS, 1984), table 4.

34. The reaction of the Ground Self-Defense Forces to the efforts of Japanese novelist and right-wing activist Yukio Mishima to spark a coup d'état is compelling evidence of just how strong civilian control of the Japanese military was during the Cold War. On November 25, 1970, Mishima and four of his followers took over the Eastern Command headquarters of the Ground Self-Defense Force at Ichigaya outside of Tokyo. Not only did the garrison not respond favorably to Mishima's entreaties, it ridiculed them. On this incident, see Tetsuo Maeda, *The Hidden Army: The Untold Story of Japan's Military Forces* (Chicago: Edition Q, 1995), 150–55.

For a discussion of how the Cold War fostered civilian control of the Bundeswehr, see Donald Abenheim, *Reforging the Iron Cross: The Search for Tradition in the West German Armed Forces* (Princeton: Princeton University Press, 1988), 46.

35. Alan Cowell, "Pro-Nazi Incidents in German Army Raise Alarm," *New York Times*, Nov. 5, 1997, 4.

36. This section draws heavily on Vincent Cable, "The Diminished Nation-State: A Study in the Loss of Sovereignty," in "What Future for the State?" *Daedalus* 124, no. 2 (1995): 23–54.

37. Kenechi Ohmae, "The Rise of the Regional State," *Foreign Affairs* 72, no. 2 (1993): 78–86.

38. A useful discussion of this is Frederick M. Nunn, "The South American Military and (Re)Democratization: Professional Thought and Self-Perception," *Journal of Inter-American Studies and World Affairs* 37, no. 2 (1995): 27.

39. For a discussion of the withering of the Argentine Fabricaciones Militares, see "Argentina Restructures Defense Industry: Plan for Decentralization and Partial Privatization," *Latin American Regional Reports—Southern Cone* (hereafter *LARR—SC*) RS-88-05 (June 30, 1988), 4–5.

40. "Survival Depends on Exports," *LARR—Brazil* (hereafter *LARR—B*) RB-83-05 (June 3, 1983), 6.

41. "Foreign Stake in Defense Companies," *LARR—B* RB-91-07 (Aug. 15, 1991), 3.

42. James Brooke, "Peace Unhealthy for Brazilian Arms Industry," *New York Times*, Feb. 25, 1990, 19.

43. "'Internationalization' of Amazon Is Rallying-Point for Military Hardliners," *LARR—B* RB-92-03 (Mar. 19, 1992), 1.

44. "Franco Responds to Military Concerns: Go-Ahead for Amazon Watch System," *LARR—B* RB-93-08 (Sept. 16, 1993), 1.

45. Andrew F. Krepinevich, "Cavalry to Computer: The Pattern of Military Revolutions," *National Interest*, no. 37 (Fall 1994): 30.

46. There was some discussion of the impact on domestic politics in David Jablonsky, "U.S. Military Doctrine and the Revolution in Military Affairs," *Parameters* 24, no. 3 (1994): 18–36.

47. This was the initial impact of the nuclear revolution, too. See Peter D. Feaver, *Guarding the Guardians: Civilian Control of Nuclear Weapons in the United States* (Ithaca: Cornell University Press, 1992), 87–106.

48. "Lessons of the Falklands," *LARR—SC* RS-82-07 (Sept. 10, 1982), 7.

49. "Military Re-think Is in Progress," *LARR—SC* RS-82-06 (July 30, 1982), 6.

50. "Malvinas Post-mortem Hits the Fan," *LARR—SC* RS-83-07 (Sept. 9, 1983), 6.

51. "Services Ponder 'Reform' Policies," *LARR—SC* RS-84-06 (Aug. 3, 1994), 6.

52. "Survival Depends on Exports," 7; and "Electronic Warfare Centre Established," *LARR—B* RB-84-06 (Aug. 10, 1984), 6.

53. Thomas M. Nichols, *The Sacred Cause: Civil-Military Conflict over Soviet National Security, 1917–1992* (Ithaca: Cornell University Press, 1993), 23. This is also a theme in Samuel Huntington's *The Common Defense: Strategic Programs in National Politics* (New York: Columbia University Press, 1961), 1–12.

54. See Michael C. Desch, "War and Strong States, Peace and Weak States?" *International Organization* 50, no. 2 (1996): 237–68.

55. Peter Gourevitch, "The Second Image Reversed: The International Sources of Domestic Politics," *International Organization* 32, no. 4 (1978): 881–911; and Peter Katzenstein, "International Relations and Domestic Structures: Foreign Economic Policies of Advanced Industrial States," *International Organization* 30, no. 1 (1976): 1–45. Steven R. David, *Choosing Sides: Alignment and Realignment in the Third World* (Baltimore: Johns Hopkins University Press, 1991) is a notable exception in the security studies subfield.

56. See the debate sparked in *International Security* by John J. Mearsheimer's "Back to the Future: Instability in Europe after the Cold War," *International Security* 15, no. 1 (1990): 5–56.

57. See Kenneth N. Waltz, *Theory of International Politics* (Reading, Mass.: Addison-Wesley, 1979), 18–78.

58. See Jack Snyder, "The Concept of Strategic Culture: Caveat Emptor," in Carl G. Jacobsen et al., eds., *Strategic Power: USA/USSR* (New York: St. Martin's Press, 1990), 4–6.

59. See the various essays in Peter J. Katzenstein, ed., *The Culture of National Security* (New York: Columbia University Press, 1996), esp. 190, 279, and 325.

60. W. Brian Arthur, "Competing Technologies and Lock-in by Historical Events," *Economic Journal* 99, no. 394 (1989): 116–31; and Paul David, "Understanding the Necessity of QWERTY: The Necessity of History," in W. N. Parker, ed., *Economic History and the Modern Economist* (London: Blackwell, 1986), 30–49.

61. Alexander Wendt, "Anarchy Is What States Make of It: The Social Construction of Power Politics," *International Organization* 46, no. 2 (1992): 391–425.

62. Richard Ned Lebow, "The Long Peace, the End of the Cold War, and the Failure of Realism," *International Organization* 48, no. 2 (1994): 277.

Index

The Library of Congress has cataloged the hardcover edition
of this book as follows:

Desch, Michael C. (Michael Charles), 1960–
    Civilian control of the military : the changing security
environment / Michael C. Desch.
      p. cm.
    Includes bibliographical references and index.
    ISBN 0-8018-6059-8 (alk. paper)
    1. Civil supremacy over the military.   2. Civil-military
relations.   I. Title.
JF195.D47   1999
322′.5—dc21   98-46418

ISBN 0-8018-6639-1 (pbk.)